T. T. Carter

The Treasury of Devotion

A Manual of Prayer for General and Daily Use

T. T. Carter

The Treasury of Devotion
A Manual of Prayer for General and Daily Use

ISBN/EAN: 9783337275167

Printed in Europe, USA, Canada, Australia, Japan

Cover: Foto ©Lupo / pixelio.de

More available books at **www.hansebooks.com**

THE
Treasury of Devotion

A MANUAL OF PRAYER

For General and Daily Use

COMPILED BY A PRIEST

EDITED BY THE
REV. T. T. CARTER, M.A.
RECTOR OF CLEWER, BERKS

RIVINGTONS
London, Oxford, and Cambridge
1871

[Fourth Edition]

RIVINGTONS

LONDON	*Waterloo Place*
OXFORD	*High Street*
CAMBRIDGE	*Trinity Street*

Preface.

TO the loving care and unsparing diligence of a Priest who desires to withhold his name, we are indebted for this, as the Editor believes, very important addition to the series of our devotional Manuals. The difficulty of course in such a work, is to select out of the mass of materials what is likely to be adapted to many different minds under many varying circumstances; and arrange what is selected in the order most easily followed in familiar use. Such use only can be a real test of its success. But the greatest care has been bestowed in aiming at the desired result.

For the ordinary daily devotions as great variety has been given as the compass of the work admitted; and in the case of special devotions, where doubt was felt as to their introduction, the rule observed has been to adopt such as are found in the greater number of manuals, as being a guarantee of their popularity. In all important cases where the devotions are derived from ancient sources, the translation has been carefully compared with the original. In doctrinal statements, for the most part, the words of some recognised authority has been employed; in one or two cases the authorities are given in the text.

The compiler has drawn his materials from whatever sources were accessible to him. The aid given in the case of individual prayers or Litanies, etc., it is scarcely possible to acknowledge; but for the most important assistance in his work, his thanks are specially due to Dr. Pusey for the kind permission to use his translation of the "Paradise of the Christian Soul;" to the Editors of the "Priest to the Altar," the "Encheiridion, or Hours of Sarum," and of the "Hours of the Passion," for kindly placing their works at his disposal. He is also indebted for a few important additions to "The Manual for Sisters of Mercy," also kindly allowed. The translations of the hymns, "Rerum DEUS tenax vigor," "Nunc Sancte nobis SPIRITUS," "Rector potens verax DEUS," "Pange lingua," "Verbum Supernum prodiens," "O Esca Viatorum," are taken from "Hymns Ancient and Modern," through the kind permission of the Editors.

In venturing to commend this Manual, of which his own share has chiefly been in suggesting what occurred to him as likely to enhance its value and usefulness, the Editor feels the momentous responsibility of promoting what, if it become popular, must exercise a vital and lasting influence on the character of the devotional life now, through the mercy of God, deeply stirred within the Church of England. But he believes that, according to the best judgment he is able to form, the "Treasury" contains all the great principles which are important to cherish, in perfecting our communion with God, and the things which are of God; and this according to the teaching of those who have been mercifully given to us, as our authoritative guides in the ways of faith and piety. In conclusion, he would ask of those who use this book that they may sometimes remember before the Throne of Grace him to whose labours for his brethren's sake, we are indebted for so great an aid, as well as those who have assisted him in his work.

T. T. C.

CLEWER RECTORY, *Lent* 1869.

PREFACE TO THE THIRD EDITION

IN preparing the "Treasury," the desire was to supply a body of devotions in faithful accordance with the truest standards of the mind of the Church of England, and, in trust that this rule had been observed, it was thought better to commit the book to the test of general approval rather than seek any authoritative sanction to its contents. It had not, however, been long published before the Compiler received a testimony to the value of his work, which, since death has set its seal to the faithful witness of the life and teaching of the writer, has now a sacredness which could not attach to any ordinary "imprimatur."

The Editor therefore feels it due to the Church to make known the estimate at which the book was held by one, lately ruling amongst us as a Father in God, whose entire heartfelt anxiety consistently and loyally to uphold our Church's doctrine and devotional life in the affectionate fervour of a most simple faith, cannot be questioned. In the fourth month of his last illness, and rather more than four months before his death, he wrote the following letter.

T. T. C.

Whitsun Tide 1870.

Palm Sunday, 1869.

I have looked through your book, and have begun to use it. In fact I feel that I am now in a position to do more than acknowledge your gift; I thank you heartily for it, and assure you that it is to me a blessed thought that one, who was one of my own clergy, should now give me such effectual help to prepare for my account. May God bless and keep you in your blessed work. This is the hearty prayer and wish of your affectionate brother in Christ,

W. K. SARUM.

Contents.

Tables: (1) *Lesser Holy Days;* (2) *Feasts to be observed;* (3) *Vigils, Fasts, Days of Abstinence;* (4) *Times when Marriages are not solemnized.*

I.

DOCTRINE AND INSTRUCTION.

PAGE

Apostles' Creed—Lord's Prayer—Gloria Patri—Ten Commandments—Precepts of the Church—Two Sacraments generally necessary to Salvation—The other Five ordained for certain Persons or States of Life—Three Theological Virtues—Four Cardinal Virtues—Seven Gifts of the HOLY GHOST—Twelve Fruits of the HOLY GHOST—Seven Spiritual Works of Mercy—Seven Corporal Works of Mercy—Eight Beatitudes—Seven Capital or Deadly Sins and the Contrary Virtues—Nine ways of Participating in another's Sin—Six Sins against the HOLY GHOST—Three Notable Duties—Three Parts of true Repentance—Penitential Psalms—Gradual Psalms—Evangelical Counsels—Seven Words on the Cross—Four Last Things—Subjects for Daily Meditation—Anima CHRISTI 1–6

II.

DAILY DEVOTIONS.

Morning Prayer—Evening Prayer—Ejaculations—Acts of Faith, Hope, and Love—Occasional Prayers—Memorials for a Week—

Prayers for the Third, Sixth, and Ninth Hours, and Compline—Intercessory Prayers 7-65

III.

DEVOTIONS FOR HOLY COMMUNION.

PAGE

Preparation for Communion—Daily Preparation during a Week—Prayers before the Service—The Order of the Administration with Private Devotions—Prayers after the Service—Thanksgiving after Communion—Acts of Devotion before or during the Service—Acts of Devotion after Communion—Litany of the Holy Eucharist—Hymns 66-118

IV

PENITENTIAL DEVOTIONS.

Prayers before Examination of Conscience—Acts of Faith, Hope, and Love—Method of Self-Examination by the Ten Commandments—Method of Self-Examination by the Seven Deadly Sins—Considerations to excite Contrition—Ejaculations—Prayers for Confession—Prayers for Pardon and Amendment—Prayers against Deadly Sins—Litany of Repentance—Penitential Psalms 119-150

V.

DEVOTIONS FOR THE CHURCH'S SEASONS.

Advent—Christmas—S. Stephen's Day—S. John the Evangelist Day—Holy Innocents' Day—The Circumcision—The Epiphany—Septuagesima—Lent—Holy Week—Easter—Rogation Days—Ascension-Tide—Whitsun-Tide—Trinity—Saints' Days—

Golden Litany—Mysteries of the Incarnation—Mysteries of the Redemption—Mysteries of the Resurrection—Litany for the Church 151–268

VI.

MEDITATION.

PAGE

Explanation of the Four Parts of Meditation, viz. : 1. The Preparation; 2. The Considerations; 3. The Affections and Resolutions; 4. The Conclusion—A Meditation on our Sins—Advice as to making Resolutions—Prayer before Meditation . . 269–274

VII.

DEVOTIONS FOR THE OCCASIONAL OFFICES.

Holy Baptism—Confirmation—Holy Matrimony—Devotions for the Sick—Commendatory Office—Prayers for Mourners—Communion of the Sick—Thanksgiving for Recovery . . 275–318

A TABLE
OF THE
LESSER HOLY DAYS.

January.
- 8. S. Lucian, Pr. M.
- 13. S. Hilary, Bp. C.
- 18. S. Prisca, V. M.
- 20. S. Fabian, Bp. M.
- 21. S. Agnes, V. M.
- 22. S. Vincent, Dea. M.

February.
- 3. S. Blasius, Bp. M.
- 5. S. Agatha, V. M.
- 14. S. Valentine, Bp. M.

March.
- 1. S. David, Abp.
- 2. S. Chad, Bp.
- 7. S. Perpetua, M.
- 12. S. Gregory, M. Bp. C.
- 18. S. Edward, K.
- 21. S. Benedict, Abbot.

April.
- 3. S. Richard, Bp.
- 4. S. Ambrose, Bp.
- 19. S. Alphege, Abp.
- 23. S. George, M.

May.
- 3. Invention of the Cross.
- 6. S. John E. ante Port Lat.
- 19. S. Dunstan, Abp.
- 26. S. Augustine, Abp.
- 27. Ven. Bede, Pr.

June.
- 1. S. Nicomede, Pr. M.
- 5. S. Boniface, Bp. M.
- 17. S. Alban, M.
- 20. Trans. S. Edw., K.

July.
- 2. Visitation B. V. M.
- 4. Trans. S. Martin, Bp. C.
- 15. Trans. S. Swithun, Bp.
- 20. S. Margaret, V. M.
- 22. S. Mary Magdalene.
- 26. S. Anne.

August.
- 1. Lammas Day.
- 6. Transfig. of Our Lord.
- 7. Name of Jesus.
- 10. S. Laurence, Archdeac. M.
- 28. S. Augustine, Bp. C. D.
- 29. Beheading S. John Bapt.

September.
- 1. S. Giles, Ab. C.
- 7. S. Enurchus, Bp.
- 8. Nativity, B. V. M.
- 14. Holy Cross Day.
- 17. S. Lambert, Bp. M.
- 26. S. Cyprian, Abp. M.
- 30. S. Jerome, Pr. C. D.

October.
- 1. S. Remigius, Bp.
- 6. S. Faith, V. M.
- 9. S. Denys, Bp. M.
- 13. Transl. S. Edward, K. C.
- 17. S. Etheldreda, V.
- 25. S. Crispin, M.

November.
- 6. S. Leonard, C.
- 11. S. Martin, Bp. C.
- 13. S. Britius, Bp.
- 15. S. Machutus, Bp.
- 17. S. Hugh, Bp.
- 20. S. Edmund, K. M.
- 22. S. Cecilia, V. M.
- 23. S. Clement, Bp. M.
- 25. S. Catherine, V. M.

December.
- 6. S. Nicolas, Bp.
- 8. Conception B. V. M.
- 13. S. Lucy, V. M.
- 31. S. Silvester, Bp.

A TABLE OF ALL THE FEASTS

THAT ARE TO BE OBSERVED IN THE

CHURCH OF ENGLAND THROUGHOUT THE YEAR.

All Sundays in the Year.
The Circumcision of Our Lord Jesus Christ.
The Epiphany.
The Conversion of S. *Paul*.
The Purification of the Blessed Virgin.
S. *Matthias* the Apostle.
The Annunciation of the Blessed Virgin.
S. *Mark* the Evangelist.
S. *Philip* and S. *James* the Apostles.
The Ascension of Our Lord Jesus Christ.
S. *Barnabas*.

The Nativity of S. *John* Baptist.
S. *Peter* the Apostle.
S. *James* the Apostle.
S. *Bartholomew* the Apostle.
S. *Matthew* the Apostle.
S. *Michael* and all Angels.
S. *Luke* the Evangelist.
S. *Simon* and S. *Jude* the Apostles.
All Saints.
S. *Andrew* the Apostle.
S. *Thomas* the Apostle.
The Nativity of Our Lord.
S. *Stephen* the Martyr.
S. *John* the Evangelist.
The Holy Innocents.

Monday and *Tuesday* in *Easter-Week*.
Monday and *Tuesday* in *Whitsun-Week*.

Note.— *EASTER-DAY* (on which all the other moveable feasts depend) is always the First *Sunday* after the Full Moon which happens upon, or next after the Twenty-first Day of *March*; and if the Full Moon happens upon a *Sunday*, *Easter-Day* is the *Sunday* after.

Advent-Sunday is always the nearest *Sunday* to the Feast of *Saint Andrew*, whether before or after.

Septuagesima
Sexagesima
Quinquagesima
Quadragesima
} *Sunday* is { Nine, Eight, Seven, Six } Weeks before *Easter*.

Rogation-Sunday
Ascension-Day
Whitsun-Day
Trinity-Sunday
} is { Five Weeks, Forty Days, Seven Weeks, Eight Weeks } after *Easter*.

A TABLE
OF THE
VIGILS, FASTS, AND DAYS OF ABSTINENCE,
TO BE OBSERVED IN THE YEAR.

The Eves or Vigils before
- The Nativity of Our Lord.
- The Purification of the Blessed Virgin *Mary*.
- The Annunciation of the Blessed Virgin.
- *Easter-Day.*
- *Ascension-Day.*
- *Pentecost.*
- *S. Matthias.*

The Eves or Vigils before
- *S. John* Baptist.
- *S. Peter.*
- *S. James.*
- *S. Bartholomew.*
- *S. Matthew.*
- *S. Simon* and *S. Jude.*
- *S. Andrew.*
- *S. Thomas.*
- All Saints.

Note.—That if any of these Feast-Days fall upon a *Monday*, then the Vigil or Fast-Day shall be kept upon the *Saturday*, and not upon the *Sunday* next before it.

DAYS OF FASTING, OR ABSTINENCE.

I. The Forty Days of Lent.
II. The Ember-Days at the Four Seasons, being the *Wednesday*, *Friday*, and *Saturday* after ....
   1. The First *Sunday* in Lent.
   2. The Feast of *Pentecost*.
   3. September 14.
   4. December 13.
III. The Three *Rogation-Days*, being the *Monday*, *Tuesday*, and *Wednesday*, before *Holy Thursday*, or the *Ascension* of Our Lord.
IV. All the *Fridays* in the Year, except CHRISTMAS-DAY.

THE TIMES WHEREIN MARRIAGES ARE NOT SOLEMNIZED.

From
- Advent Sunday
- Septuagesima Sunday
- Rogation Sunday

until
- Eight Days after the Epiphany.
- Eight Days after Easter.
- Trinity Sunday.

Some of these being times of solemn fasting and abstinence, some of holy festivity and joy, both fit to be spent in such sacred exercises, without other avocations.   (*Bp. Cosin.*)

Doctrine and Instruction

The Apostles' Creed.

I BELIEVE in GOD the FATHER Almighty, Maker of Heaven and earth:

And in JESUS CHRIST His only SON our LORD: Who was conceived by the HOLY GHOST, born of the Virgin Mary: Suffered under Pontius Pilate, was crucified, dead, and buried: He descended into Hell, the third day He rose again from the dead: He ascended into Heaven, and sitteth on the right hand of GOD the FATHER Almighty: From thence He shall come to judge the quick and the dead:

I believe in the HOLY GHOST: The Holy Catholick Church, the Communion of Saints: The Forgiveness of sins: The Resurrection of the body: And the Life everlasting. Amen.

The Lord's Prayer.

OUR FATHER, Which art in Heaven, Hallowed be Thy Name: Thy Kingdom come: Thy Will be done in earth, as it is in Heaven: Give us this day our daily Bread: And forgive us our trespasses, as we forgive them that trespass against us: And lead us not into temptation: But deliver us from evil. Amen.

The Gloria Patri.

GLORY be to the FATHER, and to the SON, and to the HOLY GHOST:

As it was in the beginning, is now, and ever shall be, world without end. Amen.

The Ten Commandments.

I. God spake these Words and said; I am the LORD

thy GOD: Thou shalt have none other gods but Me.

II. Thou shalt not make to thyself any graven image, nor the likeness of any thing that is in Heaven above, or in the earth beneath, or in the water under the earth. Thou shalt not bow down to them, nor worship them: for I the LORD thy GOD am a Jealous GOD, and visit the sins of the fathers upon the children, unto the third and fourth generation of them that hate Me, and shew mercy unto thousands in them that love Me, and keep My Commandments.

III. Thou shalt not take the Name of the LORD thy GOD in vain: for the LORD will not hold him guiltless that taketh His Name in vain.

IV. Remember that thou keep holy the Sabbath-day. Six days shalt thou labour, and do all that thou hast to do; but the seventh day is the Sabbath of the LORD thy GOD. In it thou shalt do no manner of work, thou, and thy son, and thy daughter, thy man-servant, and thy maid-servant, thy cattle, and the stranger that is within thy gates. For in six days the LORD made Heaven and earth, the sea, and all that in them is, and rested the seventh day; wherefore the LORD blessed the seventh day, and hallowed it.

V. Honour thy father and thy mother, that thy days may be long in the land which the LORD thy GOD giveth thee.

VI. Thou shalt do no murder.

VII. Thou shalt not commit adultery.

VIII. Thou shalt not steal.

IX. Thou shalt not bear false witness against thy neighbour.

X. Thou shalt not covet thy neighbour's house, thou shalt not covet thy neighbour's wife, nor his servant, nor his maid, nor his ox, nor his ass, nor any thing that is his.

The Precepts of the Church.

1. To observe the Festivals and Holy-days appointed.
2. To keep the Fasting-days with devotion and abstinence.
3. To observe the Ecclesiastical Customs and Ceremonies established, and that without frowardness or contradiction.
4. To repair unto the public Service of the Church for

Matins and Evensong, with other holy Offices at times appointed, unless there be a just and unfeigned cause to the contrary.

5. To receive the Blessed Sacrament of the Body and Blood of CHRIST with frequent devotion, and three times a year at least, of which times Easter to be always one. And for better preparation thereunto, as occasion is, to disburden and quiet our consciences of those sins that may grieve us, or scruples that may trouble us, to a learned and discreet Priest, and from him to receive advice, and the benefit of absolution. (*Bp. Cosin.*)

The Two Sacraments generally necessary to Salvation.

1. Baptism.
2. The Holy Eucharist.

The Other Five ordained for certain Persons or States of Life.

1. Confirmation.
2. Penitence.
3. Orders.
4. Matrimony.
5. Visitation of the Sick or Extreme Unction.
(*Bp. Cosin.*)

The Three Theological Virtues.

1. Faith.
2. Hope.
3. Charity.

The Four Cardinal Virtues.

1. Justice.
2. Prudence.
3. Temperance.
4. Fortitude.

The Seven Gifts of the Holy Ghost.

1. Wisdom.
2. Understanding.
3. Counsel.
4. Ghostly strength.
5. Knowledge.
6. True Godliness.
7. Holy Fear.

The Twelve Fruits of the Holy Ghost.

1. Love.
2. Joy.
3. Peace.
4. Long-suffering.
5. Gentleness.
6. Goodness.
7. Faith.
8. Meekness.
9. Patience.
10. Modesty.
11. Temperance.
12. Chastity.

The Seven Spiritual Works of Mercy.

1. To instruct the ignorant.
2. To correct offenders.
3. To counsel the doubtful.
4. To comfort the afflicted.
5. To suffer injuries with patience.
6. To forgive offences and wrongs.
7. To pray for others.

The Seven Corporal Works of Mercy.

1. To feed the hungry, and give drink to the thirsty.
2. To clothe the naked.
3. To harbour the stranger and needy.
4. To visit the sick.
5. To minister unto prisoners and captives.
6. To visit the fatherless and widows.
7. To bury the dead.

The Eight Beatitudes.

1. Blessed are the poor in spirit: for theirs is the Kingdom of Heaven.
2. Blessed are they that mourn: for they shall be comforted.
3. Blessed are the meek: for they shall inherit the earth.
4. Blessed are they which do hunger and thirst after righteousness: for they shall be filled.
5. Blessed are the merciful: for they shall obtain mercy.
6. Blessed are the pure in heart: for they shall see GOD.
7. Blessed are the peacemakers: for they shall be called the Children of GOD.
8. Blessed are they which are persecuted for righteousness' sake: for theirs is the Kingdom of Heaven.

The Seven Capital or Deadly Sins, and the Contrary Virtues.

Sins	Contrary Virtues
1. Pride	1. Humility
2. Covetousness	2. Liberality
3. Lust	3. Chastity
4. Envy	4. ~~Gentleness~~
5. Gluttony	5. Temperance
6. Anger	6. Patience
7. Sloth	7. Diligence

Nine Ways of Participating in another's Sin.

1. By counsel.
2. By command.
3. By consent.

4. By provocation.
5. By praise or flattery.
6. By concealment.
7. By partaking.
8. By silence.
9. By defence of the ill done.

Six Sins against the Holy Ghost.

1. Presuming on GOD's mercy.
2. Despair.
3. Impugning a known truth.
4. Envy at another's good.
5. Obstinacy in sin.
6. Final impenitence.

Three Notable Duties.

1. Prayer.
2. Fasting.
3. Almsgiving.

The Three Parts of True Repentance.

1. Contrition.
2. Confession.
3. Satisfaction.

The Penitential Psalms.

Pss. vi., xxxii., xxxviii., li., cii., cxxx., cxliii.

The Gradual Psalms.

Pss. cxx. to cxxxiv.

The Evangelical Counsels.

1. Voluntary Poverty.
2. Perpetual Chastity, *i.e.*, Perpetual Virginity or Widowhood.
3. Holy Obedience.

The Seven Words on the Cross.

JESUS said :

1. FATHER, forgive them; for they know not what they do.
2. Verily I say unto thee, To-day shalt thou be with me in Paradise.
3. Woman, behold thy SON! Behold thy Mother!
4. My GOD, my GOD, why hast Thou forsaken me?
5. I thirst.
6. It is finished.
7. FATHER, into Thy hands I commend my spirit.

The Four Last Things.

1. Death.
2. Judgment.
3. Heaven.
4. Hell.

Subjects for Daily Meditation and Prayer.

Remember, Christian Soul, that thou hast this day, and every day of thy life,

> God to glorify.
> Jesus to imitate.
> A soul to save.
> A body to mortify.
> Sins to repent of.
> Virtues to acquire.
> Hell to avoid.
> Heaven to gain.
> Eternity to prepare for.
> Time to profit by.
> Neighbours to edify.
> The world to despise.
> Devils to combat.
> Passions to subdue.
> Death, perhaps, to suffer.
> Judgment to undergo.

Anima Christi.

SOUL of CHRIST, sanctify me!
Body of CHRIST, save me!
Blood of CHRIST, inebriate me!
Water from the Side of CHRIST, wash me!
Passion of CHRIST, strengthen me!
O Good JESU, hear me!
Within Thy Wounds hide me!
Suffer me not to be separated from Thee!
From the malicious enemy defend me!
In the hour of my death, call me,
And bid me come to Thee;
That with Thy Saints I may praise Thee
For ever and ever. Amen.

Daily Devotions

MORNING PRAYER

As soon as you are awake, make the Sign of the Cross, and say:

Glory be to the FATHER, Who hath created me.
Glory be to the SON, Who hath redeemed me.
Glory be to the HOLY GHOST, Who sanctifieth me.

Blessed be the Holy and Undivided TRINITY, now and for evermore, Who hath preserved me during the night past, and saved me from the sleep of death.

On rising from your bed, say:

IN Thy Name, O LORD JESUS CHRIST, do I rise from sleep: do Thou bless, guide, and guard me, and lead me to everlasting life. Amen.

While you are dressing, be on your guard against admitting worldly thoughts into your mind; fix your thoughts on some point in the Life or Passion of our Blessed Lord, on the particular subject fixed for your morning's meditation, on God's mercies to you, on some daily duty, or probable temptation, on the shortness of life, on eternity, or say a Psalm or a Hymn.

As soon as you are dressed, calling to mind the greatness of God and your own nothingness, place yourself in His presence, and kneel down and say:

IN the Name ✠ of the FATHER, and of the SON, and of the HOLY GHOST. Amen.

Blessed be the Holy and Undivided TRINITY, now and for evermore. Amen.

Come, HOLY GHOST, and fill the hearts of Thy faithful people, and kindle in them the fire of Thy love.

Send forth Thy SPIRIT, and they shall be made, and Thou shalt renew the face of the earth.

The Lord's Prayer.

OUR FATHER.

The Angelic Salutation, or Memorial of the Incarnation.

THE Angel said unto Mary, Hail, thou that art highly favoured. The LORD is with thee. Blessed art thou among women. Amen.

The Apostles' Creed.

I BELIEVE in GOD.

Confession.

I CONFESS to Thee, O LORD JESU CHRIST, all my sins that I have committed from my childhood even unto this hour, whether knowingly or ignorantly, by day or by night, either sleeping or waking, in word or in deed, in thought or in neglect, through the assaults of the devil, or the frailty of my flesh, against Thy divine will; beseeching Thee that Thy wrath may not come upon me, but that Thy grace may visit me now and for ever. Amen.

May the Almighty and most merciful LORD grant to me ✠ pardon, absolution, and remission of all my sins. Amen.

Act of Thanksgiving.

O ETERNAL GOD, I praise Thee, and I thank Thee from my inmost heart, because Thou hast created me after Thine own Image; and hast redeemed me with the precious Blood of Thy dear SON; and in addition to other countless blessings, hast so mercifully preserved me, bringing me safely to the beginning of another day, and keeping me from evils and dangers during the past night. What return, O LORD, shall I make to Thee, for these and all the other manifold mercies which Thou hast bestowed upon me?

Act of Self-Dedication.

BEHOLD, O LORD, I cheerfully give up all to Thee, from Whom alone cometh all that I have. I truly and entirely dedicate, to the greater glory of Thy Name, my body and soul, with all their powers and faculties, and all the thoughts, words, and actions of this day, that in them all Thy blessed Name may be for ever praised and glorified: and this I do in union with all the works which, in the most perfect love, our SAVIOUR wrought on earth for our salvation; so that out of the abundant merits of Thine Only-Begotten SON, in Whom Thou art ever well-pleased, my offerings may be accepted, my weakness strengthened, and my defects supplied.

Renew your sorrow for the sins of your past life; form good resolutions to avoid sin, resist temptation throughout the day, and to do your duty towards God and towards Man.

Act of Contrition, with good Resolutions.

O GOD of infinite mercy, I grieve for love of Thee that I have ever offended Thee. I love Thee with my whole heart. I beseech Thee to give me the continual increase of Thy love, by preventing and directing all my thoughts, words, and actions to Thy glory. O most Mighty GOD, Who knowest that by the light of Thy grace I am taught and bound to do good works, to follow after virtue, and to flee from sin, help me in this my resolve, for I entirely distrust myself, and lean wholly upon Thy heavenly grace. I do purpose never more to commit sin, but to avoid all occasions of evil, and whatsoever displeases Thee; for what Thou willest I will, and what Thou hatest I hate; and do Thou, O LORD, grant that I may abide steadfast in this purpose, and by Thy continual aid be fully master of all the desires and motions of my heart.

Petition for Divine Grace.

O LORD, Thou knowest my frailty, that I am poor and miserable, and that without Thee I can neither do nor think anything that is good, but that all my sufficiency is of Thee. Arise Thou, therefore, and help me, and by Thy effectual grace give me strength, that the good I will, I may be able to bring to good effect, and that the evil I would not I may overcome and avoid; that by Thy guidance I may so pass this day, that together with all Thine Elect, whether living or departed, I may live with Thee, and rejoice in Thee, and praise Thee throughout eternity. Amen.

℣ O LORD, hear my prayer,

℟ And let my crying come unto Thee.

℣ Have mercy upon me, O LORD, for I am weak.

℟ O LORD, heal me, for my bones are vexed.

℣ Vouchsafe, O LORD,

℟ To keep me this day without sin.

℣ Our help is in the Name of the LORD.

℟ Who hath made Heaven and earth.

Intercession.

ALMIGHTY and Everlasting GOD, Who hast promised to hear the petitions of those who ask in Thy SON's Name, I commend unto Thee my Parents, my Brothers, and Sisters, my Wife (or Husband), my Children and Godchildren, and all my Relations, Friends, Dependants, and those for whom I have been asked to pray. Let Thy Fatherly hand, I beseech Thee, ever be over them, let Thy HOLY SPIRIT ever be with them, and so lead them in the knowledge and obedience of Thy word, that in the end they may obtain everlasting life. Pity, O LORD, and have mercy upon all men, for JESUS CHRIST's sake, Who with Thee and the HOLY GHOST, liveth and reigneth, ever One GOD, world without end. Amen.

May the intercessions of the holy Mother of GOD, of the Prophets, of the holy Apostles, of the Martyrs, help me! May all the Saints and Elect of GOD pray for me, that I may be worthy with them to possess the Kingdom of God. Amen.

May the holy Angels, especially my own Guardian, keep watch around me throughout this day, to protect me against the assaults of the evil one, to suggest to me holy thoughts, to defend me against all dangers, to lead me in the perfect way of peace, and to bring me safe, at length, to my home in Heaven.

Benediction.

✠ MAY the power of the FATHER govern and protect me! May the wisdom of the SON teach and enlighten me! May the influence of the HOLY GHOST renew and quicken me! May the blessing of the Everlasting and All-Holy TRINITY be with me, now and for evermore. Amen.

Now, or at some convenient time, occupy yourself with your morning meditation, or with reading a portion of Holy Scripture, or some spiritual book.

A SECOND FORM OF MORNING PRAYER.

As soon as you are awake, make the Sign of the Cross, and say:

Glory be to the FATHER, and to the SON, and to the HOLY GHOST, Three Persons in One GOD: Blessed for evermore: all love, all praise be to Thee.

On rising from your bed, kneel down and say:

GLORY be to Thee, O LORD, all glory be to Thee, for the sleep which Thou hast graciously given me this night: a seasonable recruit to the wastings, and a kind intermission to the labours of this poor, weak, and wearied body.

While dressing, think of what occasions you may meet with during the day,—Of serving God and doing good—Of offending God and doing evil; and form good resolutions. Think too of the glorious qualities of the bodies of those who shall rise to a joyful resurrection, and the misery and shame and horror of those who shall rise to the resurrection of damnation.

When dressed, kneel down and say:

IN the Name ✠ of the FATHER, and of the SON, and of the HOLY GHOST. Amen.

Come, HOLY GHOST, and fill the hearts of Thy faithful people, and kindle in them the fire of Thy love.

Send forth Thy SPIRIT, and they shall be made, and Thou shalt renew the face of the earth.

GOD, Who didst teach the hearts of Thy faithful people by the sending to them the light of Thy HOLY SPIRIT: grant us by the same SPIRIT to have a right judgment in all things, and evermore to rejoice in His holy comfort, through the merits of CHRIST JESUS our Saviour, Who liveth and reigneth with Thee in the Unity of the same SPIRIT, One GOD, world without end. Amen.

The Lord's Prayer.

OUR FATHER.

The Angelic Salutation, or Memorial of the Incarnation.

THE Angel said unto Mary: Hail, thou that art highly favoured. The LORD is with thee. Blessed art thou among women. Amen.

The Apostles' Creed.

I BELIEVE in God.

Place yourself in the presence of God.

O MY GOD! I firmly believe that Thou art here present, and perfectly seest me: that Thou observest all my actions and knowest all my thoughts. I acknowledge that I am not worthy to come into Thy presence, nor to lift up mine eyes in Thy sight, because I have so often sinned against Thee. But, O LORD, of Thy mercy give me pardon for all my sins, and assist me with Thy HOLY SPIRIT that I may pray to Thee as I ought.

Then say:

BLESSED art Thou, O LORD my GOD, Who hast enlightened my eyes that I should not sleep in death, Who hast delivered me from the terror by night, and from the pestilence that walketh in darkness : For that I laid me down and slept, and rose up again, because Thou, LORD, didst make me dwell in safety.

And now that Thou hast added to the number of my days, that this and every day may be employed to the perfecting of holiness in Thy fear, and sweetened with the comforts of health, of peace, and innocence; Grant, O Good LORD.

That all the sins, offences, and neglects of my days already gone, may, by Thy mercy, be freely pardoned and entirely done away ; Grant, O Good LORD.

That it may please Thee to bless the world with prosperity and peace, but chiefly with such mercies as Thou knowest to be most expedient for the good of all our souls; Grant, O Good LORD.

Whatsoever things are true, whatsoever things are honest, whatsoever things are just, whatsoever things are pure, whatsoever things are lovely, whatsoever things are of good report, if there be any virtue, and if there be any praise that I may think on these things and may do these things; Grant, O Good LORD.

That the Angel of Peace, the holy guide of Thy children, the faithful guard set by Thee over their souls and bodies, may encamp round about me, and continually suggest to my mind such things as conduce to Thy glory, and to my salvation; Grant, O Good LORD.

That since this life must shortly have an end; that mine may be concluded with a truly Christian death, a death perfectly void of sin and shame, and, if such be Thy good pleasure, as free from pain as may be; Grant, O Good LORD.

But above all, in regard it is appointed unto all men once to die, and after that the judgment; that I may appear with comfort, and find a favourable account, at the great and terrible tribunal of Thy SON JESUS CHRIST, Who, I believe, shall come to be our Judge; Grant, O Good LORD.

Intercession.

O LORD, I commend unto Thy protection and mercy all those for whom I ought to pray (especially N.), beseeching Thee to supply all their needs, to comfort and support them in all their troubles, to deliver them in all their temptations, to guide them through this life, to be with them in the hour of death, and to bring them safely to Thy Heavenly Kingdom, through JESUS CHRIST our LORD. Amen.

O LORD JESUS, in union with Thy most perfect actions, I commend to Thee my works of this day, to be directed according to Thy will. Amen.

Benediction.

THE peace of our LORD JESUS CHRIST, and the virtue of His most sacred Passion, the Sign of the ✠ Holy Cross, and the triumphant title JESUS of Nazareth, King of the Jews; His immaculate Birth of the Blessed Virgin Mary, the guardianship of holy Angels, especially of my peculiar guardian, and the prayers of all the Elect of God, be between me and all my enemies, visible and invisible, both now and at the hour of my death. Amen.

In the Name ✠ of the FATHER, and of the SON, and of the HOLY GHOST. Amen.

A THIRD FORM OF MORNING PRAYER.

As soon as you are awake, make the Sign of the Cross, and say:

O GOD, Thou art my God, early will I seek Thee, my soul thirsteth for Thee, my flesh longeth after Thee.

On rising from your bed, say:

AWAKE, O my Soul, and give glory to GOD. I laid me down and slept, and rose up again; for the LORD sustained me. Glory be to Thee, O LORD, for watching over me this night. LORD, raise me up at the last day to life everlasting.

While washing and dressing:

MAKE me a clean heart, O GOD: wash me, and I shall be whiter than snow. Clothe me in Thy righteousness, and give me the ornament of a meek and quiet spirit.

When dressed, kneel down and say:

IN the Name ✠ of the FATHER, and of the SON, and of the HOLY GHOST. Amen.

Blessed be the Holy and Undivided TRINITY now and for evermore. Amen.

The Lord's Prayer.

OUR FATHER.

The Angelic Salutation, or Memorial of the Incarnation.

THE Angel said unto Mary: Hail, thou that art highly favoured.

~~The Lord is with thee. Blessed art thou among women. Amen.~~

The Apostles' Creed.

I BELIEVE in God.

Collects.

WE give Thee thanks, Holy Lord, Almighty Father, Eternal God, Who hast guarded us through the hours of the night, and hast vouchsafed to bring us safely to another day: grant us we pray Thee to pass this day without sin, that at eventide we may again give thanks unto Thee.

O Lord, mercifully incline Thy ears to hear our morning prayers, and of Thy loving-kindness enlighten the depths of our hearts, that no evil desires may rule those hearts which have been renewed by the light of Thy heavenly grace.

We beseech Thee, O Lord, in Thy loving-kindness, to pour Thy holy light into our souls; that we may ever be devoted to Thee, by Whose wisdom we were created, and by Whose providence we are governed. Amen.

Veni Creator.

COME, Holy Ghost, our souls inspire,
And lighten with celestial fire;
Thou the anointing Spirit art,
Who dost Thy seven-fold gifts impart:
Thy blessed Unction from above,
Is comfort, life, and fire of love;
Enable with perpetual light
The dulness of our blinded sight:
Anoint and cheer our soilèd face
With the abundance of Thy grace;
Keep far our foes, give peace at home;
Where Thou art guide, no ill can come.
Teach us to know the Father, Son,
And Thee, of Both, to be but One;
That, through the ages all along,
This may be our endless song;
   Praise to Thy eternal merit,
   Father, Son, and Holy Spirit.
              Amen.

Act of Faith.

I FIRMLY believe, O my God, that Thou art One God in Three Persons, the Father, the Son, and the Holy Ghost, and that God the Son was made Man and died for us. Moreover, I believe all the truths which the Church believes and teaches, because Thou hast revealed them, Who canst neither deceive nor be deceived.

Act of Hope.

O MY God, relying upon Thy infinite power and mercy, and the precious Blood of my Lord and Saviour Jesus Christ, I hope to obtain the forgiveness of my sins and everlasting life: and I hereby resolve, by Thy grace, to perform all that Thou hast revealed to me of Thy holy will.

Act of Love.

O MY God, because Thou art of infinite goodness, and most worthy of all love, I love Thee with my whole heart, and above all things: and for Thy sake I love my neighbour as myself.

Act of Contrition.

O MY God, I repent from my heart of all the sins which, from my youth up, I have committed against Thee: since Thou art infinitely Holy, and utterly abhorrest all sin, I resolve, O my Lord and Saviour, by Thy help, never more to offend Thee wilfully: do Thou wash away my past sins in Thy precious Blood, and have mercy upon me now and at the hour of my death. Amen.

Benediction.

✠ MAY God Almighty bless me, and of His mercy vouchsafe to defend me from all wickedness, and may His presence and His love sustain and direct me throughout this day. Amen.

EVENING PRAYER.

IN the Name ✠ of the FATHER, and of the SON, and of the HOLY GHOST. Amen.

Blessed be the Holy and Undivided TRINITY, now and for evermore. Amen.

Come, HOLY GHOST, and fill the hearts of Thy faithful people, and kindle in them the fire of Thy love.

Send forth Thy SPIRIT, and they shall be made, and Thou shalt renew the face of the earth.

The Lord's Prayer.

OUR FATHER.

The Angelic Salutation, or Memorial of the Incarnation.

THE Angel said unto Mary, Hail, thou that art highly favoured. The LORD is with thee. Blessed art thou among women. Amen.

The Apostles' Creed.

I BELIEVE in GOD.

Thanksgiving.

O INFINITE Goodness! I thank Thee from my inmost heart for all Thy blessings, which this day, and through my whole life, Thou hast so bountifully bestowed upon me, who am so utterly unworthy of them. Praise and glory be to Thee, from me and from Thine Elect in Heaven and in earth, and from all Thy creatures for ever and ever.

Prayer for Light.

O ETERNAL Wisdom! in many things, alas! we all offend; but who can understand his errors? Do Thou, O true Light, enlighten my darkness, that I may see and know what is wanting in me. Thou knowest all the secrets of my heart, and markest all my steps. Grant, therefore, that in bitterness of my soul, I may fully recall before Thee all wherein I have this day offended against Thee, in thought, word, or deed.

Here examine your conscience; consider well where you have been; with whom you have had anything to do; what you have thought, said, or done during the day. Examine yourself with respect to your station, office, or calling. Consider what progress you have made in the practice of the grace you most need, and in rooting out the fault that most besets you: put to yourself such questions as these:

DID I say my prayers this morning reverently and carefully?

Have I wasted my time?

Have I injured the character of any one?

Have I led any one to commit sin?

Have I been angry or impatient with any one?

Have I earnestly put away any evil, bitter, or impure thoughts that may have occurred?

Have I done to-day, or have I not done, what I determined yesterday to do or not to do?

When you have finished your self-examination and confession, say:

Prayer for Pardon.

O FATHER of Mercies! Who hast no pleasure in the death of a sinner, look upon me in the multitude of Thy mercies. I cast all the offences of this day, and of my whole life, into the depths of Thine eternal love wherewith Thou hast loved us. I grieve from my inmost heart that I have been so ungrateful for Thy many blessings to me, and that I have so often offended Thee, my GOD, and my chief Good. I beseech Thee, by the Death and by the love of Thy SON, JESUS CHRIST, spare me, a wretched sinner, and of Thine exceeding mercy, forgive me all that I have this day, or ever committed, either against Thee, my neighbour, or myself.

Here you may say the Miserere or any other Act of Contrition.

Resolution of Amendment.

O ALMIGHTY GOD, without Whose power man is nothing, I firmly resolve, before Thee and all the Company of Heaven, to follow more closely the rule of Thy will; to amend my ways; to attend more diligently to the duties of my calling; to avoid all sin, and its occasions. This, indeed, is my will; but without Thee I am unable to perform it.

Do Thou, then, Who givest me the will, give me also the power to accomplish it. Grant what Thou commandest, and command what Thou wilt; that so I may live soberly, righteously, and godly in this present world, and in the world to come may, with all Thy Saints, praise Thee eternally. O Lord, let my desire come up before Thee as incense. Of Thine infinite mercy, despise not Thou this my evening sacrifice.

℣ Vouchsafe, O Lord.
℟ To keep us this night without sin.
℣ O Lord, have mercy upon us.
℟ Have mercy upon us.
℣ O Lord, let Thy mercy lighten upon us,
℟ As our trust is in Thee.
℣ O Lord, hear our prayer.
℟ And let our cry come unto Thee.

Intercession.

O LORD GOD, give unto us the increase of faith, hope, and charity. Root out from among us all sin and wickedness, all discord and infidelity, all errors and false opinions. Rebuke the erring, convert the unbelieving. Bring back into the unity of the Church all those that are in schism, and show unto them the light of Thy grace. Defend from all adversity, both of body and soul, the Bishops, Pastors, and Governors of Thy Church, all Emperors, Kings, Princes, and all who are in authority. Convert sinners to true repentance. Preserve the righteous in the good way. Confirm all their thoughts, words, and works. Have mercy, O Lord, upon all men, and strengthen in Thy service those who are dedicated to Thee. Provide for all those who labour with their hands; raise up those who are oppressed with grief; heal the sick; supply the wants of all who are in need; grant unto travellers a return to their home; bring to a haven of safety those in perils of the sea; give joy to those who are labouring with child; and deliverance to captives. Forgive all who have sinned with me, or whom I have led into sin. Recompense one hundredfold those whom I have injured, offended, or deceived. Direct in the way of life all united to me by kindred or friendship, my Parents, Brothers, and Sisters, all whose labour or help I make use of; all who pray for me, or desire my prayers, and all who think kindly of me. Hear them in whatsoever trouble they call upon Thee. Vouchsafe both to our enemies and to ourselves constant charity. May we all have patience, kindness, and pity; and may envy, wrath, and bitterness be far from us. O most Merciful FATHER, have mercy upon the souls of all who have fallen asleep in CHRIST, especially on my Parents and Relations, and on those with whom I have been intimate, or whose possessions I have inherited; to all who have departed in Thy faith, Grant, O LORD, eternal rest, and let perpetual light shine upon them. Amen.

May the intercessions of the holy Mother of God, of the Prophets, of the holy Apostles, of the Martyrs, help me! May all the Saints and Elect of GOD pray for me, that I may be worthy with them to possess the Kingdom of GOD. Amen.

May the holy Angels, especially my own Guardian, keep watch around me throughout this night, to protect me against the assaults of the evil one, to suggest to me holy thoughts, to defend me against all dangers, to lead me in the perfect way of peace, and to bring me safe, at length, to my home in Heaven. Amen.

Benediction.

MAY GOD the FATHER bless me; JESUS CHRIST defend and keep me; the power of the HOLY GHOST enlighten me and sanctify me, this night and for ever. Amen.

Read over the matter for your morning's meditation from Holy Scripture, or a portion of some spiritual book: while undressing occupy your mind with thoughts about what you have been reading.

On composing yourself to sleep.

✠ INTO Thy hands, O LORD, I commend my spirit, for Thou hast redeemed me, O LORD, Thou GOD of Truth. I will lay me down in peace, and take my rest, for it is Thou LORD only Who makest me dwell in safety.

A SECOND FORM OF EVENING PRAYER.

IN the Name ✠ of the FATHER, and of the SON, and of the HOLY GHOST. Amen.

Abide with us, O LORD!
For it is towards evening, and the day is far spent.
May my evening prayer ascend up unto Thee, O LORD!
And Thy mercy descend upon me.
Keep me, O LORD, as the apple of an eye, hide me under the shadow of Thy wings.

The Lord's Prayer.

OUR FATHER.

The Angelic Salutation, or Memorial of the Incarnation.

THE Angel said unto Mary: Hail, thou that art highly favoured. The LORD is with thee. Blessed art thou among women. Amen.

The Apostles' Creed.

I BELIEVE in GOD.

Thanksgiving.

I GIVE Thee thanks, O HOLY FATHER Almighty! Eternal GOD! Who not for mine own merits, but of Thy most holy grace, hast vouchsafed to keep me, Thine unworthy servant, safe throughout this day. Of Thy goodness, O most Merciful GOD, I intreat Thee that I may so pass through the ensuing night with a pure heart and body, that, arising in the morning, I may be enabled to offer Thee a grateful and obedient service, through CHRIST our LORD Amen.

Prayer for Light.

COME HOLY GHOST, and send forth from Heaven the rays of Thy light: enlighten the darkness of my mind, that I may see and know the sins which I have this day committed in thought, word, or deed, and whatsoever good I have left undone; and give me the grace of true contrition, that I may acknowledge them and hate them, as I ought. Amen.

Examine yourself by the following questions in order to discover how you have sinned during the day in thought, word or deed.

1. At what time did I get up this morning? Was I sluggish in doing so? Did I think of GOD the first thing? Did I say my prayers fully, reverently, and with devotion?

2. How did I employ myself until breakfast time?

3. What did I do between breakfast and dinner? Whom did I see? Whom did I talk with? What did I talk about? Did I do my work diligently, honestly, and good-temperedly?

4. What did I do at or after dinner?

5. Have I during the day been guilty of gluttony, envy, pride, jealousy? Have I used any bad words? Have I judged my neighbour? Have I had unkind feelings towards any one? Have I had impure thoughts? Have I lost my temper, and been put out by little cross accidents? Have I thought of GOD; how often during the day, and lifted up my heart to Him?

Confession.

I CONFESS to Thee, O LORD GOD! Almighty Creator of Heaven and earth! all my sins which I have ever committed from my childhood, even to this hour, whether knowingly or ignorantly, and especially what I have done this day (. . .) in thought, word, or deed, against Thy Divine Majesty. To Thee, O LORD! I confess from my heart; and I intreat of Thee forgiveness; most humbly I beseech Thee to pardon all mine offences whatsoever Thou knowest me to have been guilty of. Kindle within me the flame of Thy love, and inspire me with fear, and grant me a real amendment of my whole life, with true faith, hope, and love. Amen.

Prayer for Pardon.

O GOD of Mercy and of Pity, of Thy goodness pardon and have compassion upon me Thy servant; vouchsafe graciously to receive my supplications: of Thy great kindness and long suffering forgive me all the sins into which I have fallen this day; grant me space for repentance, so that I may receive at Thy hand remission of all my sins, through JESUS CHRIST our LORD. Amen.

Intercession.

REMEMBER, Gracious GOD, for good my dear Parents, Brothers, Sisters, Husband [Wife], Children, God-children. Bless all my Relations, Benefactors, and Friends (especially N.). Hear me, Good LORD, who commend unto Thy tender mercy all that labour under trials and afflictions. Have mercy upon this household; and grant that humility and meekness, peace and charity, chastity and purity, may rule therein. Grant that we may so correct and amend ourselves, that we may love, and fear, and serve Thee faithfully all our days; through our LORD and SAVIOUR JESUS CHRIST. Amen.

O Eternal FATHER, I beseech Thee, of Thy boundless mercy, and by the Life and Passion of Thy dear SON, enable me to persevere unto the end, and to die in Thy grace.

O Blessed JESUS, by the love of Thy Eternal FATHER, and by Thy last words upon the Cross, whereby Thou didst commend Thy Spirit into His hands, I pray Thee to receive my soul at my last hour.

O Holy SPIRIT, true GOD, have mercy upon me; and guard me with Thy holy inspirations now and in the hour of my death.

O most Holy TRINITY, One GOD, have mercy upon me, now and in the hour of death, and in the Day of Judgment. Amen.

May the Souls of the Faithful, through the mercy of GOD, rest in peace. Amen.

On going into bed.

☩ IN the Name of our LORD JESUS CHRIST crucified, I lay me down to rest; may He bless, save, and defend me, and bring me to everlasting life. Amen.

On composing yourself to sleep, say,

HOLY, Holy, Holy, LORD GOD of Hosts: Heaven and earth are full of Thy glory. Glory be to Thee, O LORD most High. Amen.

A THIRD FORM OF EVENING PRAYER.

IN the Name ✠ of the FATHER, and of the SON, and of the HOLY GHOST. Amen.

Blessed be the Holy and Undivided TRINITY, now and for evermore. Amen.

OUR FATHER.

Give Thanks.

BLESSED be Thou, O GOD of Infinite Goodness! for all Thy mercies which Thou hast bestowed upon me this day, and through my whole life. Praise and glory be to Thee for ever and ever.

Pray for Light.

O GOD of Infinite Majesty! Grant that I may now recall whereinsoever I have offended Thee this day.

Here examine your conscience on

What you have been, and How you have failed,
{
1. At your prayers and at Church,
2. In your business,
3. In your conversation,
4. At your meals,
}
This day.

Confess one by one the sins that you have committed during the day.

Pray for Pardon.

O GOD of Infinite Mercy! pardon all my past sins; behold I cast all my offences of this day and of my whole life into the abyss of Thy love, and I beseech Thee, O my GOD, by the Death of Thy dear SON, do Thou forgive me wheresoever I have sinned against Thee in thought, word, or deed.

Resolve to Amend.

O Eternal Wisdom! I do most firmly purpose, by Thy grace, not to offend Thee any more.

Pray for Others.

O LORD, I commend unto Thy protection and mercy all those for whom I ought to pray (especially N.), beseeching Thee to supply all their needs, to comfort and support them in all their troubles, to deliver them from all temptations, and to bring them to everlasting life, through JESUS CHRIST our LORD. Amen.

Pray for a Happy Death.

O LORD JESU CHRIST, through that Agony which Thou sufferedst when Thou didst give up the ghost upon the Cross, have mercy on my sinful soul when it shall depart from the body. Amen.

Collect.

VISIT, we beseech Thee, O LORD, this habitation, and drive far from it all snares of the enemy. Let Thy holy Angels dwell herein, to preserve us in peace, and let Thy blessing be upon us evermore, through CHRIST our LORD. Amen.

Benediction.

✠ MAY the LORD bless me, and defend me from all evil, and bring me to everlasting life; and of His boundless mercy grant unto me, and all His faithful servants, eternal rest and peace. Amen.

On lying down to sleep.

SAVE us, O LORD, while waking, and defend us while sleeping; that, when we are awake, we may watch with CHRIST, and when we sleep, we may rest in peace.

Ejaculations

When Lying Sleepless.

WITH my soul have I desired Thee in the night: yea, with my spirit within me will I seek Thee early.

I come to Thee, my GOD, for quiet and repose, and new supplies of strength to drooping nature, wearied with the labours and cares of the past day.

Take me under the covering of Thy wings, and let Thy loving-kindness and Thy truth always preserve me.

Preserve my lying down and my rising up, from this time forth for evermore.

When Lying Awake in Pain.

O LORD, by Thy Cross and Passion strengthen me: LORD, let this cup pass from me; nevertheless, not my will, but Thine be done.

At Midnight.

O THOU, Who didst at midnight raise the Prophet David, and Paul and Silas, to sing praises to Thee because of Thy righteous judgments: make me to think upon Thee with gladness in my bed, whose presence makes our darkness to be light, and save me.

At Sun-Rising.

O THOU, Who very early in the morning, about the rising of the sun, wast pleased to leave Thy empty tomb, and return again from the dead; raise me, I pray Thee, to walk in newness of life, by such daily exercise of repentance and virtue, as may keep me dead unto sin, but alive unto GOD, through Thee, and save me.

On Entering Church.

I WILL come into Thine House, even upon the multitude of Thy mercy, and in Thy fear will I worship toward Thy holy Temple.

My soul hath a desire and longing to enter into the Courts of the LORD.

Blessed are they that dwell in Thy House; they will be alway praising Thee.

Hear the voice of my prayer, O LORD, when I cry unto Thee, when I lift up my hands towards the mercy-seat of Thy holy Temple.

At Going forth from your House.

THE LORD preserve my going out and my coming in: from this time forth for evermore.

O give Thine Angels charge over me, to keep me in all my ways.

Order my steps according to Thy Word, so shall no wickedness have dominion over me.

At Hearing the Clock strike.

MY time is in Thy hand, O LORD.

Watch ye, therefore, for ye know not when the Master of the House cometh, at even, or at midnight, or at the cock-crowing, or in the morning.

Have mercy upon me, O LORD, now and at the hour of my death.

At Meals.

LORD, grant that whether I eat or drink, or whatsoever I do, I may do all to Thy glory.

Before Conversation.

SET a watch, O LORD, before my mouth, and keep the door of my lips.

LORD, keep my tongue from evil, and my lips that they speak no guile.

When Alone.

HELP me now, O GOD, to do all things in Thy sight, Who seest in secret.

Shut out, O GOD, from my heart everything that offends Thee.

By Thy mighty power, repress all my wandering thoughts, and tread down Satan under my feet.

In the Shop or Market.

LORD, give me grace to use this world, as not abusing it.

LORD, grant that I may never go beyond or defraud my brother in any matter, for Thou art the Avenger of all such.

At the Beginning of every Wor[k]

PROSPER Thou th[e] work of my hand[s] O LORD; O prosper Tho[u] my handywork.

Guide me with Thy counsel

To the greater glory of Th[y] Name, O GOD, I approac[h] this work, and offer it t[o] Thee in union with the infinite merits of JESUS CHRIST.

Whatsoever I do in wor[d] or deed, may I do all in th[e] Name of the LORD JESUS.

In the Midst of any Work.

LORD JESU, grant tha[t] I may accomplish thi[s] work to Thy glory, and m[y] salvation, as may be pleasing unto Thee.

Wherever I am, whateve[r] I do, Thou, LORD, seest me.

O keep me in Thy fear al[l] the day long.

On Completing any Work.

O JESU, I commend unto Thee this work o[f] mine to be perfected and finished by Thee, and I offe[r] it unto Thee in union with Thine own works.

When Tempted.

HOW can I do this great wickedness and sin against GOD.

Lord, help me with Thy grace, that I may overcome this temptation.

Oh! help me now in the fiery trial.

O God, make speed to save me. O Lord, make haste to help me.

I believe in ✠ Jesus Christ; leave me not to myself, O Lord.

O Christ, save me: bid the tempter depart from me.

Help me to persevere in this and every trial.

Gladden me with the joy of Thy countenance.

I can do all things through Christ, Who strengtheneth me.

When Tempted to Impurity.

SPIRIT of evil: In the Name of ✠ Jesus Christ of Nazareth, I bid thee depart.

O Blessed Spirit of purity, quench in me this evil thought.

For Custody of the Eyes.

TURN away mine eyes, lest they behold vanity, and quicken Thou me in Thy way.

Mine eyes shall be ever looking unto the Lord: for He shall pluck my feet out of the net.

After Falling into Sin.

O GOD, against Thee only have I sinned, and done this evil in Thy sight.

I acknowledge my transgression: and am sorry for my sin.

Turn Thy face from my sins: and put out all my misdeeds.

Lord, be merciful to me, for the merits of Thy Son Jesus Christ: lay not this sin to my charge.

To Cultivate a Sense of God's Presence.

THOU God seest me.
I am Thine, O save me.

Wherever I am, whatever I do, Thou Lord seest me: O keep me in Thy fear all the day long.

When in Spiritual Deadness.

WHY art Thou so full of heaviness, O my Soul, and why art Thou so disquieted within me?

Put thy trust in God: for I will yet give Him thanks for the help of His countenance.

My soul cleaveth unto the dust. O quicken Thou me in Thy way.

O show me the light of Thy

Countenance, and I shall be whole.

When in Sorrow.

IT is the LORD, let Him do what seemeth Him good.
Not my will, but Thine be done.
He hath done all things well.
LORD, what wilt Thou have me to do?

When the Temper is Disturbed.

BLESSED JESU, Who didst bear to be smitten on the cheek, and to be reviled, give me grace to be like unto Thee, and to be patient under this trial.
Learn of Me, for I am meek and lowly in heart, and ye shall find rest unto your souls.
O LORD, make me to rest in meekness and lowliness of mind.

After Doing any Good.

NOT unto me, O LORD, not unto me, but unto Thy Name give the praise.

Short Thanksgivings.

GLORY be to Thee, O LORD, for Thy mercy.
Praise the LORD, O my Soul, and all that is within me praise His holy Name.
What reward shall I give unto the LORD: for all the benefits that He hath done unto me.
I will thank Thee, for Thou hast heard me: and art become my salvation.

A Prayer.

Be, LORD,

within	}	to strengthen me.
without		to guard me.
over		to shelter me.
beneath	} me {	to stablish me.
before		to guide me.
after		to forward me
round about	}	to secure me.

Acts of Faith, Hope, and Love

Acts of Faith.

I BELIEVE in Thee, O LORD, that Thou art Almighty, infinitely Wise, and supremely Good; True and Faithful to Thy promises, yea, Truth itself.
LORD increase my faith, help Thou mine unbelief.

O Truth, O Goodness! Who both here and everywhere art most present with me; I believe in Thee.

Thou art All-Mighty, All-Wise, All-Good, shall I not believe Thee?

Henceforth, even for ever, I will believe in Thee, and love Thee in deed and in truth.

I believe in Thee, Almighty, Eternal GOD, my FATHER, my Redeemer, my Sanctifier! Thou hast made me in Thine own Image. Thou hast redeemed me with Thy precious Blood. Thou sanctifiest me with Thy ever-renewing Presence.

Acts of Hope.

I HOPE to see the goodness of the LORD in the land of the living, O Thou, Who hast of Thine infinite Love, made me an heir of Thy Kingdom, even a joint-heir with CHRIST.

I, dust and ashes, flee unto Thee, O GOD, that by Thee, and through patience and comfort of Thy Scriptures, I may have hope.

O Goodness and Truth, Thou Who hast prevented me with so many blessings, Who hast so often commanded me to ask and promised to give, surely Thou wilt give me that which I shall ask, that I may hope in Thee with my whole heart.

Though the hosts of this world rise against me, O my Hope, my Life, yet will I hope in Thee.

Whither shall I go from Thee, O Good JESU? Art not Thou my Life? Hast not Thou the words of eternal Life?

I hope in Thy faithfulness, Thy pity, Thy love, yea, LORD, I have a good hope, because of Thy word.

My heart is fixed, O GOD, my heart is fixed. I will hope in the LORD, I will abide patiently in Him.

O my Soul, wait Thou still upon GOD, for my hope is in Him: in GOD is my health and my glory, the rock of my might, and in GOD is my trust.

Acts of Love.

O MOST Loving FATHER, inflame my heart with love of Thee, that I may do Thy will and obey Thy commandments.

O Eternal FATHER, for the love of JESUS give me Thy love.

O Eternal FATHER, Who hast so loved the world as to give Thine Only Begotten SON to die for us, I will love Thee, O GOD, my Strength.

O JESU, grant me to love Thee, not in word and in tongue, but in deed and in truth; give Thyself to me, Who art my Hope, my Refuge, and my Salvation.

O LORD, who am I, that Thou hast so loved me, and sought to be loved by me? Unite Thyself to me, LORD: let not the loathesomeness of my sins drive Thee from me.

O GOD, whom would I love, if I love not Thee, my Life, my Love, my All.

I love Thee, and will never cease to love Thee.

Chasten me as Thou wilt, but take not from me the power to love Thee.

O my JESUS! Whoso loves Thee not, knows Thee not.

Who shall separate me from the love of CHRIST?

My JESUS! despised for me, make me to be despised for Thee.

O Love, my GOD, I believe in Thee, I hope in Thee, and with my whole heart I love Thee, and my neighbour for Thy sake.

Occasional Prayers

Prayers before Service.

O LORD, open Thou our lips, that we may bless Thy holy Name; cleanse also our hearts from all vain, evil, and wandering thoughts; enlighten our understandings, enkindle our affections, that we may worthily and devoutly offer up our prayers and praises to Thee, and so be meet to be heard in the presence of Thy Divine Majesty, through JESUS CHRIST our LORD. Amen.

O LORD JESU CHRIST, in union with the divine intention with which Thou didst perform all Thine actions in this world, I offer up these prayers and praises to Thee, Who livest and reignest with the FATHER, and the HOLY GHOST, One GOD, world without end. Amen.

Prayers after Service.

ALMIGHTY FATHER, mercifully accept these our unworthy prayers, which we have offered unto Thy Divine Majesty; look not, we pray Thee, on our faltering lips, but heal our infirmities, and receive our prayers, for Thine own mercies' sake, in CHRIST JESUS our LORD, Who liveth and reigneth with Thee, and the HOLY GHOST, One GOD, world without end. Amen.

Accept, most Merciful GOD, through the merits of Thine Only-Begotten Son JESUS CHRIST, this my duty and service. Whatsoever has been offered aright, graciously regard; wherein I have been negligent, mercifully pardon. Who in the perfect Trinity, livest and reignest, One GOD for ever and ever. Amen.

Grace before Meals.

BLESS us, O LORD, and these Thy gifts, of which through Thy bounty we partake: through JESUS CHRIST our LORD. Amen.

Grace after Meals.

WE give Thee thanks, Almighty GOD, for these and all Thy mercies, Who livest and reignest, world without end. Amen.

Before Commencing a Work.

O GOD, Who knowest that we are not sufficient of ourselves to think anything as of ourselves, but that all our sufficiency is of Thee, assist us with Thy grace in this work which we are about to undertake, direct us in it by Thy wisdom, support us by Thy power, that, doing our duty diligently, we may bring it to a good end, so that it may be profitable to our souls, and tend to the greater glory of Thy Name; through JESUS CHRIST our LORD. Amen.

Before a Journey.

O GOD, Who didst cause the Children of Israel to pass with dry feet through the midst of the sea, and Who, by the guidance of a star, didst show to the three Wise Men the way that led to Thyself: grant to us, we beseech Thee, a prosperous journey and a peaceful time; that, accompanied by Thy holy Angels, we may arrive safely at the place whither we are going, and finally, through Thy mercy, enter the haven of eternal rest. Amen.

For the Choice of a Vocation.

O JESUS, Eternal Wisdom, and most Mighty Counsellor, grant me the light of Thy HOLY SPIRIT, that I may know what Thou wouldest have me do; I offer myself entirely to Thee, do with me what seemeth good in Thy sight: not my will but Thine be done. Correct whatsoever Thou seest amiss in me, strengthen my weak resolutions, restrain my wayward desires: remove all hindrances to the fulfilment of Thy will, and give me grace so to follow the leadings of Thy Providence, that my life may be spent to Thy honour and glory, in whatsoever way it pleases Thee; Who livest and reignest God for ever and ever. Amen.

✠ *Before Study.*

O GOD, Who art the Fountain of Light, and Author of all knowledge, vouchsafe, we beseech Thee, to enlighten our understandings, and to remove from us all darkness of sin and ignorance. Give us diligence in studying, quickness of apprehension, the power to retain what we hear or learn, that what we acquire by Thy help, we may apply to Thy honour and the eternal salvation of our souls; through JESUS CHRIST our LORD. Amen.

✠ *Before Teaching.*

O INEFFABLE Creator, my LORD, and my GOD, Who art the true Fountain and one essential Principle of light and wisdom, deign to shed the brightness of Thy light on the darkness of my understanding. O Thou, Who madest eloquent the tongues of the speechless, instruct my tongue and pour forth on my lips the grace of Thy blessing. Grant to me readiness and acuteness in understanding what I am about to teach, and power, clearness, and ease in expressing it. Give me, I pray Thee, the help of Thy grace, that I may please Thee in this that I would do for Thy honour and glory; through JESUS CHRIST our LORD. Amen.

For a Happy Death.

O LORD JESU CHRIST, to Whom only we

belong in life and in death; grant that I may so live now that I may never be unprepared to die. Forsake me not, O LORD, in my last hour, and when Thou callest me, do Thou confirm my faith, deepen my repentance, and strengthen me with Thy most blessed Body and Blood. Let Thy holy Angels then be with me to shield me from temptation, to comfort me in suffering, to support me in my last agony; may they receive my soul cleansed from all offences, and place me among Thy Saints and Elect, where light abides and life reigns; world without end. Amen.

Prayer for various Graces.

O MIGHTY GOD, O GOD All-powerful, All-gracious, Whom all must believe and know Unchangeable, Incorruptible; O TRINITY in Unity, by the Catholic Church worshipped and adored, I dedicate myself unto Thee; O make me Thine, and keep me Thine for ever. Grant me, Gracious LORD, a pure intention of my heart, and a single eye to Thy glory, in all my actions; possess my soul with Thy presence, and ravish it with Thy love.

Be Thou a Light unto mine eyes, and Music to mine ears: Sweetness to my taste, and a full Contentment to my heart. Be Thou my Sunshine in the daytime, my Repose at night, a Shadow in the heat, and a Shelter from the cold, my Food in hunger, my Clothing in nakedness, and a Refuge in every time of trouble.

O LORD GOD, I give unto Thee my body, soul, and spirit, to be Thine for ever, in sickness and in health, in poverty and wealth, in fulness and in want, in life and in death. I give Thee my substance and my friends, and all that I have. Use me for Thyself, and for the glory of Thy blessed Name. Dispose of me, as seemeth good unto Thee; I am not mine own, but Thine, therefore claim me as Thy right, keep me as Thy charge, and love me as Thy child. Fight for me when I am assaulted, heal me when I am wounded, revive me when I am destroyed.

My LORD and my GOD! I beseech Thee to give me patience in adversities, humility in comforts, constancy in temptations, and victory over all my ghostly enemies.

Grant me sorrow for my sins, thankfulness for Thy benefits, fear of Thy judgments, love of Thy mercies, and mindfulness of Thy presence. Make me humble to my superiors, and friendly to my equals, charitable to my enemies, and loving to my friends, ready to please all, and loath to offend any.

Give me modesty in my countenance, gravity in my behaviour, deliberation in my speech, holiness in my thoughts, and righteousness in all my actions; let Thy mercy cleanse me from my sins, and Thy grace produce in me the fruits of everlasting life.

Give me, O LORD, an obedient spirit, and a teachable mind; let me be cheerful without lightness, sorrowful yet rejoicing, fearing Thee without doubting, and trusting Thee without presumption. Let me be joyful at nothing but that which pleaseth Thee, and sorrowful for nothing but that which doth displease Thee; let labour for Thee be my delight, and all rest be a weariness out of Thee. Give me a waking spirit, and a diligent soul, that I may seek to know Thy will, and when I know it, may perform it faithfully, to the honour and glory of Thy ever-blessed Name. Amen.

A Prayer of S. Thomas Aquinas.

GRANT me, I beseech Thee, Almighty and most Merciful GOD, fervently to desire, wisely to search out, wholly to acknowledge, and perfectly to fulfil, all that is well-pleasing unto Thee. Order Thou my worldly condition to the honour and glory of Thy Name; and of all that Thou requirest me to do, grant me the knowledge, the desire, and the ability, that I may so fulfil it as I ought, and as is expedient for the welfare of my soul.

May my path to Thee, I pray, be safe, straightforward, and perfect to the end, failing not either amid prosperity or adversity, that I may not be elated in the one, nor depressed in the other. But may I in prosperity give thanks to Thee, and in adversity preserve my patience, rejoicing in nought save what advances me towards Thee, grieving for nought save what withdraws me from Thee; neither seeking to please, nor fearing to displease, any save only Thee.

Grant me to do all I do in charity, and to regard as dead all that belongeth not to the service of Thee.

Let all that is transitory be worthless in my eyes because of Thee, and all that is Thine dear and precious, and Thou, my GOD, more than all. Let all toil that is for Thee be delightful to me, and all rest irksome that is not in Thee.

Grant me, O Sweetest LORD, frequently and with fervency to direct my heart to Thee, and sadly, with full purpose of amendment, to think over my shortcomings.

Make me, O my GOD, humble without pretence, cheerful without levity, serious without dejection, grave without moroseness, active without frivolity, truthful without duplicity, fearful of Thee without despair, trustful in Thee without presumption, chaste without depravity, able to correct my neighbour without angry feeling, and by word and example to edify him without pride, obedient without gainsaying, patient without murmuring. Give me, O Sweetest JESUS, a wakeful heart, which no curious imaginations may withdraw from Thee : give me a steadfast heart, which no unworthy affection may drag downwards : give me an unconquered heart, which no tribulation can wear out : give me a free and disengaged heart, which the violence of no absorbing fascination may enslave : give me an upright heart, which no unworthy purpose may tempt aside.

Bestow upon me, also, O LORD my GOD, understanding to know Thee, diligence to seek Thee, wisdom to find Thee, a behaviour that may please Thee, a perseverance that may happily and trustfully await Thee, and a faithfulness that may finally embrace Thee. Grant me on my pilgrimage to suffer Thy punishments with contrition, to make good use of Thy blessings through Thy grace, and at length in Heaven to be admitted to Thy joys in glory. Who livest and reignest, with the FATHER and the HOLY SPIRIT, now and ever. Amen.

Prayer for Every Need.

LORD, I believe, but would believe more firmly. I hope, O LORD, but would hope more securely. O LORD, I love, but yet would love more warmly. I grieve, O LORD, but yet would grieve more deeply.

Thee I adore, Who art my first Beginning; Thee I desire, Who art my final End. I praise Thee, Who art my continual Benefactor; I call on Thee, Who art my kind Defender.

By Thy wisdom do Thou direct me, by Thy righteousness do Thou keep me, by Thy sweet mercy comfort and protect me.

I offer unto Thee, my GOD, my thoughts, that they may be towards Thee; my words, that they may be of Thee; my deeds, that they may be according to Thee; my sufferings, that they may be for Thee.

I will whatsoever Thou willest; I will because Thou willest; I will in that manner Thou willest; I will as long as Thou willest.

I pray Thee, O LORD, that Thou wouldest give to my understanding enlightenment, to my will fervency, to my body purity, to my soul holiness.

Let pride never corrupt me, nor flattery move me: let the world never entice me, nor Satan beguile me.

Grant me grace to cleanse my memory, to check my tongue, refrain my eyes, restrain my senses.

Let me bewail my past transgressions, and for the future resist temptation: let me correct my sinful inclinations, and labour after all needful virtues.

Grant me, Good LORD, love of Thee, hatred of self, love of my neighbour, contempt of the world.

Let me study to obey my superiors, to help my inferiors, to serve my friends, to envy no man.

Let me keep in mind, O JESUS, Thy precept and example, by loving mine enemies, by patiently suffering wrong, by doing good to those that persecute me, by praying for those that falsely speak evil against me.

Let me overcome love of pleasure by self-denial, love of money by freely giving, heat of temper by gentleness, lukewarmness by earnestness.

Make me prudent in counsel, steadfast in danger, patient in adversity, humble in prosperity.

Grant me, O LORD, to be instant in prayer, temperate in meat and drink, diligent in duty, unwavering in purpose.

Let me be careful to preserve inward holiness, outward propriety, an exemplary conversation, a well-ordered life.

Let me take watchful heed to tame nature, to cherish grace, to keep Thy law, to work out my salvation.

Let me strive after holiness by sincere confession of sin, by worthy receiving of the Body and Blood of CHRIST, by continual recollection of mind and pure intention of heart.

Let me learn from Thee, O GOD, how little is all that is earthly, how great all that is Heavenly, how short all that is of time, how lasting all that is of eternity.

Grant me, O LORD, to be prepared for death, to stand in awe of judgment, to escape from hell, and to attain to Heaven; through JESUS CHRIST our LORD. Amen.

Memorials for a Week

SUNDAY.

Of the Holy Trinity.

WE praise Thee, we adore Thee, we glorify Thee, O Blessed TRINITY.

℣ Let us bless the FATHER, and the SON, and the HOLY GHOST.

℟ Let us praise and exalt Him for ever.

Almighty and Everlasting God! I, Thy suppliant, beseech Thee that Thou wouldest make me so firmly and faithfully to believe, so truthfully and simply to confess the HOLY TRINITY in this world, that in the life to come I may be enabled perfectly to know, and with all joy face to face to behold the Same, Who livest and reignest GOD, world without end. Amen.

℣ May the souls of the faithful departed, through the mercy of GOD, rest in peace. Amen.

℟ Blessed be the most sweet Name of our LORD JESUS CHRIST, and Blessed be the Ever-Virgin Mary, His Mother, and may all the Company of Heaven be blessed now and for ever and for evermore. Amen.

MONDAY.

Of the Faithful Departed.

I HEARD a voice from Heaven saying, Blessed are the dead which die in the LORD.

℣ Eternal rest grant unto them, O LORD;

℟ And let perpetual light shine upon them.

GOD Who didst form man from the dust of the earth after Thy likeness, to repair the loss of the Angels, and didst suffer death upon the Cross to restore him when fallen, have pity, I beseech Thee, upon the souls of all the faithful departed, Thy mercy rejoicing against judgment; so that the works of Thy hands become frail and prone to evil through falling from Thee, may not be condemned for their sins in the flesh, Who livest and reignest GOD, world without end. Amen.

May the souls of the faithful departed, through the mercy of GOD, rest in peace. Amen.

TUESDAY.

Of the Holy Spirit.

COME, HOLY GHOST, and fill the hearts of Thy faithful people, and kindle in them the fire of Thy love. Alleluia.

℣ Send forth Thy Spirit, and they shall be made;

℟ And Thou shalt renew the face of the earth.

Grant, we beseech Thee, Almighty GOD, that the radiance of Thy brightness may shine forth upon us, so that the beams of Thy light, through the illumination of Thy HOLY SPIRIT, may confirm our hearts and renew them, by Thy grace through CHRIST our LORD. Amen.

WEDNESDAY.

Of the Saints.

THE Saints shall be joyful in glory; they shall rejoice in their beds.

℣ Wonderful is GOD in His Saints;

℟ And glorious in His Majesty.

O LORD, we beseech Thee, mercifully regard our infirmities, and do Thou avert from us all the evils which we justly deserve, for the intercession of Thy SON, and in Him of all Thy Saints, through the Same JESUS CHRIST our LORD. Amen.

O Lord! we beseech Thee, purify our consciences by Thy Visitation; that when Jesus Christ, Thy Son our Lord shall come with all His Saints, He may find in us a mansion prepared for Himself, through the Same Jesus Christ our Lord. Amen.

Of the Angels.

ALL the heavenly citizens do praise the Son of the Supreme King, to Whom Cherubim and Seraphim continually do cry, Holy! Holy! Holy!

℣ Bless ye the Lord, all ye His Angels.

℟ Ye servants of His, that do His pleasure.

O God, Who in the beginning didst create divers orders of Blessed Spirits to know Thine everlasting Divinity, and after the fall of mankind didst wonderfully redeem mankind; grant unto us to be so fulfilled with the gifts of Thy grace by the Spirit of Thy mouth, that going on from strength to strength, we may be enabled to attain to the happy society of the choirs of Thy blessed Angels, through Christ our Lord. Amen.

THURSDAY.

Of the Blessed Sacrament.

O SACRED Feast! wherein Christ is received; the memory of His Passion is brought to our remembrance; our souls are filled with grace, and a pledge of eternal glory is given unto us. Alleluia.

℣ Thou didst give them Bread from Heaven,

℟ Having in Itself every delight.

O God, Who, in this wonderful Sacrament, hast left us a Memorial of Thy Passion; Grant us, we beseech Thee, so to venerate the Sacred Mysteries of Thy Body and Blood, that we may ever feel within ourselves the fruit of Thy Redemption, Who livest and reignest with the Father, in the Unity of the Holy Spirit, God, for ever and ever. Amen.

FRIDAY.

Of the Holy Cross.

CHRIST crucified, to the Jews a stumbling-block, and to the Greeks foolishness; but unto them which are called, both Jews and

Greeks, CHRIST the Power of GOD, and the Wisdom of GOD.

℣ We adore Thee, O CHRIST! and we bless Thee.

℟ Because by Thy Cross, and precious Blood Thou hast redeemed the world.

O LORD JESU CHRIST! SON of the Living GOD! Who for the redemption of mankind didst vouchsafe to ascend the wood of the Cross, that the whole world which lay in darkness might be enlightened; we beseech Thee, pour such light into our souls and bodies, that we may be enabled to attain to that light which is eternal, and through the merits of Thy Passion, may after death joyfully enter within the gates of Paradise, Who with the FATHER and the HOLY GHOST livest and reignest, One GOD, world without end. Amen.

SATURDAY.

Of the Incarnation.

O WONDERFUL exchange. The Creator of mankind, taking upon Him a living body, vouchsafed to be born of the Virgin Mary, and proceeding forth as Man bestowed upon us His Divinity.

℣ Beautiful is His Form before the Sons of Men.

℟ Grace is poured forth upon Thy lips.

Almighty and Everlasting GOD, Who, by the co-operation of Thy HOLY SPIRIT, didst wonderfully prepare the body and soul of the Blessed Virgin Mary to become a fit habitation for Thy SON, grant that we, who have been gladdened by His Incarnation, by His merits and intercession, may be delivered from all the evils which threaten us, and from everlasting death, Who livest and reignest, GOD, world without end. Amen.

℣ May the souls of the faithful departed, through the mercy of GOD, rest in peace.

℟ Blessed be the most sweet Name of our LORD JESUS CHRIST, and Blessed be the Ever-Virgin Mary, His Mother, and may all the Company of Heaven be blessed, now and for ever and for evermore. Amen.

Prayers for the Third, Sixth, Ninth Hours, and Compline

THE THIRD HOUR.

IN the Name ✠ of the Father, and of the Son, and of the Holy Ghost. Amen.

Our Father.

℣ O God, make speed to save us.

℟ O Lord, make haste to help us.

℣ Glory be to the Father, and to the Son : and to the Holy Ghost ;

℟ As it was in the beginning, is now, and ever shall be : world without end. Amen.

Alleluia.

From Septuagesima Sunday to Wednesday in Holy Week, inclusive, is said, instead of Alleluia:

Praise to Thee, O Lord, we sing,
Of Glory the Eternal King.

HYMN.
Nunc sancte nobis Spiritus.

COME, Holy Ghost, Who ever One
Art with the Father and the Son ;
Come, Holy Ghost, our souls possess
With Thy full flood of holiness.

In word and deed, by heart and tongue,
With all our powers, Thy praise be sung ;
May love enwrap our mortal frame,
And others catch the living flame.

Almighty Father, hear our cry
Through Jesus Christ our Lord most High,
Who, with the Holy Ghost and Thee,
Doth live and reign eternally. Amen.

Antiphon. O let Thy loving mercies.

Ps. cxix. *Legem pone.*

TEACH me, O Lord, the way of Thy statutes : and I shall keep it unto the end.

34 Give me understanding, and I shall keep Thy law : yea, I shall keep it with my whole heart.

35 Make me to go in the path of Thy commandments : for therein is my desire.

36 Incline my heart unto Thy testimonies : and not to covetousness.

37 O turn away mine eyes, lest they behold vanity : and quicken Thou me in Thy way.

38 O stablish Thy word in Thy servant : that I may fear Thee.

39 Take away the rebuke that I am afraid of : for Thy judgements are good.

40 Behold, my delight is in Thy commandments : O quicken me in Thy righteousness.

41 Let Thy loving mercy come also unto me, O LORD: even Thy salvation, according unto Thy word.

42 So shall I make answer unto my blasphemers : for my trust is in Thy word.

43 O take not the word of Thy truth utterly out of my mouth : for my hope is in Thy judgements.

44 So shall I alway keep Thy law : yea, for ever and ever.

45 And I will walk at liberty : for I seek Thy commandments.

46 I will speak of Thy testimonies also, even before kings : and will not be ashamed.

47 And my delight shall be in Thy commandments : which I have loved.

48 My hands also will I lift up unto Thy commandments, which I have loved : and my study shall be in Thy statutes.

Glory be to the FATHER.

Memor esto servi tui.

O THINK upon Thy servant, as concerning Thy word : wherein Thou hast caused me to put my trust.

50 The same is my comfort in my trouble : for Thy word hath quickened me.

51 The proud have had me exceedingly in derision : yet have I not shrinked from Thy law.

52 For I remembered Thine everlasting judgements, O LORD : and received comfort.

53 I am horribly afraid : for the ungodly that forsake Thy law.

54 Thy statutes have been my songs : in the house of my pilgrimage.

55 I have thought upon Thy Name, O Lord, in the night-season : and have kept Thy law.

56 This I had : because I kept Thy commandments.

57 Thou art my portion, O Lord : I have promised to keep Thy law.

58 I made my humble petition in Thy presence with my whole heart : O be merciful unto me, according to Thy word.

59 I called mine own ways to remembrance : and turned my feet unto Thy testimonies.

60 I made haste, and prolonged not the time : to keep Thy commandments.

61 The congregations of the ungodly have robbed me: but I have not forgotten Thy law.

62 At midnight I will rise to give thanks unto Thee : because of Thy righteous judgements.

63 I am a companion of all them that fear Thee : and keep Thy commandments.

64 The earth, O Lord, is full of Thy mercy : O teach me Thy statutes.

Glory be to the Father.

Bonitatem fecisti.

O LORD, Thou hast dealt graciously with Thy servant : according unto Thy word.

66 O learn me true understanding and knowledge : for I have believed Thy commandments.

67 Before I was troubled, I went wrong : but now have I kept Thy word.

68 Thou art good and gracious : O teach me Thy statutes.

69 The proud have imagined a lie against me : but I will keep Thy commandments with my whole heart.

70 Their heart is as fat as brawn : but my delight hath been in Thy law.

71 It is good for me that I have been in trouble : that I may learn Thy statutes.

72 The law of Thy mouth is dearer unto me : than thousands of gold and silver.

73 Thy hands have made me and fashioned me : O give me understanding, that I may learn Thy commandments.

74 They that fear Thee will be glad when they see me : because I have put my trust in Thy word.

75 I know, O Lord, that Thy judgements are right : and that Thou of very faithfulness hast caused me to be troubled.

76 O let Thy merciful kindness be my comfort : according to Thy word unto Thy servant.

77 O let Thy loving mercies come unto me, that I may live : for Thy law is my delight.

78 Let the proud be confounded, for they go wickedly about to destroy me : but I will be occupied in Thy commandments.

79 Let such as fear Thee, and have known Thy testimonies : be turned unto me.

80 O let my heart be sound in Thy statutes : that I be not ashamed.

Glory be to the FATHER.

Antiphon. O let Thy loving mercies come unto me, that I may live.

THE CHAPTER.

Jer. xvii. 14.

HEAL me, O LORD, and I shall be healed; save me, and I shall be saved; for Thou art my praise.

℟ Heal my soul, for I have sinned against Thee.

℣ I said, LORD, be merciful unto me.

℟ For I have sinned against Thee.

℣ Glory be to the FATHER, and to the SON, and to the HOLY GHOST.

℟ Heal my soul, for I have sinned against Thee.

℣ Thou hast been my succour.

℟ Leave me not, neither forsake me, O GOD of my salvation.

℣ The LORD be with you.

℟ And with thy spirit.

Let us pray:

ALMIGHTY GOD, Who as at this hour didst teach the hearts of Thy faithful people, by the sending to them the light of Thy HOLY SPIRIT : Grant us by the Same SPIRIT to have a right judgment in all things, and evermore to rejoice in His holy comfort; through the merits of JESUS CHRIST our SAVIOUR, Who was also at this hour contented to receive the bitter sentence of death for us, and now liveth and reigneth with Thee in the Unity of the Same Blessed Spirit, One GOD, world without end. Amen.

THE SIXTH HOUR.

IN the Name ✠ of the FATHER, and of the SON, and of the HOLY GHOST. Amen.

OUR FATHER.

℣ O GOD, make speed to save us.

℟ O LORD, make haste to help us.

℣ Glory be to the FATHER, and to the SON : and to the HOLY GHOST.

℟ As it was in the beginning, is now, and ever shall be : world without end. Amen.

Alleluia.

From Septuagesima Sunday to Wednesday in Holy Week, inclusive, is said, instead of Alleluia :

Praise to Thee, O LORD, we sing,
Of Glory the Eternal King.

HYMN.

Rector potens verax Deus.

O GOD of truth, O LORD of might,
Who orderest time and change aright,
Brightening the morn with golden gleams,
Kindling the noon-day's fiery beams;

Quench Thou in us the flames of strife,
From passion's heat preserve our life,
Our bodies keep from perils free,
And give our souls true peace in Thee.

Almighty FATHER, hear our cry
Through JESUS CHRIST our LORD most High,
Who, with the HOLY GHOST and Thee,
Doth live and reign eternally. Amen.

Antiphon. Let me not.

Ps. cxix. *Defecit anima mea.*

MY soul hath longed for Thy salvation : and I have a good hope because of Thy word.

82 Mine eyes long sore for Thy word : saying, O when wilt Thou comfort me?

83 For I am become like a bottle in the smoke : yet do I not forget Thy statutes.

84 How many are the days

of Thy servant: when wilt Thou be avenged of them that persecute me?

85 The proud have digged pits for me: which are not after Thy law.

86 All Thy commandments are true: they persecute me falsely; O be Thou my help.

87 They had almost made an end of me upon earth: but I forsook not Thy commandments.

88 O quicken me after Thy loving-kindness: and so shall I keep the testimonies of Thy mouth.

89 O LORD, Thy word: endureth for ever in Heaven.

90 Thy truth also remaineth from one generation to another: Thou hast laid the foundation of the earth, and it abideth.

91 They continue this day according to Thine ordinance: for all things serve Thee.

92 If my delight had not been in Thy law: I should have perished in my trouble.

93 I will never forget Thy commandments: for with them Thou hast quickened me.

94 I am Thine, O save me: for I have sought Thy commandments.

95 The ungodly laid wait for me to destroy me: but I will consider Thy testimonies.

96 I see that all things come to an end: but Thy commandment is exceeding broad.

Glory be to the FATHER.

Quomodo dilexi!

LORD, what love have I unto Thy law: all the day long is my study in it.

98 Thou through Thy commandments hast made me wiser than mine enemies: for they are ever with me.

99 I have more understanding than my teachers: for Thy testimonies are my study.

100 I am wiser than the aged: because I keep Thy commandments.

101 I have refrained my feet from every evil way: that I may keep Thy word.

102 I have not shrunk from Thy judgements: for Thou teachest me.

103 O how sweet are Thy words unto my throat: yea, sweeter than honey unto my mouth.

104 Through Thy commandments I get understanding: therefore I hate all evil ways.

105 Thy word is a lantern unto my feet : and a light unto my paths.

106 I have sworn and am stedfastly purposed : to keep Thy righteous judgements.

107 I am troubled above measure : quicken me, O LORD, according to thy word.

108 Let the free-will offerings of my mouth please Thee, O LORD : and teach me Thy judgements.

109 My soul is alway in my hand : yet do I not forget Thy law.

110 The ungodly have laid a snare for me : but yet I swerved not from Thy commandments.

111 Thy testimonies have I claimed as mine heritage for ever : and why? they are the very joy of my heart.

112 I have applied my heart to fulfil Thy statutes alway : even unto the end.

Glory be to the FATHER.

Iniquos odio habui.

I HATE them that imagine evil things : but Thy law do I love.

114 Thou art my defence and shield : and my trust is in Thy word.

115 Away from me, ye wicked : I will keep the commandments of my GOD.

116 O stablish me according to Thy word, that I may live : and let me not be disappointed of my hope.

117 Hold Thou me up, and I shall be safe : yea, my delight shall be ever in Thy statutes.

118 Thou hast trodden down all them that depart from Thy statutes : for they imagine but deceit.

119 Thou puttest away all the ungodly of the earth like dross : therefore I love Thy testimonies.

120 My flesh trembleth for fear of Thee : and I am afraid of Thy judgements.

121 I deal with the thing that is lawful and right : O give me not over unto mine oppressors.

122 Make Thou Thy servant to delight in that which is good : that the proud do me no wrong.

123 Mine eyes are wasted away with looking for Thy health : and for the word of Thy righteousness.

124 O deal with Thy servant according unto Thy loving mercy : and teach me Thy statutes.

125 I am Thy servant, O grant me understanding :

that I may know Thy testimonies.

126 It is time for Thee, LORD, to lay to Thine hand : for they have destroyed Thy law.

127 For I love Thy commandments : above gold and precious stone.

128 Therefore hold I straight all Thy commandments : and all false ways I utterly abhor.

Glory be to the FATHER.

Antiphon. Let me not be disappointed of my hope.

THE CHAPTER.

1 Thess. v. 21.

PROVE all things ; hold fast that which is good. Abstain from all appearance of evil.

℟ I will alway give thanks unto the LORD.

℣ His praise shall ever be in my mouth.

℟ I will alway give thanks.

℣ Glory be to the FATHER, and to the SON : and to the HOLY GHOST.

℟ I will alway give thanks unto the LORD.

℣ The LORD is my Shepherd, therefore shall I lack nothing.

℟ He shall feed me in a green pasture.

℣ The LORD be with you.

℟ And with Thy spirit.

Let us pray:

O MOST Gracious JESUS, our LORD and our GOD, Who as at this Hour didst bear our sins in Thine Own Body on the Tree, that we, being dead to sin, might live unto righteousness : have mercy upon us we beseech Thee, both now and at the hour of our death ; and grant unto us Thy humble servants, with all other Christian people, that have this Thy blessed Passion in devout remembrance, a godly and peaceful life in this present world, and through Thy grace, eternal glory in the life to come ; where, with the FATHER, and the HOLY GHOST, Thou livest and reignest, ever One GOD, world without end. Amen.

THE NINTH HOUR.

IN the Name ✠ of the FATHER, and of the SON, and of the HOLY GHOST. Amen.

OUR FATHER.

℣. O GOD, make speed to save us.

℟. O LORD, make haste to help us.

℣. Glory be to the FATHER, and to the SON, and to the HOLY GHOST.

℟. As it was in the beginning, is now, and ever shall be, world without end. Amen.

Alleluia.

From Septuagesima Sunday to Wednesday in Holy Week, inclusive, is said instead of Alleluia:

Praise to Thee, O LORD, we sing,
Of Glory the Eternal King.

HYMN.

Rerum Deus tenax vigor.

O GOD of all the Strength and Power,
Who dost, unmoved, each passing hour
Through all its changes guide the day,
From early morn to evening's ray;

Brighten life's eventide with light
That ne'er shall set in gloom of night;
Till we a holy death attain
And everlasting glory gain.

Almighty FATHER, hear our cry
Through JESUS CHRIST our LORD most High,
Who, with the HOLY GHOST and Thee,
Doth live and reign eternally. Amen.

Antiphon. Give me understanding.

Ps. cxix. *Mirabilia.*

THY testimonies are wonderful : therefore doth my soul keep them.

130 When Thy word goeth forth : it giveth light and understanding unto the simple.

131 I opened my mouth and drew in my breath : for

my delight was in Thy commandments.

132 O look Thou upon me, and be merciful unto me : as Thou usest to do unto those that love Thy Name.

133 Order my steps in Thy word : and so shall no wickedness have dominion over me.

134 O deliver me from the wrongful dealings of men : and so shall I keep Thy commandments.

135 Shew the light of Thy countenance upon Thy servant : and teach me Thy statutes.

136 Mine eyes gush out with water : because men keep not Thy law.

137 Righteous art Thou, O LORD, and true is Thy judgement.

138 The testimonies that Thou hast commanded : are exceeding righteous and true.

139 My zeal hath even consumed me : because mine enemies have forgotten Thy words.

140 Thy word is tried to the uttermost : and Thy servant loveth it.

141 I am small, and of no reputation : yet do I not forget Thy commandments.

142 Thy righteousness is an everlasting righteousness : and Thy law is the truth.

143 Trouble and heaviness have taken hold upon me : yet is my delight in Thy commandments.

144 The righteousness of Thy testimonies is everlasting : O grant me understanding, and I shall live.

Glory be to the FATHER.

Clamavi in toto corde meo.

I CALL with my whole heart : hear me, O LORD, I will keep Thy statutes.

146 Yea, even unto Thee do I call : help me and I shall keep Thy testimonies.

147 Early in the morning do I cry unto Thee : for in Thy word is my trust.

148 Mine eyes prevent the night-watches : that I might be occupied in Thy words.

149 Hear my voice, O LORD, according unto Thy loving-kindness : quicken me, according as Thou art wont.

150 They draw nigh that of malice persecute me : and are far from Thy law.

151 Be Thou nigh at hand,

O Lord : for all Thy commandments are true.

152 As concerning Thy testimonies, I have known long since : that Thou hast grounded them for ever.

153 O consider mine adversity, and deliver me : for I do not forget Thy law.

154 Avenge Thou my cause, and deliver me : quicken me according to Thy word.

155 Health is far from the ungodly : for they regard not Thy statutes.

156 Great is Thy mercy, O Lord : quicken me as Thou art wont.

157 Many there are that trouble me, and persecute me : yet do I not swerve from Thy testimonies.

158 It grieveth me when I see the transgressors : because they keep not Thy law.

159 Consider, O Lord, how I love Thy commandments : O quicken me according to Thy loving-kindness.

160 Thy word is true from everlasting : all the judgements of Thy righteousness endure for evermore.

Glory be to the Father.

Principes persecuti sunt.

PRINCES have persecuted me without a cause : but my heart standeth in awe of Thy word.

162 I am as glad of Thy word : as one that findeth great spoils.

163 As for lies, I hate and abhor them : but Thy law do I love.

164 Seven times a day do I praise Thee : because of Thy righteous judgements.

165 Great is the peace that they have who love Thy law : and they are not offended at it.

166 Lord I have looked for Thy saving health : and done after Thy commandments.

167 My soul hath kept Thy testimonies : and loved them exceedingly.

168 I have kept Thy commandments and testimonies : for all my ways are before Thee.

169 Let my complaint come before Thee, O Lord : give me understanding, according to Thy word.

170 Let my supplication come before Thee : deliver me, according to Thy word.

171 My lips shall speak of

Prayers for the Ninth Hour

Thy praise : when Thou hast taught me Thy statutes.

172 Yea my tongue shall sing of Thy word : for all Thy commandments are righteous.

173 Let Thine hand help me : for I have chosen Thy commandments.

174 I have longed for Thy saving health, O LORD : and in Thy law is my delight.

175 O let my soul live, and it shall praise Thee : and Thy judgements shall help me.

176 I have gone astray like a sheep that is lost : O seek Thy servant, for I do not forget Thy commandments.

Glory be to the FATHER.

Antiphon. Give me understanding according to Thy Word.

THE CHAPTER.

Gal. vi. 2.

BEAR ye one another's burdens, and so fulfil the law of CHRIST.

℟ O deliver me, and be merciful unto me.

℣ My foot standeth right : I will praise the LORD in the congregations.

℟ And be merciful unto me.

℣ Glory be to the FATHER, and to the SON, and to the HOLY GHOST.

℟ O deliver me, and be merciful unto me.

℣ O cleanse Thou me from my secret faults.

℟ Keep Thy servant also from presumptuous sins.

℣ The LORD be with you.

℟ And with Thy spirit.

Let us pray:

HEAR us, O Merciful LORD JESUS CHRIST, and remember now the hour in which Thou didst commend Thy blessed Spirit into the hands of Thy Heavenly Father, and so assist us by this Thy most precious Death, that being dead unto the world we may live only unto Thee : and at the hour of our departing from this mortal life, we may be received into Thine everlasting Kingdom, there to reign with Thee, world without end.   Amen.

COMPLINE.

IN the Name ✠ of the FATHER, and of the SON, and of the HOLY GHOST. Amen.

OUR FATHER.

℣ Turn Thou us, O GOD, our SAVIOUR.
℟ And let Thine anger cease from us.
℣ O GOD, make speed to save us.
℟ O LORD, make haste to help us.
℣ Glory be to the FATHER, and to the SON, and to the HOLY GHOST.
℟ As it was in the beginning, is now, and ever shall be, world without end. Amen.

Alleluia.

From the Compline before Septuagesima to Wednesday in Holy Week, inclusive, is said instead of Alleluia:

Praise to Thee, O LORD, we sing,
Of Glory the Eternal King.

Antiphon. Have mercy.

Psalm iv. *Cum invocarem.*

HEAR me when I call, O GOD of my righteousness : Thou hast set me at liberty when I was in trouble ; have mercy upon me, and hearken unto my prayer.

2 O ye sons of men, how long will ye blaspheme Mine honour : and have such pleasure in vanity, and seek after leasing ?

3 Know this also, that the LORD hath chosen to Himself the man that is godly : when I call upon the LORD, He will hear me.

4 Stand in awe, and sin not : commune with your own heart, and in your chamber, and be still.

5 Offer the sacrifice of righteousness : and put your trust in the LORD.

6 There be many that say : Who will shew us any good ?

7 LORD, lift Thou up : the light of Thy countenance upon us.

8 Thou hast put gladness in my heart : since the time that their corn, and wine, and oil, increased.

9 I will lay me down in peace, and take my rest : for it is Thou, LORD, only that makest me dwell in safety.

Glory be to the FATHER.

Ps. xxxi. In te, Domine, speravi.

IN Thee, O LORD, have I put my trust : let me never be put to confusion, deliver me in Thy righteousness.

2 Bow down Thine ear to me : make haste to deliver me.

3 And be Thou my strong Rock, and House of defence : that Thou mayest save me.

4 For Thou art my strong Rock, and my Castle : be Thou also my Guide, and lead me for Thy Name's sake.

5 Draw me out of the net, that they have laid privily for me : for Thou art my Strength.

6 Into Thy hands I commend my spirit : for Thou hast redeemed me, O LORD, Thou GOD of truth.

Glory be to the FATHER.

Psalm xci. Qui habitat.

WHOSO dwelleth under the defence of the most High : shall abide under the shadow of the Almighty.

2 I will say unto the LORD, Thou art my Hope, and my Strong Hold : my GOD, in Him will I trust.

3 For He shall deliver thee from the snare of the hunter : and from the noisome pestilence.

4 He shall defend thee under His wings, and thou shalt be safe under His feathers : His faithfulness and truth shall be thy shield and buckler.

5 Thou shalt not be afraid for any terror by night : nor for the arrow that flieth by day ;

6 For the pestilence that walketh in darkness : nor for the sickness that destroyeth in the noon-day.

7 A thousand shall fall beside thee, and ten thousand at thy right hand : but it shall not come nigh thee.

8 Yea, with thine eyes shalt thou behold : and see the reward of the ungodly.

9 For Thou, LORD, art my Hope : Thou hast set Thine house of defence very high.

10 There shall no evil happen unto thee : neither shall any plague come nigh thy dwelling.

11 For He shall give His Angels charge over thee : to keep thee in all thy ways.

12 They shall bear thee in their hands : that thou hurt not thy foot against a stone.

13 Thou shalt go upon the lion and adder : the young lion and the dragon shalt Thou tread under Thy feet.

14 Because He hath set His love upon me, therefore will I deliver him : I will set him up, because he hath known My Name.

15 He shall call upon Me, and I will hear him : yea, I am with him in trouble ; I will deliver him, and bring him to honour.

16 With long life will I satisfy him : and shew him My salvation.

Glory be to the FATHER.

Psalm cxxxiv. *Ecce nunc.*

BEHOLD now, praise the LORD : all ye servants of the LORD;

2 Ye that by night stand in the house of the LORD : even in the courts of the house of our GOD.

3 Lift up your hands in the sanctuary : and praise the LORD.

4 The LORD that made Heaven and earth : give thee blessing out of Sion.

Glory be to the FATHER.

Antiphon. Have mercy upon me, and hearken unto my prayer.

THE CHAPTER.

Jer. xiv. 9.

THOU, O LORD, art in the midst of us, and we are called by Thy Name; leave us not.

℟ Thanks be to GOD.

Hymn.

Te Lucis ante terminum.

NOW that the daylight dies away,
Ere we lie down and sleep,
Thee, Maker of the world, we pray,
To own us and to keep.

Let dreams depart and visions fly,
The offspring of the night :
Keep us, as shrines beneath Thine eye,
Pure in our foes despite.

This grace on Thy redeem'd confer,
FATHER, co-equal SON,
And HOLY GHOST, the Comforter;
Eternal Three in One. Amen.

℣ Keep me as the apple of an eye.

℟ Hide me under the shadow of Thy wings.

Antiphon. Save us.

Nunc Dimittis.

S. Luke ii. 29.

LORD, now lettest Thou Thy servant depart in peace : according to Thy Word.

For mine eyes have seen : Thy Salvation,

Which Thou hast prepared : before the face of all people ;

To be a light to lighten the Gentiles : and to be the glory of Thy people Israel.

Glory be to the FATHER.

Antiphon. Save us, O LORD, while waking, guard us while sleeping, that awake we may be with CHRIST, and may sleep in peace.

LORD, have mercy upon us.

CHRIST, have mercy upon us.

LORD, have mercy upon us.

OUR FATHER.

I BELIEVE in GOD.

℣ Let us bless the FATHER, and the SON, and the HOLY GHOST.

℟ Let us praise and exalt Him for ever.

℣ Blessed art Thou, O LORD, in the firmament of Heaven.

℟ Greatly to be praised, and glorified, and highly exalted for ever.

℣ May the Almighty and most Merciful GOD bless us and keep us.

℟ Amen.

Confession.

WE confess to Thee, Almighty GOD, the FATHER, the SON, and the HOLY GHOST, and before the whole Company of Heaven, that we have sinned exceedingly in thought, word, and deed, through our fault, through our fault, through our grievous fault : therefore we pray GOD to have mercy upon us.

May the Almighty GOD have mercy upon us, pardon all our sins, deliver us from all evil, preserve and strengthen us in all good, and bring us to everlasting life. Amen.

If a Priest be present let him add:

[May the Almighty and Merciful LORD grant to us absolution and remission of all our sins, time for true repentance, amendment of life, and the grace and comfort of His HOLY SPIRIT. Amen.]

℣ Wilt Thou not turn again and quicken us, O LORD.

℟ That Thy people may rejoice in Thee.

℣ Show us Thy mercy, O Lord.

℟ And grant us Thy salvation.

℣ Vouchsafe, O Lord.

℟ To keep us this night without sin.

℣ O Lord, have mercy upon us.

℟ Have mercy upon us.

℣ O Lord, let Thy mercy lighten upon us.

℟ As our trust is in Thee.

℣ Turn us again, Thou God of Hosts.

℟ Shew the Light of Thy countenance, and we shall be whole.

℣ O Lord, hear our prayer.

℟ And let our cry come unto Thee.

℣ The Lord be with you.

℟ And with Thy Spirit.

Let us pray:

LIGHTEN our darkness, we beseech Thee, O Lord; and by Thy great mercy defend us from all perils and dangers of this night; for the love of Thy only Son, our Saviour, Jesus Christ. Amen.

℣ The Lord be with you.

℟ And with Thy spirit.

℣ Let us bless the Lord.

℟ Amen.

Intercessory Prayers

☩ *For the Church.*

O HOLY Jesus, King of the Saints, and Prince of the Catholic Church, preserve Thy Spouse whom Thou hast purchased with Thy right hand, and redeemed and cleansed with Thy Blood, even Thy whole Catholic Church from one end of the earth to the other, founded upon a Rock, but planted in the sea. O preserve her safe from schism, heresy, and sacrilege. Unite all her members with the bands of faith, hope, and charity: and also of an external communion, when it shall seem good in Thine eyes. Let the daily Sacrifice of Prayer and Sacramental Thanksgiving never cease, but be for ever presented unto Thee, and for ever united to the Intercession of her dearest Lord, and for ever prevail for the obtaining for every of its members grace and blessing, pardon and salvation; for Thy most tender mercy's sake. Amen.

✝ *For the Visible Unity of the Church.*

O LORD JESU CHRIST, Who saidst unto Thine Apostles, Peace I leave with you, My Peace I give unto you; regard not my sins, but the faith of Thy Church, and grant her that peace and unity which is agreeable to Thy will, Who livest and reignest, GOD, for ever and ever. Amen.

✝ *For the Queen.*

O LORD, Who, of Thy favour towards us, hast set Victoria our Queen to reign over us: keep her, we beseech Thee, under Thy almighty protection; save and defend her from all her enemies, both ghostly and bodily; give her grace to rule Thy people according to Thy will, that she may here govern to Thy honour and glory, and after this life receive and enjoy the inheritance of Thy Heavenly Kingdom, in the life and bliss that never shall have an end: through JESUS CHRIST our LORD. Amen.

For all Estates of Men.

ALMIGHTY and Everlasting GOD, by Whose SPIRIT the whole body of the Church is governed and sanctified, receive our supplications and prayers, which we offer before Thee for all estates of men in Thy Holy Church, that every member of the same, in his vocation and ministry, may truly and godly serve Thee; through our LORD and SAVIOUR JESUS CHRIST. Amen.

For Bishops and Clergy.

O HOLY and Eternal JESUS, Thou great Shepherd and Bishop of our souls, send down upon Thy servants, the Bishops and Pastors of Thy Church, Thy heavenly blessing. Give them the Spirit of wisdom and holiness, patience and charity, zeal and watchfulness, that they may faithfully declare Thy will, boldly rebuke vice, rightly and duly administer Thy holy Sacraments, and intercede with Thee acceptably for Thy people. Support and comfort them under all suffering and opposition for the cause of Thy truth, and grant that after turning many to righteousness, they may shine as the stars for ever and ever; for Thy tender mercy's sake. Amen.

For the Bishop of the Diocese.

O GOD, the Pastor and Ruler of Thy faithful servants, look down in mercy on Thy servant N. our Bishop, to whom Thou hast given charge over this Diocese, and evermore guide, defend, comfort, sanctify, and save him; and grant him by Thy grace so to advance in word and good example, that he may with the flock committed to him, attain to everlasting life; through JESUS CHRIST our LORD. Amen.

For the Parish Priest.

O GOD, the Pastor and Guide of all Thy people, look favourably on Thy servant N., whom Thou hast willed to preside as Pastor over Thy Church in this Parish; grant, we beseech Thee, that both by word and by example he may profit those over whom he is set, that, together with his flock, he may attain eternal life; through JESUS CHRIST our LORD. Amen.

☩ *For the Parish.*

ALMIGHTY and Everlasting GOD, Who dost govern all things in Heaven and earth, mercifully hear the supplication of us Thy servants; and grant unto this Parish all things that are needful for its spiritual welfare (especially N.), Strengthen and confirm the faithful; visit and relieve the sick; turn and soften the wicked: rouse the careless; recover the fallen; restore the penitent; remove all hindrances to the advancement of Thy truth, and bring all to be of one heart and mind within the fold of Thy Holy Church, to the honour and glory of Thy Blessed SON, JESUS CHRIST, our LORD. Amen.

For Brotherhoods and Sisterhoods.

VOUCHSAFE, we beseech Thee, Merciful LORD, to prosper with Thy blessing the work of N. and all others designed to promote Thy glory and the good of souls. Grant that those who serve Thee there, may set Thy holy will ever before them, and do that which is well pleasing in Thy sight, and persevere in Thy Service unto the end ; through JESUS CHRIST our LORD. Amen.

For Home and Foreign Missions.

O LORD JESUS CHRIST, Who didst charge Thine Apostles that they should preach the Gospel to every nation ; prosper, we pray Thee, all Missions both at home and abroad (especially N.) ; give them all things needful for their work, making them to be centres of spiritual life, to the quickening of many souls, and the glory of Thy holy Name. Support, guide, and bless the Clergy, who are called to labour in those parts of Thy vineyard, give them grace to witness to the Faith, endue them with burning zeal and love, make them patient under all disappointments, and meekly submissive under all persecutions, that they may turn many to righteousness, and may themselves win a Crown of everlasting glory, Who livest and reignest God for ever and ever. Amen.

For a Parent or Benefactor.

O GOD, Merciful and Gracious, Who hast made my Parents (or Benefactors) Ministers of Thy mercy, and instruments of providence to Thy servant, I humbly beg a blessing to descend upon them. Depute Thy holy Angels to guide their souls, Thy providence to minister to their necessities : let Thy grace and mercy preserve them from the bitter pains of eternal death, and bring them to everlasting life ; through JESUS CHRIST our LORD. Amen.

For Friends and Kindred.

ALMIGHTY, Everlasting GOD, have mercy on Thy Servants N. Keep them continually under Thy protection, and direct them according to Thy gracious favour in the way of everlasting salvation : that they may desire such things as please Thee, and with all their strength perform the same. And forasmuch as they trust in Thy mercy, vouchsafe, O LORD, graciously to assist them with Thy heavenly help, that they may ever diligently serve Thee, and by no temptations be separated from Thee; through JESUS CHRIST our LORD. Amen.

A Master's Prayer.

GRACIOUS FATHER, bless my servants, and make them Thine; give them grace to serve Thee first, with faithfulness, soberness, and diligence. Make me ever willing, and in some measure able, to repay unto them the time and the strength which they either have spent or shall spend to do me service, even for JESUS CHRIST His sake. Amen.

A Servant's Prayer.

BLESS, O LORD, my Master and Mistress, and all my fellow-servants, with all temporal and spiritual blessings; make me obedient to those who are set over me, considerate and kind to those who are under me. Grant that I may endure reproof with humility and gentleness, and without murmuring or discontent faithfully fulfil the duties of my calling; through JESUS CHRIST our LORD. Amen.

For Widows and Orphans.

O HEAVENLY FATHER, Who wilt not leave comfortless such as faithfully seek Thee, protect with Thine almighty power all Widows and Orphans, (especially N.); and grant that the loss of their natural Guardians may lead them to rely the more entirely on Thy heavenly care; through JESUS CHRIST our LORD. Amen.

For Travellers.

O GOD of Infinite Majesty and Mercy, Whom neither distance of place nor length of time can separate from those whom Thou defendest: mercifully assist Thy servants (especially N.) who put their trust in Thee; vouchsafe to be their guide, and their companion through the way by which they are about to go. Let no misfortune harm them, no difficulty hinder them; let everything be favourable and prosperous for them: that whatsoever they shall rightly and lawfully desire, they may speedily and effectually obtain; through JESUS CHRIST our LORD. Amen.

For Sufferers in Mind or Body.

O LORD JESUS CHRIST, our Sympathising SAVIOUR, Who for man didst bear the Agony and the Cross; draw Thou near to Thy suffering servants, in their pain of body or trouble of mind (especially N.); hallow all their crosses in this life, and crown them hereafter where all tears are wiped away; where, with the FATHER and the HOLY GHOST, Thou livest and reignest, One GOD, world without end. Amen.

For the Tempted.

MERCIFUL and Faithful High Priest, Who didst deign for us to be tempted of Satan; make speed to aid Thy servants who are assaulted by manifold temptations; and as Thou knowest their several infirmities, let each one find Thee mighty to save, Who livest and reignest with the FATHER and the HOLY GHOST, One GOD, world without end. Amen.

For our Enemies.

O LORD JESUS CHRIST, Who didst pray for Thy murderers, forgive mine enemies, I beseech Thee, all their sins against Thee, and give me that measure of Thy grace, that for their hatred I may love them; for their cursing I may bless them; for their injury I may do them good; for their persecution I may pray for them: Who livest and reignest with the FATHER, and the HOLY GHOST, One GOD, world without end. Amen.

For the Removal of Schism.

O GOD, Who graciously correctest what is wrong, and gatherest together into one that which is scattered, and keepest together that which Thou hast so gathered: mercifully pour forth, we beseech Thee, the grace of union on all Christian people, that they all may forsake division, and uniting themselves to the true Pastors of Thy Church, may be enabled worthily to serve Thee; through JESUS CHRIST our LORD. Amen.

For Heretics.

ALMIGHTY and Everliving GOD, Who

hast given us the Catholic Faith of CHRIST for a light to our feet amid the darkness of this world; have pity upon all who, by doubting or denying it, are gone astray from the path of safety; bring home the Truth to their hearts, and grant them to receive it as little children; through the Same JESUS CHRIST our Lord. Amen.

For the Jews.

ALMIGHTY and Everlasting GOD, Who dost extend Thy pity even to the faithless Jews, hear our prayers which we offer to Thee for their blindness of heart, that by the knowledge of Thy Truth, which is CHRIST, they may be delivered out of their darkness, through the Same JESUS CHRIST our LORD. Amen.

For the Heathen.

ALMIGHTY and Everlasting GOD, Who willest not the death of a sinner, but rather that he should be converted and live, favourably receive our prayers which we make before Thee, that Thou wouldest deliver the Heathen from the worship of idols, and unite them to Thy Holy Church, to the praise and glory of Thy Name. Amen.

For the Conversion of Sinners.

ALMIGHTY GOD, we beseech Thee to hear our prayers for all such as sin against Thee, or neglect to serve Thee (especially N.), that Thou wouldest bestow upon them true contrition, and an earnest desire to devote themselves to Thy holy service; through JESUS CHRIST our LORD. Amen.

For the Sick and Dying.

O GRACIOUS LORD JESUS, Who didst vouchsafe to die on the Cross for us; remember, we beseech Thee, all Sick and Dying Persons (especially N.); and grant that they may omit nothing which is necessary to make their peace with Thee before they die. Deliver them, O LORD, from the malice of the Devil, and from all sin and evil, and grant them a happy end for Thy loving mercy's sake. Amen.

Intercessory Prayers

For a Sick Person's Recovery.

O GOD, by Whose ordering the moments of our life run out, accept the prayers and offerings of Thy servants and handmaids, for whom in their sickness we implore Thy mercy; that our fears on account of their danger may be changed into joy on account of their recovery; through JESUS CHRIST our LORD. Amen.

For a Father or Mother Departed.

O GOD, Who hast commanded us to honour our Father and Mother, of Thy clemency have pity upon the souls of my Father and Mother: and grant that I may live with them in the joy of eternal brightness; through JESUS CHRIST our Lord. Amen.

For a Departed Friend.

O GOD, Whose nature and property is ever to have mercy and to forgive, have mercy upon the Soul of Thy Servant (or Handmaid): and grant *him* eternal rest among Thy Saints and Elect, that *he* may enjoy their companionship in everlasting life: through JESUS CHRIST our LORD. Amen.

In time of Pestilence or any Affliction.

TURN away Thine anger, O LORD, we beseech Thee, and have pity on Thy people; and while by reason of the frailty of our nature we cannot bear Thine indignation, which for our misdeeds we have justly deserved, do Thou keep us in Thy favour with which Thou art wont to visit Thine unworthy servants; through JESUS CHRIST our LORD. Amen.

In Time of War.

ALMIGHTY and most Merciful GOD, deliver us, we beseech Thee, from the tumult of war: for in bestowing peace of mind and body, Thou dost give us all good things; through JESUS CHRIST our LORD. Amen.

ANIMA CHRISTI.

SOUL OF CHRIST, SANCTIFY ME!
BODY OF CHRIST, SAVE ME!
BLOOD OF CHRIST, INEBRIATE ME!
WATER FROM THE SIDE OF CHRIST, WASH ME!
PASSION OF CHRIST, STRENGTHEN ME!
O GOOD JESU! HEAR ME!
WITHIN THY WOUNDS HIDE ME!
SUFFER ME NOT TO BE SEPARATED FROM THEE!
FROM THE MALICIOUS ENEMY DEFEND ME!
IN THE HOUR OF MY DEATH, CALL ME!
AND BID ME COME TO THEE,
THAT WITH THY SAINTS I MAY PRAISE THEE,
FOR EVER AND EVER.
AMEN.

Devotions for Holy Communion

PREPARATION FOR COMMUNION

Antiphon. I will fear no evil : for Thou art with me.

Ps. lxxxiv. *Quam dilecta!*

O HOW amiable are Thy dwellings : Thou LORD of Hosts !

My soul hath a desire and longing to enter into the Courts of the LORD : my heart and my flesh rejoice in the living GOD.

Yea, the sparrow hath found her an house, and the swallow a nest where she may lay her young : even Thy altars, O LORD of Hosts, my King and my GOD.

Blessed are they that dwell in Thy house : they will be alway praising Thee.

Blessed is the man whose strength is in Thee : in whose heart are Thy ways.

Who going through the vale of misery use it for a well : and the pools are filled with water.

They will go from strength to strength : and unto the GOD of gods appeareth every one of them in Sion.

O LORD GOD of Hosts, hear my prayer : hearken, O GOD of Jacob.

Behold, O GOD our Defender : and look upon the face of Thine Anointed.

For one day in Thy Courts : is better than a thousand.

I had rather be a doorkeeper in the House of my GOD : than to dwell in the tents of ungodliness.

For the LORD GOD is a Light and Defence : the LORD will give grace and worship, and no good thing shall He withhold from them that live a godly life.

O LORD GOD of Hosts : blessed is the man that putteth his trust in Thee.

Glory be to the FATHER.

Antiphon. I will fear no evil : for Thou art with me. Thou shalt prepare a Table before me against them that trouble me : Thou hast anointed my head with oil, and my cup shall be full.

In Penitential Seasons.

Antiphon. Remember not, LORD.

Ps. cxxx. *De profundis.*

OUT of the deep have I called unto Thee, O LORD: LORD, hear my voice.

O let Thine ears consider well: the voice of my complaint.

If Thou, LORD, wilt be extreme to mark what is done amiss: O LORD, who may abide it?

For there is mercy with Thee: therefore shalt Thou be feared.

I look for the LORD; my soul doth wait for Him: in His word is my trust.

My soul fleeth unto the LORD: before the morning watch, I say, before the morning watch.

O Israel, trust in the LORD, for with the LORD there is mercy: and with Him is plenteous redemption.

And He shall redeem Israel: from all his sins.

Glory be to the FATHER.

Antiphon. Remember not, LORD, our offences, nor the offences of our forefathers, neither take Thou vengeance of our sins.

LORD have mercy upon us. CHRIST have mercy upon us. LORD have mercy upon us.

OUR FATHER.

℣ And lead us not into temptation.

℟ But deliver us from evil.

℣ I said, LORD, have mercy upon me.

℟ Heal my soul, for I have sinned against Thee.

℣ Turn Thee again, O LORD, at the last.

℟ And be gracious unto Thy servants.

℣ Let Thy mercy, O LORD, be showed upon us.

℟ As we do put our trust in Thee.

℣ Let Thy Priests be clothed with righteousness.

℟ And let Thy Saints sing with joyfulness.

℣ Cleanse Thou me from my secret faults.

℟ And keep Thy servant also from presumptuous sins.

℣ O LORD, hear my prayer.

℟ And let my cry come unto Thee.

Let us pray:

MOST Gracious GOD, incline Thy merciful

ears to our prayers, and enlighten our hearts by the grace of Thy HOLY SPIRIT; that we may worthily approach Thy Holy Mysteries, and love Thee with an everlasting love.

O LORD, we beseech Thee, may the Comforter Who proceedeth from Thee illuminate our minds, and lead us, as Thy SON hath promised, into all truth.

O LORD, we beseech Thee, may the power of the HOLY GHOST be with us, and both mercifully cleanse and purge our hearts, and defend us from all adversities.

Cleanse our consciences, we beseech Thee, O LORD, by Thy visitation: that Thy SON our LORD JESUS CHRIST, when He cometh, may find in us a mansion prepared for Himself; through the Same Thy SON JESUS CHRIST our LORD, Who liveth and reigneth with Thee in the Unity of the Same SPIRIT, ever One GOD, world without end. Amen.

Almighty and Everlasting GOD, behold I approach the Sacrament of Thy Only-Begotten SON, our LORD JESUS CHRIST. As one sick, I come to the Physician of life: as unclean, to the Fountain of mercy: as blind, to the Light of eternal splendour: as needy, to the LORD of Heaven and earth: as naked, to the King of glory: a lost sheep, to the Good Shepherd: a fallen creature, to its Creator: desolate, to the kind Comforter: miserable, to the Pitier: guilty, to the Bestower of pardon: sinful, to the Justifier; hardened, to the Infuser of grace. I implore therefore the abundance of Thine Infinite Majesty, that Thou wouldest vouchsafe to heal my sickness, to wash my foulness, to lighten my darkness, to enrich my poverty, and to clothe my nakedness, that I may receive the Bread of Angels, the King of Kings, and Lord of Lords, with such reverence and fear, such contrition and love, such faith and purity, such devotion and humility, as is expedient for the welfare of my soul. Grant me, I beseech Thee, to receive not only the Sacrament of the LORD's Body and Blood, but also the virtue of the Sacrament. O most Merciful GOD, grant me so to receive the Body of Thy Only-Begotten SON, our LORD JESUS CHRIST, Which He took of the Virgin Mary, that I may be incorporated in His Mystical Body, and ever reckoned among His members. And, O most Loving FATHER, grant me that Whom I now purpose to receive under a veil I may at length behold with open face, even Thy Beloved SON, Who, with Thee and the HOLY GHOST, liveth and reigneth, ever One GOD, world without end. Amen.

Joy with peace, amendment of life, time for true repentance, the grace and comfort of Thy HOLY SPIRIT, perseverance in good works, grant me, O Almighty and Merciful LORD. Amen.

Additional Devotions will be found at page 96.

DAILY PREPARATION DURING A WEEK

BLESSED JESUS, Who art about to come to us Thy unworthy servants in the Blessed Sacrament of Thy Body and Blood, prepare our hearts, we beseech Thee, for Thyself. Grant us that repentance for our past sins, that faith in the Atonement made for them by Thee upon the Cross, that full purpose of amendment of life, that perfect love to Thee and to all men, which shall fit us to receive Thee. LORD, we are not worthy that Thou shouldest come under our roof, much less that we should receive Thee into ourselves; but since Thou didst not disdain to be laid in a manger amidst unclean beasts, so vouchsafe to enter into our souls and bodies, unclean though they be through many sins and defilements.

LORD, come to us that Thou mayest cleanse us.

LORD, come to us that Thou mayest heal us.

LORD, come to us that Thou mayest strengthen us.

And grant that having received Thee, we may never be separated from Thee by our sins, but may continue Thine for ever, till we see Thee face to face in Thy heavenly Kingdom, where, with the FATHER and the HOLY GHOST, Thou livest and reignest, ever One GOD, world without end. Amen.

O sacred Feast! wherein CHRIST is received; the memory of His Passion is brought to our remembrance; our souls are fulfilled with grace, and the pledge of eternal glory is given unto us. Alleluia.

PRAYERS BEFORE THE SERVICE

Direction of the Intention.

O ALMIGHTY LORD of Heaven and earth, behold I, an unworthy sinner, desire to offer up to Thee, by the hands of this Thy Minister, the mystical and commemorative Sacrifice of the Body and Blood of Thy SON JESUS CHRIST, in union with the One True Sacrifice which He offered up to Thee upon the Cross. I desire to offer It, first, for Thine own honour, praise, adoration, and glory: secondly, in remembrance of His Death and Passion: thirdly, in thanksgiving for all Thy blessings bestowed in Him on His whole Church, whether triumphant in Heaven or militant in earth, and especially for those bestowed on me, the most unworthy of all: fourthly, for obtaining pardon and remission of all my sins, and of those of all others for whom I ought to pray: and lastly, for obtaining all graces and blessings, both for myself and for the whole Mystical Body of Thy SON, that such as are yet alive may finish their course with joy, and that such as are dead in the LORD may rest in peace and hope, and rise in glory: for the LORD'S sake Whose Death we are now about to commemorate.

A Prayer.

GRANT, O LORD, that we may be truly prepared for the offering of this great Sacrifice to Thee this day; do Thou, O LORD, I pray Thee, possess and govern my heart by Thy grace, that I may perform this act piously, religiously, and becomingly, so that this my service may be well pleasing to Thee, and profitable to my soul. Amen.

Prayer for the Priest.

THE LORD be in thy heart, and on thy lips, and make thee a worthy Minister at His Altar: the LORD be merciful to thee, and forgive thee all thy sins, and bring thee to everlasting life; the LORD accept this Holy Sacrifice at thy hands to His greater glory, and for our necessities: In the Name ✠ of the FATHER, and of the SON, and of the HOLY GHOST. Amen.

THE ORDER

OF THE ADMINISTRATION OF

The Holy Communion

The Lord's Prayer

OUR FATHER, Which art in Heaven, Hallowed be Thy Name: Thy Kingdom come: Thy Will be done in earth, as it is in Heaven: Give us this day our daily Bread: And forgive us our trespasses, as we forgive them that trespass against us: And lead us not into temptation: But deliver us from evil. Amen.

The Collect for Purity

ALMIGHTY GOD, unto Whom all hearts be open, all desires known, and from Whom no secrets are hid; cleanse the thoughts of our hearts by the inspiration of Thy HOLY SPIRIT, that we may perfectly love Thee, and worthily magnify Thy holy Name; through CHRIST our LORD. *Amen.*

The Ten Commandments

Minister. GOD spake these Words and said; I am the LORD thy GOD· thou shalt have none other gods but Me.

People. LORD, have mercy upon us, and incline our hearts to keep this Law.

Minister. Thou shalt not make to thyself any graven image, nor the likeness of any thing that is in Heaven above, or in the earth beneath, or in the water under the earth. Thou shalt not bow down to them, nor worship them: for I the LORD thy GOD am a Jealous GOD, and visit the sins of the fathers upon the children, unto the third and fourth generation of them that hate Me, and shew mercy unto thousands in them that love Me, and keep My Commandments.

People. LORD, have mercy upon us, and incline our hearts to keep this Law.

Minister. Thou shalt not take the Name of the LORD thy GOD in vain: for the LORD will not hold him guiltless, that taketh His Name in vain.

People. LORD, have mercy upon us, and incline our hearts to keep this Law.

Minister. Remember that thou keep holy the Sabbath-Day. Six days days shalt thou labour and do all that thou hast to do; but the seventh day is the Sabbath of the LORD thy GOD. In it thou shalt do no manner of work, thou, and thy son, and thy daughter, thy man-servant, and thy maid-servant, thy cattle, and the stranger that is within thy gates. For in six days the LORD made Heaven and earth, the sea, and all that in them is, and rested the seventh day: wherefore the LORD blessed the seventh day and hallowed it.

People. LORD, have mercy upon us, and incline our hearts to keep this Law.

Minister. Honour thy father and thy mother; that thy days may be long in the land which the LORD thy GOD giveth thee.

People. LORD, have mercy upon us, and incline our hearts to keep this Law.

Minister. Thou shalt do no murder.

People. LORD, have mercy upon us, and incline our hearts to keep this Law.

Minister. Thou shalt not commit adultery.

People. LORD, have mercy upon us, and. incline our hearts to keep this Law.

Minister. Thou shalt not steal.

People. LORD, have mercy upon us, and incline our hearts to keep this Law.

Minister. Thou shalt not bear false witness against thy neighbour.

People. LORD, have mercy upon us, and incline our hearts to keep this Law.

Minister. Thou shalt not covet thy neighbour's house, thou shalt not covet thy neighbour's wife, nor his servant, nor his maid, nor his ox, nor his ass, nor anything that is his.

People. LORD, have mercy upon us, and write all these Thy Laws in our hearts, we beseech Thee.

The Collect for the Queen.

Let us pray.

ALMIGHTY GOD, Whose Kingdom is everlasting, and power infinite; have mercy upon the whole Church; and so rule the heart of Thy chosen Servant *Victoria*, our Queen and Governour, that she, knowing Whose Minister she is, may above all things seek Thy honour and glory; and that we and all her subjects, duly considering Whose authority she hath, may faithfully serve, honour, and humbly obey her in Thee, and for Thee, according to Thy blessed Word and ordinance; through JESUS CHRIST our LORD, Who with Thee and the HOLY GHOST, liveth and reigneth, ever One GOD, world without end. *Amen.*

Or,

ALMIGHTY and Everlasting GOD, we are taught by Thy holy word, that the hearts of Kings are in Thy rule and governance, and that Thou dost dispose and turn them as it seemeth best to Thy godly wisdom; we humbly beseech Thee so to dispose and govern the heart of *Victoria*, Thy Servant, our Queen and Governour, that in all her thoughts, words, and works she may ever seek Thy honour and glory, and study to preserve Thy people committed to her charge in wealth, peace, and godliness: Grant this, O Merciful FATHER, for Thy dear SON'S sake, JESUS CHRIST our LORD. *Amen.*

The Collect of the Day

The Epistle

After the Epistle.

THANKS be to Thee, O GOD.

The Holy Gospel

Benediction.

THE LORD open thy mouth to read and our ears to understand the Holy Gospel of the GOD of Peace. In the Name ✠ of the FATHER, and of the SON, and of the HOLY GHOST. Amen.

Before the Holy Gospel.

GLORY be to Thee, O LORD.

After the Holy Gospel.

PRAISE be to Thee, O CHRIST.

The Creed

I BELIEVE in One God, the FATHER Almighty, Maker of Heaven and earth, And of all things visible and invisible:

And in One LORD JESUS CHRIST, the Only-Begotten SON of GOD; Begotten of His FATHER before all worlds; GOD of GOD, Light of Light, Very GOD of Very GOD, Begotten, not made; Being of one Substance with the FATHER; By Whom all things were made; Who for us men, and for our salvation came down from Heaven, AND WAS INCARNATE BY THE HOLY GHOST OF THE VIRGIN MARY, AND WAS MADE MAN; And was crucified also for us under Pontius Pilate: He suffered and was buried; And the third day He rose again according to the Scriptures; And ascended into Heaven, And sitteth on the right hand of the FATHER. And He shall come again with glory, to judge both the quick and the dead: Whose Kingdom shall have no end.

And I believe in the HOLY GHOST, The LORD and Giver of life; Who proceedeth from the FATHER and the SON; Who, with the FATHER and the SON together, is worshipped aud glorified; Who spake by the Prophets. And I believe One, Catholick, and Apostolick Church. I acknowledge one Baptism for the remission of sins; And I look for the resurrection of the dead, And the life of the world to come. Amen.

The Offertory Sentences

LET your light so shine before men, that they may see your good works, and glorify your FATHER Which is in Heaven.

. . . . .
Blessed be the man that provideth for the sick and needy: the LORD shall deliver him in the time of trouble.

When you give your alms say,

BLESSED be Thou, O LORD GOD of Israel, our FATHER, for all that is in the Heaven and in the earth is Thine. All things come of Thee, and of Thine own do we give Thee.

At the Oblation of the Elements.

RECEIVE, O Holy TRINITY, this Oblation, which I join in offering unto Thee in memory of the Passion of our LORD JESUS CHRIST, and grant that It ascending before Thee may be acceptable in Thy sight, and promote my everlasting salvation, and that of all Thy faithful people, both living and departed, through JESUS CHRIST. Amen.

O GOD, Who didst wonderfully constitute the dignity of human nature in creating it, and hast still more wonderfully regenerated it; grant that by the Mystery of this Water and Wine we may be made partakers of His Divine Nature Who vouchsafed to become a partaker of our human nature, JESUS CHRIST, Thy SON our LORD, Who liveth and reigneth with Thee and the HOLY GHOST, ever One GOD, world without end. Amen.

Let my prayer, O LORD, be set forth in Thy sight as the incense: and let the lifting up of my hands be an evening sacrifice.

Set a watch, O LORD, before my mouth: and keep the door of my lips.

O let not mine heart be inclined to any evil thing: let me not be occupied in ungodly works with the men that work wickedness.

May the LORD kindle in our hearts the fire of His love, and the flame of everlasting charity. Amen.

Additional Devotions will be found at page 96.

The Prayer for the Church

ALMIGHTY and Everliving GOD, Who by Thy holy Apostle hast taught us to make prayers, and supplications, and to give thanks, for all men;

We humbly beseech Thee most mercifully to accept our Alms and Oblations, and to receive these our prayers, which we offer unto Thy Divine Majesty; *[Oblation of the Elements.]*

Beseeching Thee to inspire continually the Universal Church with the SPIRIT of truth, unity, and concord: And grant, that all they that do confess Thy Holy Name may agree in the truth of Thy Holy Word, and live in unity, and godly love.

We beseech Thee also to save and defend all Christian Kings, Princes, and Governours; and specially Thy Servant VICTORIA our Queen; *[Remember the Living.]* that under her we may be godly and quietly governed: And grant unto her whole Council, and to all that are put in authority under her, that they may truly and indifferently minister justice, to the punishment of wickedness and vice, and to the maintenance of Thy true religion, and virtue.

Give grace, O Heavenly FATHER, to all Bishops and Curates, (especially N.) that they may both by their life and doctrine set forth Thy true and lively Word, and rightly and duly administer Thy Holy Sacraments:

And to all Thy people give Thy heavenly grace; and especially to this congregation here present, (especially N.) that with meek heart and due reverence, they may hear, and receive Thy Holy Word; truly serving Thee in holiness and righteousness all the days of their life.

And we most humbly

beseech Thee of Thy goodness, O LORD, to comfort and succour all them, who in this transitory life are in trouble, sorrow, need, sickness, or any other adversity (especially N.).

<small>REMEMBER THE DEPARTED.</small> And we also bless Thy Holy Name for all Thy Servants departed this life in Thy faith and fear (especially N.); beseeching Thee to give us grace, so to follow their good examples, that, with them, we may be partakers of Thy Heavenly Kingdom:

Grant this, O FATHER, for JESUS CHRIST'S sake, our only Mediator and Advocate. *Amen.*

The Short Exhortation

YE that do truly and earnestly repent you of your sins, and are in love and charity with your neighbours, and intend to lead a new life, following the commandments of GOD, and walking from henceforth in His holy ways; Draw near with faith, and take this Holy Sacrament to your comfort; and make your humble confession to Almighty GOD, meekly kneeling upon your knees.

The General Confession

ALMIGHTY GOD, FATHER of our LORD JESUS CHRIST, Maker of all things, Judge of all men; We acknowledge and bewail our manifold sins and wickedness, Which we, from time to time, most grievously have committed, By thought, word, and deed, Against Thy Divine Majesty, Provoking most justly Thy wrath and indignation against us. We do earnestly repent, And are heartily sorry for these our misdoings; The remembrance of them is grievous unto us; The burden of them is intolerable. Have mercy upon us, Have mercy upon us, most Merciful FATHER; For Thy SON, our LORD JESUS CHRIST'S sake, Forgive us all that is past; And grant, that we may ever hereafter Serve and please Thee, In newness of life, To the honour and glory of Thy Name: Through JESUS CHRIST our LORD. Amen.

The Absolution

ALMIGHTY GOD, our Heavenly FATHER, Who of His great mercy hath promised forgiveness of sins, to all them that with hearty repentance and true faith turn unto Him; have mercy upon you; pardon and deliver you from all your sins; confirm and strengthen you in all goodness; and bring you to everlasting life: through JESUS CHRIST our LORD. *Amen.*

The Comfortable Words

HEAR what comfortable words our SAVIOUR CHRIST saith unto all that truly turn to Him.

Come unto Me all that travail and are heavy laden, and I will refresh you.

So GOD loved the world, that He gave His Only-Begotten SON, to the end that all that believe in Him should not perish, but have everlasting life.

Hear also what Saint Paul saith.

This is a true saying, and worthy of all men to be received: that CHRIST JESUS came into the world to save sinners.

Hear also what Saint John saith.

If any man sin, we have

an Advocate with the FATHER, JESUS CHRIST the Righteous; and He is the Propitiation for our sins.

The Sursum Corda

Priest.

LIFT up your hearts.
Answer. We lift them up unto the LORD.
Priest. Let us give thanks unto our LORD GOD.
Answer. It is meet and right so to do.

The Preface

IT is very meet, right, and our bounden duty, that we should at all times, and in all places, give thanks unto Thee, O LORD, Holy FATHER, Almighty, Everlasting GOD.

These words [Holy FATHER] must be omitted on Trinity Sunday.

Here shall follow the proper Preface, or else immediately shall follow,

THEREFORE with Angels and Archangels, and with all the Company of Heaven, we laud and magnify Thy glorious Name; evermore praising Thee, and saying,

The Sanctus

HOLY, Holy, Holy, LORD GOD of Hosts, Heaven and earth are full of Thy glory; Glory be to Thee, O LORD most High.
Amen.

Proper Prefaces

Upon Christmas Day, and seven days after.

BECAUSE Thou didst give JESUS CHRIST Thine Only SON to be born as at this time for us; Who by the operation of the HOLY GHOST, was made Very Man of the substance of the Virgin Mary His mother: and that without spot of sin, to make us clean from all sin. Therefore with Angels, &c.

Upon Easter Day, *and seven days after.*

BUT chiefly are we bound to praise Thee for the glorious Resurrection of Thy SON JESUS CHRIST our LORD: for He is the very Paschal Lamb, which was offered for us, and hath taken away the sin of the world: Who by His Death hath destroyed death, and by His Rising to life again hath restored to us everlasting life. Therefore with Angels, &c.

Upon Ascension Day, *and seven days after.*

THROUGH Thy most dearly Beloved SON JESUS CHRIST our LORD; Who after His most glorious Resurrection manifestly appeared to all His Apostles, and in their sight Ascended up into Heaven to prepare a place for us; that where He is, thither we might also ascend, and reign with Him in glory. Therefore with Angels, &c.

Upon Whitsun Day, *and six days after.*

THROUGH JESUS CHRIST our LORD, according to Whose most true promise, the HOLY GHOST came down as at this time from Heaven with a sudden great sound, as it had been a mighty wind, in the likeness of fiery tongues, lighting upon the Apostles, to teach them and to lead them to all truth; giving them both the gift of divers languages, and also boldness with fervent zeal constantly to preach the Gospel unto all nations; whereby we have been brought out of darkness and error into the clear light and true knowledge of Thee, and of Thy SON JESUS CHRIST. Therefore with Angels, &c.

Upon the Feast of Trinity *only.*

WHO art One God, One Lord; not One only Person, but Three Persons in One Substance. For that which we believe of the glory of the Father, the same we believe of the Son, and of the Holy Ghost, without any difference or inequality. Therefore with Angels, &c.

The Prayer of Humble Access

WE do not presume to come to this Thy Table, O Merciful Lord, trusting in our own righteousness, but in Thy manifold and great mercies. We are not worthy so much as to gather up the crumbs under Thy Table. But Thou art the Same Lord, Whose property is always to have mercy: Grant us therefore, Gracious Lord, so to eat the Flesh of Thy dear Son Jesus Christ, and to drink His Blood, that our sinful bodies may be made clean by His Body, and our souls washed through His most precious Blood, and that we may evermore dwell in Him, and He in us. *Amen.*

Before the Prayer of Consecration say,

HOSANNA in the Highest, Blessed is He that cometh in the Name of the Lord: Hosanna in the Highest.

Most Merciful God, look graciously upon the gifts now lying before Thee, and send down Thy Holy Spirit upon this Sacrifice: that He may make this Bread the Body of Thy Christ, and this Cup the Blood of Thy Christ. Amen.

The Prayer of Consecration

ALMIGHTY GOD, our Heavenly FATHER, Who of Thy tender mercy didst give Thine Only SON JESUS CHRIST to suffer death upon the Cross for our Redemption, Who made there, by His one Oblation of Himself once offered, a full, perfect, and sufficient Sacrifice, Oblation, and Satisfaction, for the sins of the whole world; and did institute, and in His Holy Gospel command us to continue, a perpetual Memory of that His precious Death, until His coming again;

The Invocation. Hear us, O Merciful FATHER, we most humbly beseech Thee; and grant, that we receiving these Thy creatures of Bread and Wine, according to Thy SON our SAVIOUR JESUS CHRIST'S holy Institution, in remembrance of His Death and Passion, may be partakers of His most Blessed BODY and BLOOD:

Consecration of the Bread. Who in the same night that He was betrayed, took Bread, and when He had given thanks, He brake It, and gave It to His Disciples, saying, Take, Eat, 𝔗𝔥𝔦𝔰 𝔦𝔰 𝔐𝔶 𝔅𝔬𝔡𝔶 𝔚𝔥𝔦𝔠𝔥 𝔦𝔰 𝔤𝔦𝔳𝔢𝔫 𝔣𝔬𝔯 𝔶𝔬𝔲: Do This in Remembrance of Me.

Consecration of the Cup. Likewise after Supper He took the Cup; and when He had given thanks, He gave It to them, saying: Drink ye all of this; 𝔉𝔬𝔯 𝔗𝔥𝔦𝔰 𝔦𝔰 𝔪𝔶 𝔅𝔩𝔬𝔬𝔡 𝔬𝔣 𝔱𝔥𝔢 𝔑𝔢𝔴 𝔗𝔢𝔰𝔱𝔞𝔪𝔢𝔫𝔱, 𝔚𝔥𝔦𝔠𝔥 𝔦𝔰 𝔰𝔥𝔢𝔡 𝔣𝔬𝔯 𝔶𝔬𝔲 𝔞𝔫𝔡 𝔣𝔬𝔯 𝔪𝔞𝔫𝔶 𝔣𝔬𝔯 𝔱𝔥𝔢 𝔑𝔢𝔪𝔦𝔰𝔰𝔦𝔬𝔫 𝔬𝔣 𝔖𝔦𝔫𝔰: Do This as oft as ye shall drink It, in remembrance of Me. *Amen.*

After the Act of Consecration

Of the Bread.

HAIL most Holy Flesh of CHRIST! to me above all things the sum of delight!

Of the Cup.

HAIL Heavenly Drink of JESUS' BLOOD! to me above all things the sum of delight!

DEVOTIONS AFTER THE PRAYER OF CONSECRATION.

Act of Oblation.

O MOST Gracious Father, accept this Pure, this Holy Sacrifice at the hands of Thy Priest, in union with that All-Holy Sacrifice which Thy Beloved Son, throughout His whole life, at the Last Supper, and upon the Cross, offered unto Thee, for me, for (N.), and for all for whom He vouchsafed to die.

ACTS OF ADORATION.

I.

Agnus Dei.

O Lamb of God, that takest away the sins of the world : have mercy upon us.

O Lamb of God, that takest away the sins of the world : have mercy upon us.

O Lamb of God, that takest away the sins of the world : grant us Thy Peace.

II.

Ave verum Corpus.

Hail to Thee! true Body sprung
From the Virgin Mary's womb!
The Same that on the Cross was hung,
And bore for man the bitter doom!
Hear us, merciful and mild,
Jesu! Mary's gracious Child.
Amen.
From Whose Side for sinners riven
Water flowed and mingled Blood;
May'st Thou, dearest Lord! be given
In death's hour to be my Food!
Hear us, Merciful and Mild,
Jesu! Mary's gracious Child.
Amen.

III.

I ADORE Thee, O Lord my God, Whom I now behold veiled beneath these earthly forms. Prostrate I adore Thy Majesty, and because, sinful and unworthy that I am, I cannot honour Thee as I ought, I unite myself with Thy Saints and

Angels in their more perfect adoration.

Hail, most HOLY BODY of CHRIST! Hail, Living Bread, that comest down from Heaven to give life to the world! Hail, most HOLY BLOOD of JESUS, shed for sinners! Above all things the sum and fulness of delight! Hail, Saving Victim, offered for me and for all mankind! CHRIST, Eternal King! Man, crucified for man!

Behold, I praise, I bless, I glorify Thee. I would that all might glorify Thee in this Mystery of Thy love. And grant to me that, dying to the world and living here a life hidden in Thee, I may hereafter see Thy Face unveiled, to love and adore and rejoice in Thee, through all eternity. Amen.

Commemoration of the Living.

REMEMBER, O LORD, and have mercy upon the whole Church and its Rulers, upon all Christian Princes, and all Estates of men, whether serving GOD in His ministry, in special works of piety, or in the world, who have the greatest power whether to promote or to hinder Thy glory, and the good of souls:

Also upon my Parents, Brethren, Benefactors, and Friends; upon those who have especially commended themselves to me, or who have aggrieved me, whom I have aggrieved, offended, neglected to help, and whom Thou desirest that I should lead in the way of salvation:

On all these have mercy, O Thou FATHER of mercies, even as Thou knowest and willest, granting them Thy grace perfectly to please, acknowledge, fear, love, and glorify Thee with the Same Thy Beloved SON, and the HOLY GHOST, now and ever, and for endless ages. Amen.

Commemoration of the Saints.

AND here we do give unto Thee, O LORD, most high praise and hearty thanks for the wonderful grace and virtue declared in all Thy Saints, from the beginning of the world: and chiefly in the Glorious and most Blessed Virgin Mary, Mother of Thy SON JESUS CHRIST our LORD and GOD, and in the Holy Patriarchs, Prophets, Apostles, and Martyrs, whose example, O Lord, and steadfastness in Thy faith, and keeping Thy holy commandments, grant us to follow.

Commemoration of the Departed.

REMEMBER also, O Lord, the souls of Thy Servants and Handmaidens (N.) who have gone before us with the sign of faith, and sleep the sleep of peace; to them, O Lord, and to all who rest in Christ, we pray Thee, grant a place of refreshment, of light, and of peace. Through the Same Christ our Lord. Amen.

Prayer for Unity.

O LORD JESUS CHRIST, Who saidst unto Thine Apostles, Peace I leave with you, My peace I give unto you; regard not my sins, but the faith of Thy Church; and grant her that peace and unity which is agreeable to Thy will, Who livest and reignest God for ever and ever. Amen.

Devotions for those who do not Communicate will be found at page 96.

DEVOTIONS FOR COMMUNION.

Before Communicating.

GRANT me, Almighty and Everlasting God, not only to receive the Sacrament of the Body and Blood of Thy Only-Begotten Son, our Lord Jesus Christ, but also the virtue of the Sacrament to the remission of all my sins, and all other benefits of His Death and Passion. Amen.

On Approaching the Altar.

LORD, I am not worthy that Thou shouldest come under my roof, but speak the word only, and my soul shall be healed.

After Receiving the Body of our Lord.

O MY GOD, Thou art Holy; O my soul, thou art blessed.

On Making any Particular Request.

O ETERNAL FATHER! I receive this Holy Communion of Thy dear Son's Body and Blood, humbly beseeching Thee, because of It, in It, and with It, to grant me (*here name your request*).

After Receiving the Blood of our Lord.

LET my sins be washed away in Thy Blood, O LORD.

On Leaving the Altar.

THANKS be to GOD for His unspeakable Gift.

On Kneeling again in the Church.

Te Deum Laudamus.

THOU art the King of Glory : O CHRIST.

Thou art the Everlasting SON of the FATHER.

When Thou tookest upon Thee to deliver man : Thou didst not abhor the Virgin's womb.

When Thou hadst overcome the sharpness of death : Thou didst open the Kingdom of Heaven to all believers.

Thou sittest at the right hand of GOD : in the Glory of the FATHER.

We believe that Thou shalt come : to be our Judge.

We therefore pray Thee help Thy servants : whom Thou hast redeemed with Thy precious Blood.

Make them to be numbered with Thy Saints : in glory everlasting.

O LORD, save Thy people : and bless Thine heritage.

Govern them : and lift them up for ever.

Day by day : we magnify Thee.

And we worship Thy Name : ever world without end.

Additional Devotions will be found at page 106.

The Lord's Prayer

OUR FATHER, Which art in Heaven, Hallowed be Thy Name. Thy Kingdom come : Thy Will be done in earth, as it is in Heaven : Give us this day our daily Bread : And forgive us our trespasses, as we forgive them that trespass against us : And lead us not into temptation : But deliver us from evil : For Thine is the Kingdom, the power, and the glory, for ever and ever. Amen.

The Prayer of Oblation

O LORD, and Heavenly Father, we Thy humble servants entirely desire Thy Fatherly goodness mercifully to accept this our Sacrifice of Praise and Thanksgiving; *(The Oblation.)*

Most humbly beseeching Thee to grant, that by the Merits and Death of Thy SON JESUS CHRIST, and through faith in His Blood, we and all Thy whole Church may obtain remission of our sins, and all other benefits of His Passion.

And here we offer and present unto Thee, O LORD, ourselves, our souls and bodies, to be a reasonable, holy, and lively sacrifice unto Thee; humbly beseeching Thee, that all we, who are partakers of this Holy Communion, may be fulfilled with Thy grace and heavenly benediction. *(The Oblation of Ourselves.)*

And although we be unworthy, through our manifold sins, to offer unto Thee any sacrifice, yet we beseech Thee to accept this our bounden duty and service; not weighing our merits, but pardoning our offences, through JESUS CHRIST our LORD;

By Whom and with Whom, in the Unity of the HOLY GHOST, all honour and glory be unto Thee, O FATHER Almighty, world without end. *Amen.*

Or this:

The Thanksgiving

ALMIGHTY and Everliving GOD, we most heartily thank Thee, for that Thou dost vouchsafe to feed us, who have duly received these holy

Mysteries, with the spiritual food of the most precious Body and Blood of Thy SON our SAVIOUR JESUS CHRIST; and dost assure us thereby of Thy favour and goodness towards us; and that we are very members incorporate in the mystical Body of Thy SON, which is the blessed company of all faithful people; and are also heirs through hope of Thy everlasting kingdom, by the merits of the most precious Death and Passion of Thy dear SON. And we most humbly beseech Thee, O Heavenly FATHER, so to assist us with Thy grace, that we may continue in that holy fellowship, and do all such good works as Thou hast prepared for us to walk in; through JESUS CHRIST our LORD, to Whom with Thee and the HOLY GHOST, be all honour and glory, world without end. *Amen.*

The Gloria in Excelsis

GLORY be to GOD on high, and in earth peace, good will towards men. We praise Thee, we bless Thee, we worship Thee, we glorify Thee, we give thanks to Thee for Thy great glory, O LORD GOD, Heavenly King, GOD the FATHER Almighty.

O LORD, the Only-Begotten SON JESU CHRIST; O LORD GOD, Lamb of GOD, SON of the FATHER, that takest away the sins of the world, have mercy upon us. Thou that takest away the sins of the world, have mercy upon us. Thou that takest away the sins of the world, receive our prayer. Thou that sittest at the right hand of GOD the FATHER, have mercy upon us.

For Thou only art Holy; Thou only art the LORD; Thou only, O CHRIST, with the HOLY GHOST, art most High in the glory of GOD the FATHER. *Amen.*

The Peace and Blessing

The Peace. THE Peace of God, which passeth all understanding keep your hearts and minds in the knowledge and love of God, and of His Son Jesus Christ our Lord:

The Blessing And the Blessing of God Almighty, the Father, the Son, and the Holy Ghost, be amongst you and remain with you always. *Amen.*

At the Ablutions.

GRANT, O Lord, that what I have taken outwardly with my lips, I may with a pure heart inwardly receive, and that the Gift vouchsafed in this life may avail to my healing and salvation in the life to come.

May, Thy Body, O Lord, which I have eaten, and Thy Blood which I have drunk, cleave to my soul; and grant that no stain of sin may remain in me who have been refreshed with this most pure and Holy Sacrament.

PRAYERS AFTER THE SERVICE

I.

O GOD, Who in this wonderful Sacrament hast left us a Memorial of Thy Passion; grant us, we beseech Thee, so to venerate the Sacred Mysteries of Thy Body and Blood, that we may ever feel within ourselves the fruit of Thy Redemption: Who livest and reignest with the Father, in the Unity of the Holy Spirit, God, for ever and ever. Amen.

II.

O HOLY Trinity, may the performance of this my service be pleasing unto Thee; and may this Holy Sacrifice which I, though unworthy, have joined in offering up in Thy sight be accepted by Thy Divine Majesty, and through Thy mercy plead the pardon of my sins and those of all for whom It has been offered: through CHRIST our LORD. Amen.

III.

O MOST Merciful LORD GOD, ever Blessed Trinity, Who hast not disdained that we, miserable sinners, should even in this House stand in Thy sight to glorify and confess Thee, pardon me the faults of which I have been guilty even in this very time of prayer, whether through busy thoughts or wanderings of mind after vain desires, that the enemy boast not against me, seeing that not even at the very time of thanksgiving, intercession, and communion, have I been duly watchful against sin. Amen.

THANKSGIVING AFTER COMMUNION

Antiphon. Let us sing the Song of the Three Children, which they sang as they blessed the LORD in the furnace of fire.

Canticle.
Benedicite, omnia opera.

O ALL ye Works of the LORD, bless ye the LORD : praise Him and magnify Him for ever.

O ye Angels of the LORD, bless ye the LORD : praise Him and magnify Him for ever.

O ye Children of Men, bless ye the LORD : praise Him, and magnify Him for ever.

O let Israel bless the LORD : praise Him, and magnify Him for ever.

O ye Priests of the LORD, bless ye the LORD : praise Him, and magnify Him for ever.

O ye Servants of the LORD, bless ye the LORD : praise Him, and magnify Him for ever.

O ye Spirits and Souls of the Righteous, bless ye the LORD : praise Him, and magnify Him for ever.

O ye holy and humble Men of heart, bless ye the LORD : praise Him and magnify Him for ever.

O Ananias, Azarias, and

Misael, bless ye the LORD : praise Him, and magnify Him for ever.

Glory be to the FATHER.

Ps. cl. Laudate Dominum.

O PRAISE GOD in His holiness : praise Him in the firmament of His power.

Praise Him in His noble acts : praise Him according to His excellent greatness.

Praise Him in the sound of the trumpet : praise Him upon the lute and harp.

Praise Him in the cymbals and dances : praise Him upon the strings and pipe.

Praise Him upon the well-tuned cymbals : praise Him upon the loud cymbals.

Let everything that hath breath : praise the LORD.

Glory be to the FATHER.

The Song of Symeon.
Nunc Dimittis.

LORD, now lettest Thou Thy servant depart in peace : according to Thy word.

For mine eyes have seen : Thy salvation,

Which Thou hast prepared : before the face of all people ;

To be a light to lighten the Gentiles : and to be the glory of Thy people Israel.

Glory be to the FATHER.

Antiphon. Let us sing the song of the Three Children, which they sang as they blessed the LORD in the furnace of fire.

LORD have mercy upon us.
CHRIST have mercy upon us.
LORD have mercy upon us.

OUR FATHER.

℣ And lead us not into temptation.
℟ But deliver us from evil.
℣ Let all Thy works praise Thee, O LORD.
℟ And Thy Saints give thanks unto Thee.
℣ Thy Saints shall exult in glory.
℟ They shall rejoice in their beds.
℣ Not unto us, O LORD : not unto us.
℟ But to Thy Name give the praise.
℣ LORD, hear my prayer.
℟ And let my cry come unto Thee.

Let us pray.

O GOD, Who for Thy Three Servants didst

assuage the flames of fire: mercifully grant that no unholy fires may inflame us, Thy servants.

Purify, O LORD, with the fire of Thy HOLY SPIRIT our hearts and reins, that we may serve Thee with a chaste body and please Thee with a pure mind.

Prevent us, O LORD, in all our doings, with Thy most gracious favour, and further us with Thy continual help; that in all our works, begun, continued, and ended in Thee, we may glorify Thy holy Name; and finally, by Thy mercy, obtain everlasting life. Through JESUS CHRIST our LORD, Who liveth and reigneth with Thee, in the Unity of the Same Spirit, ever One GOD, world without end. Amen.

I YIELD Thee thanks, O LORD, Holy FATHER, Almighty, Everlasting GOD, Who, not for any merit of mine, but of the condescension of Thy mercy only, hast vouchsafed to feed me a sinner, Thy unworthy servant, with the precious Body and Blood of Thy SON, our LORD JESUS CHRIST. And I humbly entreat Thy boundless clemency, Almighty and Merciful Lord, that this Holy Communion may not bring guilt upon me to condemnation, but may be unto me for pardon and salvation. Let it be unto me an armour of faith, and a shield of good resolution. Let it be unto me a riddance of of all vices, an extermination of all evil desires and lusts, and an increase of love and patience, of humility and obedience, and all virtues, especially . . . : a firm defence against the wiles of all enemies, visible or invisible: a perfect quieting of all sinful impulses, fleshly or spiritual, especially . . . : a firm adherence to Thee, the One True GOD, and a blessed consummation of my end. And I pray Thee, that Thou wouldest vouchsafe to bring me a sinner to that ineffable feast, where Thou with Thy SON and the HOLY GHOST, art to Thy Saints true Light, full and everlasting Joy, and perfect Happiness; through the Same our LORD JESUS CHRIST. Amen.

O most Sweet LORD JESU, transfix the affections of my inmost soul with that most joyous and most healthful wound of Thy love, with true, serene, most holy, apostolic charity; that my soul may ever languish and melt with entire love and longing for Thee. Let it desire Thee, and faint for Thy courts; long to be dissolved and be with Thee. Grant that my soul may hunger after Thee, the Bread of Angels, the Refreshment of holy souls, our daily supersubstantial Bread, Who hast all sweetness and savour, and every pleasurable delight. Thee, Whom the Angels desire to look into, may my heart ever hunger after and feed upon, and may the appetite of my soul be filled with the sweetness of Thy savour. May it ever thirst for Thee, the Fountain of life, the Fountain of wisdom and knowledge, the Fountain of eternal light, the Torrent of pleasure, the Richness of the house of GOD. Let it ever compass Thee, seek Thee, find Thee, stretch towards Thee, arrive at Thee, meditate upon Thee, speak of Thee, and do all things to the praise and glory of Thy holy Name, with humility and discretion, with love and delight, with readiness and affection, with perseverance to the end; and be Thou ever my Hope, my whole Confidence, my Riches, my Delight, my Pleasure, my Joy, my Rest and Tranquillity, my Peace, my Sweetness, my sweet Savour, my Food, my Refreshment, my Refuge, my Help, my Wisdom, my Portion, my Possession, my Treasure, in Whom my mind and my heart may ever remain fixed and firm, and rooted immoveably. Amen.

ACTS OF DEVOTION

BEFORE OR DURING THE SERVICE

Seven Prayers ascribed to S. Ambrose.

I.

O GREAT High Priest, the true Priest, JESU CHRIST, Who didst offer Thyself to GOD the FATHER a pure and Spotless Victim upon the Altar of the Cross, for us miserable sinners, and didst give us Thy Flesh to eat and Thy Blood to drink, and didst ordain this Mystery in the Power of Thy HOLY SPIRIT, saying, "Do this in Remembrance of Me;" I pray Thee, by the same Thy Blood, the great Price of our Salvation; I pray Thee, by that wonderful and unspeakable love wherewith Thou deignedst so to love us miserable and unworthy as to wash us from our sins in Thy Own Blood: teach me, Thy unworthy servant, by Thy HOLY SPIRIT, to approach so great a Mystery with that reverence and honour, that devotion and fear, which is due and fitting. Make me, through Thy grace, always so to believe and understand, to conceive and firmly to hold, to think and to speak, of that exceeding Mystery, as shall please Thee, and be good for my soul.

Let Thy Good SPIRIT enter my heart, and there be heard without utterance, and without the sound of words speak all Truth. For Thy Mysteries are exceeding deep, and covered with a sacred veil. For Thy great mercy's sake, grant me to approach Thy Holy Mysteries with a clean heart and a pure mind. Free my heart from all defiling and unholy, from all vain and hurtful thoughts. Fence me with the holy and faithful guard and mighty protection of Thy blessed Angels, that the enemies of all good may go away ashamed. By the virtue of this mighty Mystery, and by the hand of Thy holy Angel, drive away from me and from all Thy servants, the hard spirit of pride and vain-glory, of envy and blasphemy, of impurity and uncleanness, of doubting and mistrust. Let them be ashamed and confounded together that seek after my soul to destroy it. Let them be driven backward and put to rebuke that wish me evil; For Thy mercy's sake. Amen.

II.

O GREAT High Priest, the true Priest, JESU CHRIST, King of virgins, Lover of chastity and innocence, extinguish in my body, by the heavenly dew of Thy blessing, the fuel of evil concupiscence, that so a calm purity of mind and body may abide in me. Mortify in my members the lusts of the flesh and all wrongful emotions, and grant me true and persevering chastity with Thy other gifts, which are well-pleasing unto Thee, that I may be able with chaste body and pure heart to join in offering to Thee the Sacrifice of Praise and Thanksgiving. For with what exceeding contrition of heart and flow of tears, with what reverence and awe, with what chastity of body and purity of soul, should that divine and heavenly Sacrifice be celebrated, wherein Thy Flesh is our Meat indeed, and Thy Blood is our Drink indeed, wherein the lowest are joined with the highest, things earthly with divine, where is present the company of Thy holy Angels, wherein in a wonderful and unspeakable way, Thou art Thyself both Sacrifice and Priest; For Thy mercy's sake. Amen.

III.

O GREAT High Priest, the true Priest, JESU CHRIST, who can worthily draw nigh unto this Holy Sacrament, unless Thou, O GOD Almighty, makest him worthy? I know, O LORD, yea, truly do I know, and do confess it to Thy lovingkindness, that I am not worthy to approach so high a Mystery by reason of my very many sins, especially . . . , and numberless negligences and omissions, especially . . .. But I know, and truly do believe with my whole heart and confess with my lips, that Thou canst make me worthy, Who alone canst make him clean that is conceived in sin, or sinners to be righteous and holy. By this Thine almighty power, I beseech Thee, O my GOD, that Thou wouldest grant to me, a sinner, to approach this Holy Sacrifice with fear and trembling, with purity of heart and plenteous tears, with spiritual gladness and heavenly joy. May my mind feel the sweetness of Thy most blessed Presence, and the love of Thy holy Angels, keeping watch around me; For Thy mercy's sake. Amen.

IV.

O GREAT High Priest, the true Priest, JESU CHRIST, mindful of Thy venerable Passion, I approach Thine Altar, sinner though I am, to join in offering unto Thee that Sacrifice which Thou hast instituted and commanded to be offered in remembrance of Thee for our well-being. May it be accepted, O GOD Most High, for Thy Holy Church, and for the people whom Thou hast purchased with Thine Own Blood. Let not, through our unworthiness, the Price of their salvation be wasted, whose saving Victim and Redemption Thou didst Thyself vouchsafe to be. Also pitifully behold, O LORD, the sorrows of Thy people, which we bring before Thee; the perils of Thy servants; the sorrowful sighing of prisoners; the miseries of widows and orphans, and all that are desolate and bereaved; the necessities of strangers and travellers; the helplessness and sadness of the weak and sickly; the depressions of the languishing; the weakness of the aged and of children; the trials and aspirations of young men; and the vows of virgins; For Thy mercy's sake. Amen.

V.

O GREAT High Priest, the true Priest, JESU CHRIST, Who hast mercy upon all, and hatest nothing that Thou hast made, remember how frail our nature is, and that Thou art our SAVIOUR and our GOD. Be not angry with us for ever, and shut not up Thy tender mercies in displeasure. For we humbly present our prayers before Thy face, not trusting in our own righteousness, but in Thy manifold and great mercies. Take away from me, O LORD, my iniquities, especially . . . , and mercifully kindle in me the fire of Thy HOLY SPIRIT. Take away from me the heart of stone, and give me an heart of flesh, an heart to love and adore Thee, an heart to delight in, to follow and to enjoy Thee. And I entreat Thy mercy, O LORD, that Thou wouldest favourably look down upon Thy family, as it pays its vows to Thy most holy Name; and that the desire of none may be in vain, nor their petitions unfulfilled, do Thou inspire our prayers, that they may be such as Thou delightest to hear and answer; For Thy mercy's sake. Amen.

VI.

O GREAT High Priest, the true Priest, JESU CHRIST, I pray Thee, for the souls of the faithful departed (especially N.), that this great Sacrament of Thy love may be to them health and salvation, joy and refreshment. O LORD, my GOD, grant them this day a great and abundant feast of Thee, the Living Bread, Who camest down from Heaven, and givest life unto the world; even of Thy holy and blessed Flesh, the Lamb without spot, Who takest away the sins of the world; even of that Flesh, which was taken of the Blessed Virgin Mary, and conceived by the HOLY GHOST; and of that Fountain of mercy which, by the soldier's lance, flowed from Thy most Sacred Side; that they be thereby enlarged and satisfied, refreshed and comforted; and may rejoice in Thy praise and in Thy glory.

I pray Thy clemency, O LORD, that on the Bread and Wine to be offered unto Thee may descend the fulness of Thy blessing and the sanctification of Thy Divinity. May there descend also the invisible and incomprehensible Majesty of Thy HOLY SPIRIT, as it descended of old on the sacrifices of the Fathers, which may make our oblations Thy Body and Blood; and may our prayers and offering be acceptable unto Thee, through Him Who offered Himself a Sacrifice to Thee, O FATHER, even JESUS CHRIST, Thine Only SON our LORD, Who liveth and reigneth with Thee in the Unity of the HOLY GHOST, ever One GOD, world without end. For Thy mercy's sake. Amen.

VII.

O GREAT High Priest, the True Priest, JESU CHRIST, I pray Thee, by the holy Mystery of Thy Body and Blood, whereby in Thy Church we are evermore fed, washed, and sanctified, and made partakers of Thy Divine Nature, grant to me the graces which are well pleasing unto Thee, especially . . . with which fulfilled I may so with a clean conscience approach Thy Altar, that the Sacramental Gifts may be made to me health and life. For Thou with Thy holy and blessed Mouth hast said, "The Bread that I will give is My Flesh, which I will give for the life of the world; I am the Living Bread Which came down from Heaven; if any man eat of this Bread, he shall live for ever."

O Bread most sweet, heal Thou the palate of my heart, that I may feel the sweetness of Thy love. Heal it of all weakness and frailty, that it may be set upon no sweetness but Thyself. O Bread most fair, full of all delight and sweetness, that ever refreshest us and never failest, may my heart feed on Thee, and may my inmost parts be filled with the sweetness of Thy savour. The Angel Host feeds on Thee with full satisfaction; may man in his pilgrimage so feed on Thee according to his measure, that he may not fail on the way, being refreshed with such food for his journey.

O Holy Bread, O Living Bread, O Bread most Pure, Which camest down from Heaven, and givest life unto the world, come into my heart, and cleanse me from all defilement of flesh and spirit. Enter Thou into my soul, and heal and cleanse me within and without, especially from . . . Be Thou the succour and abiding defence of my soul and body. Drive far from me all the snares of the enemy. Let them be scattered afar from Thy powerful Presence, that being both outwardly and inwardly guarded by Thee, I may attain by a straight course to Thy Kingdom, where, no more as now, in Mysteries, but face to face, we shall see Thee; when Thou shalt have delivered up the Kingdom to GOD even the FATHER, that GOD may be All in all. For then shalt Thou wondrously satisfy me from Thyself, so that I shall neither hunger nor thirst any more; For Thy mercy's sake, Who, with the Same FATHER and the HOLY GHOST, livest and reignest, ever One GOD, world without end. Amen.

O Gracious LORD JESU CHRIST, I, a sinner, nothing presuming on my own deserts, but trusting in Thy mercy and goodness, with fear and trembling approach to the Table of Thy most sweet Feast. For my heart and body are stained with many sins; my thoughts and lips not diligently kept. Wherefore, O Gracious GOD, O awful Majesty, in my extremity I turn to Thee, the Fount of Mercy; to Thee I hasten to be healed, and take refuge under Thy protection; and Thee, before Whom as my Judge I cannot stand, I long for as my SAVIOUR. To Thee, O LORD, I show my wounds, to Thee I lay bare my shame. I know my sins are many and great, for which I am afraid. My trust is in Thy mercies, of which there is no end. Look therefore upon me with the eye of Thy mercy, O LORD JESU CHRIST, GOD and Man, crucified for man; hearken unto me whose trust is in Thee; have mercy upon me, who am full of sin and misery, O Thou Fount of mercy, that wilt never cease to flow. Hail Saving Victim, offered for me and all mankind on the Cross of suffering and shame. Hail, noble and precious Blood, flowing from the wounds of my crucified LORD and SAVIOUR JESUS CHRIST, and washing away the sins of the whole world. Be mindful, O LORD, of Thy creature, whom Thou hast redeemed with Thine Own Blood. It repents me that I have sinned; I desire to amend what I have done. Take therefore away from me, O most Merciful SAVIOUR, all my iniquities and sins, especially . . . , that, being cleansed both in body and soul, I may worthily taste the Holy of Holies; and grant that this holy feeding on Thy Body and Blood, of which, unworthy as I am, I purpose to partake, may be for the remission of my sins, and the perfect cleansing of all my offences, for the driving away of all evil thoughts, and the renewal of all holy desires, for the healthful bringing forth of fruit well-pleasing unto Thee, and the most sure protection of my soul and body against the wiles of all my enemies. Amen.

Act of Contrition.

I DESIRE, O my SAVIOUR, humbly to offer to Thee the sacrifice of a troubled, a broken, and a contrite heart. I grieve from my inmost heart that I have ever offended Thee by my sins, Thee my GOD and my chief Good, Thee Who art so gracious to me, and so oft refreshest me in Thy Blessed Sacrament. I grieve especially for the sins of . . . which Thou knowest, Thou Searcher of our hearts, and which I, a miserable sinner, do confess in the bitterness of my soul. Would that I had never offended Thee! Yet a broken and contrite heart, O GOD, Thou wilt not despise; Thou, Who for love of us, didst give to us Thine Only-Begotten SON, to wash us from our sins in His Own Blood.

Resolution of Amendment.

I DESIRE, O LORD, earnestly longing for the help of Thy grace, to renew all my Baptismal Vows to Thee, to renounce all that displeaseth Thee, and to walk more perfectly in newness of life. I renounce the devil and all his works, and the vain pomp and glory of the world, with all covetous desires, all sinful excesses in things lawful, and whatsoever may lead my heart from Thee, or hinder my duty towards Thee; also, I renounce all the sinful lusts of the flesh, with everything in thought, word, or deed, which displeaseth Thee, especially . . . from all which let it be Thy good pleasure to deliver me, and to turn the whole stream of my affections to the love of Thee, that Thy will and Thy love may be the sole rule and guide of my life, and I may love whatever Thou lovest, and hate whatever Thou hatest.

Act of Faith.

OF a truth I firmly believe, O Good JESU, and with lively faith confess, that Thou Thyself, equal to GOD the FATHER in glory and in power, true GOD and Man, art verily and indeed present in this Sacrament. For Thou, the Very Truth Itself, hast said, This is My Body, This is My Blood. I believe whatever the SON of GOD hath said. Nothing can be truer than this word of Him Who is the Truth. LORD, I believe, help Thou mine unbelief, increase my faith.

Act of Hope.

O CHRIST JESUS, I am sinful dust and ashes, but Thou callest to Thee them that labour and are heavy laden, that Thou mayest refresh them. Art not Thou my Refuge? To whom else should I go? Thou alone hast the words of eternal life, Thou alone canst comfort me in every trouble. LORD, I am weak and sick, but Thou art my Salvation. They that are whole need not a physician, but they that are sick. Therefore I come to Thee, my Physician and my Refuge, hoping that this Communion may be to me the increase of Faith, Hope, and Charity; a firm defence against the snares of my enemies; a help to the removal of the fault and defect of . . . and to the bringing forth of works well-pleasing unto Thee, especially . . . and a pledge of future glory. This is the hope and desire which I cherish in my heart, for Thou art pitiful and of tender mercy, and in all Thy promises most faithful.

Act of Love.

O MOST Sweet SAVIOUR, JESUS CHRIST, how great was Thy love, which drew Thee from the bosom of the FATHER to this vale of tears, to take our flesh, and endure infinite miseries and wrongs, yea, even the Death of the Cross, and that only for us miserable sinners, and for our salvation. O how great was Thy love? Thou mightest have condemned us, and Thou didst rather choose to save us: we were guilty, and Thou, the Sinless One, didst endure our punishment to set us free.

Out of love it was that Thou camest down to take our flesh; and when about to depart from this world to the FATHER, Thou didst leave to us this Sacrament as a pledge of Thy love; that after a new and wondrous manner, Thou mightest abide with us for ever; Thou, Whose delights are to be with the sons of men.

O LORD, how worthy art Thou of love, Who dost so much for love of us! Wherefore I will love Thee, O LORD, my Strength, my Refuge, and my Deliverer.

O GOD, Thou art very Love! He that dwelleth in love dwelleth in Thee. I desire to receive Thee in this Sacrament, that I may be more firmly united with Thee in the bond of love. Who shall separate me from the love of CHRIST my SAVIOUR? O that neither life, nor death, nor any creature, may have power to do so.

Act of Humility.

HOW dare I venture to approach to Thee, O LORD? Art not Thou, O GOD, my LORD, my Creator, my Redeemer, the King of Heaven and earth? and who am I? A poor worm of earth, and, what is yet more unworthy, so oft a disobedient and ungrateful sinner against Thee! Of a truth, LORD, I am not worthy that Thou shouldest come under my roof: yet remember, O LORD, that although Thou wast LORD of all, yet didst Thou take upon Thee the form of a servant, and coming unto us didst converse familiarly with publicans and sinners; and lastly didst humble Thyself even unto death. Let that, Thy humility, move Thee, I beseech Thee, not to despise me, vile and worthless as I am, but graciously to come unto me, and mercifully to receive me, who come to Thee.

Act of Spiritual Communion.

IN union, O Dear LORD, with the faithful at every Altar of Thy Church, where Thy blessed Body and Blood are being offered to the FATHER, I desire to offer Thee praise and thanksgiving. I present to Thee my soul and body, with the earnest wish that I may be always united to Thee. And since I cannot now receive Thee sacramentally, I beseech Thee to come spiritually into my heart. I unite myself to Thee, and embrace Thee with all the affections of my soul. O let nothing ever separate Thee from me. Let me live and die in Thy love. Amen.

Act of Reparation.

O LORD, my GOD and SAVIOUR, Who, as

Thou didst endure for our salvation the outrages of those who crucified Thee, so now deignest to bear with those who approach and touch Thee, "not discerning" Thee, and endurest all irreverences rather than withhold Thy Sacred Presence from our Altars; I bewail these indignities, and most earnestly desire to prevent, to the utmost of my power, whatever thus still grieves Thee.

I beseech Thee, accept this sorrow and this desire, as the only offering I can make in reparation of so great dishonour. O LORD, increase our faith, and preserve us from the least profanation of this adorable Mystery, and kindle in me and in the hearts of all Thy people, especially of all who celebrate or assist in Its ministration, such reverence and devotion, that Thy most holy Name may more and more be honoured and glorified in this Sacrament of love. Amen.

Aspirations.

O LORD JESU, what great things hast Thou done, and what didst Thou suffer, out of the power of Thy boundless love towards me! But what return have I made? and what return shall I make?

I am sorry from the bottom of my heart, that I have ever offended Thee, Who hast so greatly loved me.

I believe in Thee with a lively faith, O Eternal Truth! because Thou art Thyself GOD and Man, my LORD and SAVIOUR.

I hope in Thee, O LORD, O only Hope, and true Salvation of my soul.

I love Thee, O my sovereign Good! oh, that I may love Thee above all things with my whole heart! Oh! may the burning power of Thy love absorb me, that nothing may ever separate me from the love of CHRIST JESUS, my Saviour!

Whom have I in Heaven but Thee? and there is none upon earth that I desire in comparison of Thee!

Like as the hart desireth the water-brooks, so longeth my soul after Thee, O GOD.

What is man, that Thou art mindful of him; or the son of man that Thou visitest him?

Blessed is He that cometh in the Name of the LORD.

ACTS OF DEVOTION AFTER COMMUNION

Aspirations.

WHO art Thou, O Lord, and what am I?

Dost Thou come unto me, O King, most High, even to the very lowest of Thy servants?

Behold, O Lord, I now have Thee, Who hast all things: I possess Thee, Who possessest all things and canst do all things; therefore, O my God and my All, do Thou wean my heart from all other things beside Thee, for in them there is nothing but vanity and vexation of spirit; on Thee alone may my heart be fixed; in Thee be my rest, for in Thee is my treasure, in Thee is the sovereign truth, and true happiness, and eternal life.

Let my soul, O Lord, feel the sweetness of Thy presence. May it taste how sweet Thou art, O Lord, that allured by love of Thee, it may seek for nothing wherein to rejoice out of Thee; for Thou art the Joy of my heart, and my God, and my Portion for ever.

Thou art the Physician of my soul, Who with Thine own stripes hast healed our sickness. I am that sick soul whom Thou camest from Heaven to heal; heal my soul therefore, for I have sinned against Thee.

Thou art the Good Shepherd Who hast laid down Thy life for Thy sheep. Behold, I am that sheep which was lost, and yet Thou dost vouchsafe to feed me with Thy Body and Blood; lay me now upon Thy shoulders. What wilt Thou refuse me, Who hast given Thyself unto me? O! be Thou my Shepherd, and I shall lack nothing in the green pasture wherein Thou feedest me, until I am brought to the pastures of eternal life.

O Thou true Light, which enlightenest every man that cometh into the world, enlighten mine eyes, that I sleep not in death.

O Fire continually burning, and never failing! Behold how lukewarm and cold I am; oh! do Thou inflame my reins and my heart, that they may be on fire with the love of Thee. For Thou camest to send fire on the earth, and what wilt Thou, but that it be kindled?

O King of Heaven and earth, rich in pity! Behold, I am poor and needy; Thou knowest what I most require; Thou alone art able to enrich and help me; help me, O GOD, and out of the treasure of Thy goodness, succour Thou my needy soul.

O my LORD and my GOD! Behold, I am Thy servant: give me understanding and kindle my affections that I may know and do Thy will.

Thou art the Lamb of GOD, the Lamb without spot, Who takest away the sins of the world; take away from me whatever hurteth me and displeaseth Thee; and give me what Thou knowest to be pleasing to Thee and good for me.

Thou art my Love and all my Joy: Thou art my GOD and my All: Thou art the Portion of mine inheritance and of my cup; Thou art He Who shall maintain my lot.

O my GOD and my All! may the sweet and burning power of Thy love, I beseech Thee, absorb my soul, that I may die unto the world for the love of Thee, Who for the love of me hast vouchsafed to die upon the Cross, O my GOD and my All!

LORD, if I had lived innocently, I could not have deserved to receive the crumbs that fall from Thy Table. How great is Thy mercy, Who hast feasted me with the Bread of Virgins, with the Wine of Angels, with Manna from Heaven!

O when shall I pass from this dark glass, from this veil of Sacraments, to the vision of Thy eternal light; from eating Thy Body, to beholding Thy face in Thy eternal Kingdom?

Let not my sins crucify the LORD of life again: let it never be said concerning me, "The hand of him that betrayeth Me is with Me on the table."

O that I might love Thee as well as ever any creature loved Thee! let me think nothing but Thee, desire nothing but Thee, enjoy nothing but Thee.

O JESUS, be a Saviour unto me. Thou art all things unto me. Let nothing ever please me but what savours of Thee, and Thy miraculous sweetness.

Blessed be the mercies of our LORD, Who of GOD is made unto me wisdom, and righteousness, and sanctification, and redemption. He that glorieth, let him glory in the LORD. Amen.

Adore and Magnify the Lord.

O LORD JESUS, sweetest Guest, mayest Thou have come happily to me, Thy poor and humble servant. Mayest Thou have entered blessedly under this mean and lowly roof. Blessed art Thou, O LORD, in the Highest, for that Thou hast come into my heart, Thou Day-spring from on High. O King of Peace! drive from my heart all vain and idle thoughts, that my soul may be able to dwell on and to love Thee only, the Author of Peace. For what beside Thee, O Thou Peace, Thou Calm and Sweetness of my heart, should my soul seek for or desire.

Pray for Grace.

GRANT me Thy grace, most Merciful JESUS that it may be with me, and work with me, and continue with me even to the end. Grant me ever to will and to desire what is most pleasing unto Thee. Let Thy will be mine, and my will ever follow Thine in perfect agreement with it, that so I may neither choose nor reject, save what Thou choosest and rejectest.

Grant me to die to all that is in the world, and for love of Thee to be content to be despised and unknown in this life. Grant me above all objects of desire, to rest in Thee, and to still my heart to perfect peace in Thee. For Thou art the true Peace of the heart, Thou art its only Rest, and out of Thee all is restless and unquiet. In this Peace, that is in Thyself alone, my chiefest and eternal Good, may I lay me down and take my rest. Amen.

Give Thanks.

WHAT shall I render unto Thee, O LORD JESUS, for all that Thou hast done unto me, and this day especially? Of Thy care for me Thou hast given me Thy Body for my Food, and Thy Blood for my Drink, and both for a pledge of future glory. Would that my lips might be opened, and my mouth filled with Thy praise, that I might sing of Thy glory and honour all the day long, and tell of all Thy wondrous works. O my soul, magnify thou the LORD, from Whom thou hast received blessings so many and so great; and rejoice, my spirit, in GOD thy SAVIOUR: for He hath regarded the lowliness of His servant; and He that is mighty hath done for me great things, and hath filled me when an hungered with good things.

Let my words please Thee, O LORD; my joy shall be in Thee, and I will be exercised in Thy commandments. Hold Thou me by my right hand, and guide me with Thy counsel, that Thou mayest afterwards receive me with glory; for Thy mercy's sake. Amen.

Offer to God the Father His Son Jesus Christ.

O MOST Merciful FATHER, Who hast so loved me as to give to me Thy Only Begotten SON for my Food and Drink, and with Him all things, look upon the Face of Thine Anointed, in Whom Thou art well pleased. This Thy Beloved SON, and with Him my heart, I offer and present to Thee for all the blessings Thou hast this day given me. Mayest Thou, O FATHER, be now well pleased in Him, and through Him turn away Thine indignation from me.

Behold the One Mediator between GOD and Man, the Man CHRIST JESUS, my Advocate and High Priest, Who intercedes for me. Him do I offer and plead before Thee, Who did no sin, but bare the sins of the world, and with Whose stripes we are healed. Accept, therefore, O Holy FATHER, this Immaculate Victim, to the honour and glory of Thy Name, in thanksgiving for all Thy benefits bestowed upon me, in remission also of my sins, and supply of all my defects and shortcomings.

Offer Thyself to Christ.

O LORD, for that I am Thy Servant and the son of Thy handmaid, I therefore renounce the devil and all his works, the pomps and vanity of this wicked world, and all the sinful lusts of the flesh. Thou alone art the GOD of my heart, Thou, O GOD, art my Portion for ever. Thou art the Portion of mine inheritance and of my cup. It is Thou Who shalt restore mine heritage unto me. Do Thou therefore take for Thine own the whole powers of my soul, my memory, my intellect, and all my will. All that I am, all that I have, Thou hast bestowed upon me: Therefore I give back all to Thee, and surrender it to be wholly governed by Thy Sovereign will. Grant me but grace to love Thee alone, and I am rich enough and ask no more.

Litany of our Lord Present in the Holy Eucharist

LORD, have mercy upon us.

CHRIST, *have mercy upon us.*

LORD, have mercy upon us.

O CHRIST, hear us.

O CHRIST, *graciously hear us.*

GOD the FATHER, Creator of the world;
GOD the SON, Redeemer of mankind;
GOD the HOLY GHOST, Perfecter of the elect;
HOLY TRINITY, Three Persons, One GOD;

JESU, GOD and Man, in Two Natures and One Divine Person;

} *Have mercy upon us.*

JESU, our Wonderful GOD, Who vouchsafest to be Present upon the Altar when the Priest pronounces the words of Consecration;

JESU, our Heavenly Physician, Who vouchsafest to descend from Thy Palace of immortal bliss to our houses of clay, to visit us on beds of sickness, and to give Thyself to comfort our sorrows;

JESU, our Incomprehensible GOD, Who, though the Heaven of Heavens cannot contain Thee, art pleased to dwell among men;

JESU, our Sovereign King, Who, though Thy Throne is attended by glorified Spirits, yet declinest not the service of men;

} *Have mercy upon us.*

Litany of Holy Eucharist 111

JESU, our Glorious GOD, Who sittest at the Right Hand of Thy Eternal FATHER, adored by innumerable Angels, and encompassed with the splendours of inaccessible light;

JESU, our Gracious GOD, Who, condescending to the weakness of our nature, coverest Thy Glory under the familiar Forms of Bread and Wine, and so givest Thyself to miserable sinners;

JESU, our Merciful GOD, Who, concealing the brightness of Thy Majesty under these low and humble Veils, invitest us to approach unto Thee, to lay open our miseries before Thy eyes, and to deliver our petitions into Thy hands;

JESU, our Pitiful GOD, Who, to communicate Thy Divine Nature to sinners, humblest Thyself to descend into our hearts, and, by an inconceivable Union, to become One with us;

JESU, the Bread of Life, Which camest down from Heaven, of Which whosoever eats shall live for ever;

JESU, the Heavenly Manna, Whose sweetness nourisheth Thy elect in the desert of this world;

JESU, the Food of Angels, Whose sweetness filleth our hearts with Celestial joys;

JESU, the Lamb without spot, Who, once sacrificed, art continually offered, yet art alive for evermore; Who art continually consumed, yet still remainest Perfect;

JESU, the Good Shepherd, Who layest down Thy Life for Thy Sheep, and feedest them with Thine Own Body;

JESU, Who, in this August and Venerable Mystery, art Thyself both Priest and Victim;

JESU, Who in the Sacred Memorial of Thy Death, hast consummated all Thy wonders into one stupendous Miracle;

JESU, Who, in this Adorable Mystery, hast contracted all Thy Blessings into one inestimable Bounty;

Have mercy upon us.

JESU, Who, by this blessed Fruit of the Tree of Life, restorest us again to immortality;

JESU, Who, by becoming Thyself our Daily Food in this life, preparest us to feed on Thee for ever in the next;

JESU, Who in this Divine Banquet, givest us possession of Thy grace here, and a certain pledge of our glory hereafter;

JESU, Who art the Way, the Truth, and the Life, and through Whom alone we approach the FATHER;

Have mercy upon us.

SPARE us, Good LORD;
And pardon our sins.
Spare us, Good LORD;
And hear our prayers.

FROM presuming to measure the depth of Thy Almightiness by the short line of human reason;

From presuming to interpret the unsearchable secrets of Thy will by the fallible rule of man's judgment;

From all distraction and irreverence when present at this Awful Sacrifice;

From neglecting to approach Thy Holy Table, and from coming to It unprepared:

From an unworthy and fruitless reception of this adorable Mystery;

From all hardness of heart, and ingratitude for so unspeakable a Blessing;

BY Thine irresistible Power, which changeth the course of Nature as Thou willest;

By Thine unsearchable Wisdom, which disposeth all things in perfect order;

By Thine Infinite Goodness, which freely bestoweth Thyself in this incomprehensible Mystery;

By Thy most Sacred Body broken for us, and really given to us in the Holy Communion;

By Thy most Precious Blood poured out for us on the Cross, and really given unto us in the Cup of Blessing;

Good LORD, deliver us.

Good LORD, deliver us.

Litany of Holy Eucharist

WE sinners most humbly beseech Thee;
To hear us, O LORD JESU CHRIST.

And that it may please Thee to grant,

THAT we may always believe nothing more reasonable than to submit our reason unto Thee;

That by this Sacred Oblation we may acknowledge Thine infinite perfections in Thyself and Thy supreme dominion over all things;

That by this adorable Sacrifice we may acknowledge our perpetual dependence upon Thee, and our absolute subjection to Thy will;

That we may ever magnify Thy goodness, Who, having no need of us, hast set forth such endearing motives to make us love Thee;

That we may thankfully comply with Thy gracious desire of being united to us, by a fervent desire of being made one with Thee;

That before we approach the Banquet of Divine Love, we may endeavour to be reconciled to Thee, and to be in perfect charity with all the world;

That, at the moment of receiving Thy Sacred Body and Thy Precious Blood, our souls may dissolve in reverence and love, to attend on and entertain so Glorious a Guest;

That returning from the Holy Eucharist, we may collect all our thoughts to praise and bless Thee, and strive to live after Thy commandments;

That, by this Heavenly Medicine, our heart may be healed of all infirmities, and our will strengthened against all relapses;

That, as by faith we adore Thee Present beneath the Sacred Veils, we may hereafter behold Thee Face to face, and evermore be glad with the joy of Thy Countenance;

We beseech Thee to hear us, Good Lord.

We beseech Thee to hear us, Good Lord.

O LAMB of GOD, That takest away the sins of the world;
Have mercy upon us.

O Lamb of God, That takest away the sins of the world;
Have mercy upon us.

O Lamb of God, That takest away the sins of the world;
Grant us Thy peace.

O CHRIST, hear us.
   O CHRIST, graciously hear us.

Let us pray.

O GOD, Who in this Wonderful Sacrament has left us a Memorial of Thy Passion; Grant us, we beseech Thee, so to venerate the sacred Mysteries of Thy BODY, and BLOOD, that we may ever feel within ourselves the fruit of Thy Redemption, Who livest and reignest with the FATHER in the Unity of the HOLY SPIRIT, GOD, for ever and ever. Amen.

Hymns

Lauda, Sion, Salvatorem.

LAUD, O Sion, Thy Salvation,
Laud, with hymns of exultation,
   CHRIST, thy King and Shepherd true;
Bring Him all the praise thou knowest;
He is more than thou bestowest;
   Never canst thou reach His due.

Special theme for glad thanksgiving
Is the Living and Life-giving
   Bread, to-day before thee set;
From His hands of old partaken,
As we know by faith unshaken,
   Where the Twelve at supper met.

Full and clear ring out thy chanting,
Joy nor sweetest grace be wanting,
   From thy heart let praises burst:
For to-day the Feast is holden
When the Institution olden
   Of that Supper is rehearsed.

Here the new law's new oblation,
By the new King's revelation,
   Ends the form of ancient rite;

Now the New the old effaces,
Truth away the shadow chases,
  Light dispels the gloom of night.
WhatHedid,at supper seated,
Christ ordained to be repeated,
  His Memorial ne'er to cease;
And His rule for guidance taking, [making
Bread and Wine we hallow,
  Thus our Sacrifice of peace.

Wondrous truth by Christians learnèd,
Bread into His Flesh is turnèd,
  Into precious Blood the Wine.
Sight hath failed, nor thought conceiveth;
But a dauntless faith believeth,
  Resting on a Power Divine.

Whoso of this Food partaketh
Rendeth not the Lord, nor breaketh;
  Christ is whole to all that taste;
Thousands are, as one, receivers;
One, as thousands of believers,
  Eats of Him Who cannot waste.

Bad and good the Feast are sharing:
O what diverse dooms preparing,
  Endless death or endless life!
Life to these, to those damnation:
See how like participation
  Is with unlike issues rife.

When the Sacrament is broken,
Doubt not, but believe 'tis spoken,
That each severed outward token
  Doth the very Whole contain:
Nought the precious Gift divideth,
Breaking but the sign betideth,
Jesus still the same abideth,
  Still unbroken doth remain.

Lo, the Angels' Food is given
To the pilgrim who hath striven;
See the children's Bread from Heaven
  Which on dogs may ne'er be spent:
Truth the ancient types fulfilling,
Isaac bound a victim willing;
Paschal Lamb its Life-Blood spilling;
  Manna to the Fathers sent.

Very Bread, Good Shepherd, tend us,
Jesu, of Thy love befriend us;

Thou refresh us, Thou defend us,
Thine eternal goodness send us
 In the Land of life to see:
Thou Who all things canst and knowest,
Who on earth such Food bestowest,
Grant us with Thy saints, though lowest,
Where the Heavenly Feast Thou showest,
 Fellow-heirs and guests to be.   Amen.

Pange lingua gloriosi.

NOW, my tongue, the mystery telling
 Of the glorious Body sing,
And the Blood, all price excelling,
 Which the Gentiles' LORD and KING,
In a Virgin's womb once dwelling,
 Shed for this world's ransoming.

Given for us, and condescending
 To be born for us below,
He with men in converse blending
 Dwelt the seed of truth to sow,
Till He closed with wondrous ending
 His most patient life of woe.

That last night at supper lying,
 'Mid the twelve His chosen band,
JESUS, with the law complying,
 Keeps the Feast its rites demand;
Then more precious Food supplying,
 Gives Himself with His Own hand.

Word-made-Flesh true bread He maketh
 By His Word His Flesh to be;
Wine, His Blood; which whoso taketh
 Must from carnal thoughts be free;
Faith alone, though sight forsaketh,
 Shows true hearts the Mystery.

Therefore we, before Him bending,
 This great Sacrament revere;
Types and shadows have their ending,
 For the newer Rite is here;
Faith, our outward sense befriending,
 Makes our inward vision clear.

Glory let us give, and blessing,

To the FATHER and the SON,
Honour, might, and praise addressing,
While eternal ages run;
Ever too, His love confessing,
Who from Both with Both is One. Amen.

Verbum Supernum prodiens.

THE Heavenly WORD proceeding forth,
Yet leaving not the FATHER'S side,
Accomplishing His work on earth
Had reached at length life's eventide.

By false disciple to be given
To foemen for His life athirst,
Himself, the very Bread of Heaven,
He gave to His disciples first.

He gave Himself in either kind,
His precious Flesh, His precious Blood:
In Love's own fulness thus designed
Of the whole man to be the Food.

By Birth, their fellow-man was He;
Their Meat, when sitting at the board:
He died, their Ransomer to be;
He ever reigns, their great Reward.

O Saving Victim, opening wide
The gate of Heaven to man below;
Our foes press on from every side,
Thine aid supply, Thy strength bestow.

All thanks and praise to Thee ascend
For evermore, Blest ONE IN THREE;
O grant us life that shall not end
In our true native land with Thee. Amen.

O Esca Viatorum.

O FOOD that weary pilgrims love!
O Bread of Angel Hosts above!
O Manna of the Saints!
The hungry soul would feed on Thee;
Ne'er may the heart unsolaced be
Which for Thy sweetness faints.

O Fount of love! O cleansing Tide

Which from the SAVIOUR's
   piercèd side
And Sacred Heart dost flow!
Be ours to drink of Thy pure
   rill,
Which only can our spirits fill
And all we need bestow.

LORD JESU, Whom, by power
   divine
Now hidden 'neath the out-
   ward sign,
   We worship and adore,
Grant, when the veil away is
   roll'd,
With open face we may behold
   Thyself for evermore.
   Amen.

Adoro Te devote.

HUMBLY I adore Thee,
   hidden Deity,
Which beneath these symbols
   art concealed from me :
Wholly in submission Thee
   my spirit hails,
For in contemplating Thee
   it wholly fails.

Sight, and touch, and taste
   may nought of Thee discern,
But the soul that hearkens can
   the mystery learn :
I believe whatever GOD's own
   SON averred,
Nothing can be truer than
   the Truth's own word.

On the Cross Thy Godhead
   only was concealed,
Here not e'en Thy Manhood
   is to sight revealed :
But in both believing and
   confessing, LORD,
Ask I what the dying thief
   of Thee implored.
I do not, like Thomas, see
   Thy Wounds appear,
But with him confess my
   LORD and GOD is here.
Grant this faith in me may
   evermore increase,
And my hope in Thee and
   love may never cease.

O thrice-blest Memorial of
   my dying LORD,
This true Bread of Life doth
   life to man afford ;
Grant, O LORD, my soul may
   ever feed on Thee,
And Thy taste of all things
   to it sweetest be.

Victim for Thy people, JESU,
   LORD and GOD,
Cleanse me, wretched sinner,
   in Thy precious Blood ;
Blood whereof one drop for
   humankind outpoured,
Might from all transgression
   have the world restored.

JESU, Whom in this life
   veilèd I behold,
Grant what my soul thirsts
   for with desire untold ;
O may I, beholding Thine
   unveilèd grace,
Rest in blissful vision of
   Thine open Face. Amen.

Penitential Devotions

PRAYERS BEFORE EXAMINATION OF CONSCIENCE.

O ALMIGHTY GOD, Maker of Heaven and earth, King of Kings, and Lord of Lords, Who hast made me out of nothing in Thine Image and Likeness, and hast redeemed me with Thine Own Blood: Whom I a sinner am not worthy to name or call upon, or think of. I humbly pray Thee, I earnestly beseech Thee, mercifully to look on me, Thy wicked servant. Thou Who hadst mercy on the woman of Canaan and Mary Magdalene; Thou Who didst spare the publican and the thief upon the Cross, have mercy upon me. Thou art my Hope and my Trust: my Guide and my Succour; my Comfort and my Strength; my Defence and my Deliverance; my Life, my Health, and my Resurrection; my Light and my Longing; my Help and my Protection. I pray and entreat Thee, help me and I shall be safe: direct me and defend me; strengthen me and comfort me; confirm me and gladden me; enlighten me and come unto me. Raise me from the dead; I am Thy creature, and the work of Thy hands. Despise me not, O LORD; neither regard my iniquities; but according to the multitude of Thy Mercies, have mercy upon me, the chief of sinners, and be gracious unto me. Turn Thee unto me, O LORD, and be not angry with me. I implore Thee, most pitiful FATHER, I pray Thee meekly of Thy great mercy, to bring me to a holy death, and to true penitence, to perfect confession, and worthy satisfaction for all my sins. Amen.

O LORD GOD, Who lightenest every man that cometh

into the world, enlighten my heart, I pray Thee, with the light of Thy grace, that I may fully know my sins, shortcomings, and negligences, and may confess them with that true sorrow and contrition of heart which befits me. I desire to make full amends for all my sins, and amend them to Thy honour and glory, and to the salvation of my soul, through JESUS CHRIST our LORD. Amen.

ACTS OF FAITH, HOPE, AND LOVE.

Act of Faith.

I BELIEVE in Thee, O GOD, FATHER, SON, and HOLY GHOST, my Creator, my Redeemer, and my Sanctifier; I believe that Thou art All-Holy, Just, and Merciful. I believe that Thou art willing to pardon and to save me, if I repent and forsake my sins.

O my GOD, strengthen and increase my Faith, and grant me the grace of a true repentance, for JESUS CHRIST's sake. Amen.

Act of Hope.

I HOPE in Thee, O my GOD, because Thou art Almighty, Faithful, and Long-suffering, I humbly trust that Thou wilt pardon my sins for the sake of Thy dear SON JESUS CHRIST, Who suffered and died for me upon the Cross: and that Thou wilt cleanse my sinful soul in His precious Blood, and make me holy, and bring me safe to everlasting life.

O LORD, in Thee have I trusted, let me never be confounded. Amen.

Act of Love.

I LOVE Thee, O my GOD, above all things, because Thou hast been so good, so patient, so loving to me, notwithstanding all the sins by which I have so grievously offended Thee. I love Thee, O Blessed JESUS, my SAVIOUR, because Thou didst suffer so much for love of me, an ungrateful sinner, and didst die on the Cross for my salvation.

O make me love Thee more and more, and show my love to Thee by faithfully keeping Thy Commandments all the days of my life. Amen.

A METHOD OF SELF-EXAMINATION
BY THE
TEN COMMANDMENTS.

When you examine your conscience, seek stillness and solitude, place yourself in the presence of God, and think of the Day of Judgment, when the secrets of all hearts must be known. Then search into your life by the aid of the Holy Spirit, call up your sins since your last Confession, and accuse yourself of them, one by one, note them down in order that your Confession may be full and faithful. If you are preparing to make a First Confession, you will find it well to divide your life into periods; think with whom you have lived, acted, conversed, been intimate: where you have lived, in what town, house, street, or room.

In the case of any sin, trace out: 1. The forerunners of it, its beginnings, the length of time it lasted. 2. When it began to be more against conscience, and in spite of warnings, more deliberate. 3. Whether it was in act as well as in thought and word. 4. Any aggravations of it, as after Confirmation or Communion, and Confession. 5. Whether it was resisted or committed as often as temptations occurred; or left off for a time, and if so, why? 6. Whether it led to other sins, and if so, of what sort? 7. Whether you have led others into it, especially any under your charge or special influence. During your examination, say Psalm li., or the Ejaculations at page 132, to excite sorrow for your sin, or the "Veni Creator," as a prayer to God to show you each sin, the number of them, and their guilt.

First Commandment.

HAVE I loved any thing or person more than GOD: allowed the world and its pleasures or honours to get possession of my heart: made an idol of anything? Have I lived without GOD in the world: not remembered that my inmost thoughts are always known to GOD: resisted the good thoughts GOD has sent me: followed my own will, and pleased myself rather than obeyed the will of GOD: trusted in myself or in others and not in GOD: feared man more than God : neglected my duty toward GOD for fear of being laughed at? Have I repined, thinking that God is dealing hardly with me : been unthankful : murmured : dwelt on the troubles and difficulties of life rather than on its blessings : despaired of salvation : of forgiveness : delayed to repent : laughed at sin : spoken lightly of it? Have I refused to submit to the teaching of the Church : indulged doubts concerning any doctrine : lived in unbelief : in ignorance of the Catholic Faith : not taken pains to be instructed in it : made companions of those who might draw me from the Faith : joined in any Schismatical Worship : separated myself from the Church : consulted Fortune-tellers : used charms : given way to superstition? Have I been vain of anything belonging to me : spoken much of myself or family : been unwilling to be considered less than others, to be surpassed by others : been contemptuous of others : obstinate in not owning my faults : impatient of what humbles me : sought to be flattered, admired?

Second Commandment.

HAVE I omitted to say my Prayers, Morning or Evening : said them carelessly, unwillingly, not kneeling : wilfully let my thoughts wander in saying them : risen too late to say them : hurried over them : neglected self-examination : or reading Holy Scripture and spiritual books : or Family Prayers : not prayed for others : not said Grace before and after meals? Have I been to Church regularly : kept away from Church for any insufficient reason : been irreverent, inattentive, let my thoughts wander, looked about, talked needlessly, laughed, played in Church : been less reverent when alone in Church than when with others ; desired to attract notice in Church : acted irreverently in an empty Church? Have I delayed to receive Holy Baptism or Confirmation from sloth, negligence, or any other cause : delayed or neglected or been indifferent about becoming a Communicant : or been irregular and infrequent in attendance at the Holy Communion : communicated without due preparation, from any unworthy motive : failed to receive the Blessed Sacrament fasting, when I was able? Have I confessed to a Priest, when necessary : omitted to do so because I disliked the humiliation and restraint of it : when preparing for Confession has it been done carefully; have I made my Confession with sorrow for my sins and firm purpose of amendment : carefully performed the penance, and followed the advice given to me : have I received the grace of Confirmation, Matrimony, or Holy Orders without due preparation?

Third Commandment.

HAVE I uttered any oaths or wrong words : used the Name of GOD lightly : had a habit of calling out "On my soul," "Good heavens," "O LORD," or using such like exclamations : sworn to what I did not know to be true : taken a rash oath or vow : taken an oath to do anything sinful or unlawful : perjured myself by swearing falsely : broken an oath or vow : cursed myself or others? Have I spoken against the Clergy or Services of the Church : mocked the Clergy, turned them or anything done in Church into ridicule : scoffed at good and holy persons : spoken lightly of religion : spoken against Fasting, or any duty enjoined by the Church : enquired out of curiosity or in a wrong spirit into the mysteries of the Faith : used the words of Holy Scripture lightly : laughed at others when they have done so : read it in an improper spirit? How have I kept my Baptismal Vow, any resolution made at my Confirmation, or at the Holy Communion, or any other time : have I wilfully concealed anything in Confession, or slurred over any sin to avoid its full shame or censure?

Fourth Commandment.

HAVE I profaned Sunday by neglecting to go to Church, and to the Holy Communion : if I could not go to Church have I failed to say prayers and to read at home : done unnecessarily any ordinary business : spent the day in idleness, revelling, reading newspapers, unfit books : encouraged others in not keeping Sunday : put off until Sunday any work that might have been done in the week : travelled on Sunday without reasonable cause? Have I failed to keep the Church's Holy Days and Seasons of Christmas, Easter, Ascension Day, Whitsun Day, and other Holy Days : broken them by excess of merry making? Have I failed to observe the Fasts of the Church, such as Fridays, Ash Wednesday, Good Friday, and the days of Lent : failed to practise self-denial in food and in other things : fasted out of love of making myself singular, or to be thought devout, not from a proper motive?

Fifth Commandment.

HAVE I been proud, disobedient, disrespectful to those set over me : failed in my duty towards my Parish Priest, or Spiritual Adviser : been unwilling to learn from them what is needful for my soul : disobedient, stubborn, impertinent to my Schoolmaster or Schoolmistress : angry or sullen when corrected by them : have I broken the law of the land : spoken evil of the Queen : judged the rich or those above me rashly or uncharitably without a cause : failed in respect to aged persons : acted unkindly towards any of my family : quarrelled with them : been envious or jealous of them : made sport of idiots, or persons of weak intellect : refused to do acts of kindness to my neighbours : refused obstinately, or conceitedly, the advice of my elders?

As a Child.—Have I disobeyed my Parents openly or secretly in things which were not sinful : been obstinate in taking my own way, disregarding their wishes and advice : deceived them : done anything in their absence which I would not have done in their presence : failed in love, tenderness, gratitude to them : spoken to them with rude, disrespectful, angry, impatient words : laughed at them, at their infirmities : been sulky with them : spoken disrespectfully of them : caused them grief by my faults : squandered their substance : been an unnecessary burden to them : been ashamed of them : neglected to help them : omitted to pray for them?

As a Parent.—Have I set my Children a good example : not neglected them : been careful to train them up religiously : to have them Baptized, Confirmed, prepared for the Holy Communion : removed them from occasions of sin, bad companions, bad books : corrected their faults with patience and not with temper : not overlooked their faults : have I over indulged or spoiled my Children : been equally just to all my Children : hindered their marriage without just reason : forced them to marry : forced them into a profession of my choice : hindered their vocation when called to the religious life ?

As a Husband or Wife.—Have I broken my Matrimonial Vow : been wanting in love, kindness, obedience, duty towards my Wife (Husband) : given occasion for jealousy : been unfaithful : neglected the reasonable wishes or comfort of my Wife (Husband) : used any angry abusive words towards my Wife (Husband) : been wasteful, extravagant ?

As a Sponsor.—Have I done what I could to see that my God-Children are taught the Catholic Faith : have I neglected to pray for them ?

As a Master or Mistress.—Have I been negligent in caring for the souls of my Servants : not given them opportunities of going to Church : not had Family Prayers : treated them unkindly : without consideration made their work too hard : found fault with them harshly, hastily, or without cause : failed to reprove their faults when necessary ?

As a Servant.—Have I been in any way unfaithful to my Master or Mistress : robbed, deceived, cheated them : allowed others to do so : defrauded them by giving anything away without their knowledge : by idling my time : wilfully wasted or spoiled their property : neglected to take care of what was put under my charge : disobeyed their orders : been disrespectful to them : obeyed or flattered them in anything sinful ?

Sixth Commandment.

HAVE I been angry without a cause : given way to a sullen, hasty, passionate, pettish temper : been fretful, irritable, spiteful : done any harm to any one in anger : tried to make others angry : struck them : called them names: desired my own death through passion: used violent or abusive language? Have I borne malice or hatred: been unforgiving: refused to be reconciled to others: desired any one's death through hatred, malice, or for my temporal interest: not sought to make others happy: wished for vexations to happen to others: indulged in unkind thoughts about others: taken delight in others being evil-spoken of: thought evil of others: been quarrelsome: made mischief: stirred up quarrels amongst others? Have I been revengeful: given way to resentment in thought or deed: nourished jealousy, or personal dislike, or prejudice: had an aversion to others: neglected to show sympathy to others, to help them: been thankful to those who took trouble or bore anxiety for me: as glad for others' good as for my own. Have I hurt the soul of any one by bad example or persuasion, by provoking them or tempting them to sin: ridiculed others for being religious: not told others their faults when it was my duty to do so: been more severe than needful when correcting others? Have I been cruel to animals through wantonness, or from love of cruelty, or from anger?

Seventh Commandment.

HAVE I remembered that my body is the temple of the HOLY GHOST: delighted in or given way to impure thoughts: been guilty of beginning or joining in immodest conversation, whether before children: not avoided hearing it: kept a watch over my eyes: been curious to inquire into what is contrary to perfect modesty: read impure books, or books suggestive of evil, or immodest accounts in newspapers: delighted in dangerous songs, jests, or pictures: dressed immodestly: used improper words with double meanings: been careless whose company I have sought: been to places where indecent sights are exhibited, at immoral games, plays, dances: committed impure deeds: allowed others to make too free with me or been too free with them: persuaded or led others into such sins: immodestly attracted attention? Have I been faithful to my Husband (Wife):

not committed excess in what is lawful between Husband and Wife ? Have I eaten or drunk too much at any time : been dainty, over careful, luxurious, and self-indulgent : indulged in too much sleep : neglected self-denial ?

Eighth Commandment.

HAVE I taken anything belonging to another person : been honest in little things as well as in great : received stolen goods : aided in any fraud : disparaged the value of anything to obtain it for less than it was worth : sold anything above its value : given false or light weight or measure : knowingly passed false money : evaded paying toll or taxes : borrowed money, &c., without returning it : been careless about money : run into debt without knowing whether I could pay : kept back any money from its owner : when I have found anything have I honestly tried to find an owner for it : have I taken money from those who could not afford to give it : been negligent in administering property as a Guardian or Trustee : injured the property of another wilfully : neglected to make amends to those whom I have wronged : to make restitution when I could : given alms grudgingly and not according to my power : spent too much in trifles ? Have I rashly undertaken any situation or business without sufficient knowledge : neglected any work or business for which I was hired, or which I was bound to do by contract : destroyed the property of others by carelessness or otherwise : got at others' secrets by wrong means, by reading letters : interfered in others' business ? Have I given to others the full credit, honour, consideration due to them : pretended to be worse off than I was, or more helpless, and on that account received money ?

Ninth Commandment.

HAVE I told a lie, from what motive : have I added to or diminished from the truth : made careless statements without thinking whether they were true or false : told secrets entrusted to me : broken any confidence : concealed the truth : have I acted a lie : been guilty of hypocrisy or deceit : made false excuses so as to make another believe what is not true : been as good as my word? Have I spoken evil or idly of any one : listened to any evil speaking : said anything of another which was not strictly true : spoken unnecessarily of the faults of others : taken pleasure in hearing others do so : attributed wrong motives to others : been ready to believe ill of any one : judged harshly of others : judged any one in matters in which I was not capable of judging them : restored my neighbour's good name when I have injured it? Have I said unkind things of others behind their backs, which I would not have said to their face : been too suspicious : raised false suspicions of others?

Tenth Commandment.

HAVE I wished for things which GOD has not given me : murmured and given way to discontent : coveted anything belonging to another : been dissatisfied or complaining at anything in my lot : pleased at another's misfortunes : desired another's hurt so that I might be a gainer by it : hoarded my money : kept it for myself when I should have expended it on other things : coveted or over-estimated the praise of men : desired greater ease, success, or enjoyment?

A METHOD OF SELF-EXAMINATION BY THE SEVEN DEADLY SINS.

Pride.

DO I indulge in too good an opinion of myself : make too much of myself in any way : am I constantly thinking of myself : boasting of my deeds and life : seeking to put myself first : vain of my dress, powers, personal appearance : do I claim to be what I am not : am I self-opinionated : have I been obstinate in an opinion when I felt I was wrong :

exalted my opinion against the doctrines of the Church : am I put out when I do not receive notice : disrespectful to elders or superiors : deceitful in order to get the good opinion of others : have I made false excuses to hide faults : am I over-confident in myself : have I rashly attempted to do anything for which I was unfit : determined to have my own way : desired to assert my independence : despised others : taken pleasure when they were spoken of disparagingly : felt sore when they were praised, admired : scoffed at others : indulged in satire : turned everything into ridicule : been censorious, touchy, resentful, easily offended : unwilling to be reconciled to others : impatient when humbled : obstinate in not owning my faults : disliked to be told my faults : have I indulged in display : done good actions merely to gain applause : been overbearing, sharp, imperious in exercising authority : have I put myself forward : desired power in order to exalt myself : made myself conspicuous in Church at my devotions :. been proud of my humility, of my repentance : avoided the means of humiliation which GOD has sent me ?

Covetousness.

HAVE I wished for things which GOD has not intended for me : taken unfair means to get anything : coveted anything belonging to another : given way to a grasping spirit : have I loved money for its own sake : made an idol of it : sold myself to commit sin, or wished another's death for the sake of money : gained money by gambling or any dishonest games : obtained money on any false pretence : wished for anything entrusted to me : hoarded money : been stingy or niggardly : unwilling to give a fair price for work done or purchases made : given alms according to my power : has my covetousness led me to envy others, to complain, or be discontented ?

Lust.

HAVE I remembered that my body is the temple of the HOLY GHOST : given way to wrong impulses, imaginations, desires : done anything to excite them : kept a guard over my eyes, my hands, my conversation : have I read books or looked at objects to encourage impure thoughts : have I tempted others or encouraged them to do so : have I been modest, reserved, and restrained in manner : guarded myself against too much familiarity and freedom ?

Envy.

HAVE I been envious or jealous of another because he possessed riches, beauty, temporal or spiritual gifts, worldly position or good qualities, or has been more liked than myself : given way through envy to mischief making, evil speaking, backbiting : done any one an injury by thought, word, or deed : am I pained at another's success : vexed to hear others well spoken of : rejoiced at others' adversity : do I like to hear the faults of others spoken of : have I joined in such talk : interpreted persons' sayings or doings in the worst sense : kept back the good I know of any one out of any secret dislike or grudge : reaped any gain or advantage by doing harm to others through envy ?

Gluttony.

HAVE I been careful not to eat or drink more than I needed : been greedy, indulged desires of eating and drinking : dainty : complained of my food from daintiness, &c. : spent too much money on my food : stolen anything out of greediness : persuaded others to give me anything : talked or thought over much about eating and drinking : lived a self-indulgent or luxurious life : not practised mortification of my appetite : neglected to fast ?

Anger.

AM I passionate : have I injured any person or thing when in a passion : used abusive language : been angry without a cause : disliked persons without reason : picked quarrels : refused to forgive any one who has injured me : to speak to any one who has offended me : to be reconciled to any one who is willing to be so : has anger, malice, or revenge cherished against another kept me from the Holy Communion : have I over severely corrected or reproved those under my care : been impatient or fretful about trifles : sullen, peevish, when tried by sickness, sorrow, poverty, or disappointment ?

Sloth.

HAVE I been idle or lazy at my work : done it imperfectly : done it at any other than the right time : put off doing any work through sloth : failed to rise at the appointed time and so missed saying my morning prayers : have I come to Communion as often as I might : come without preparation : omitted self-examination : performed it carelessly : given up meditation : wished I could sin with a good conscience : made light of little sins : neglected through sloth to pray for others : yielded to what is wrong rather than exert myself : gained my living by sin rather than exert myself : not spoken the truth for fear of displeasing others : neglected to amend faults through idleness : failed to persevere in a good resolution : chosen to live on other's means rather than exert myself : allowed those dependent on me to suffer by my sloth ?

CONSIDERATIONS TO EXCITE CONTRITION.

1. *Place before yourself, as distinctly as you can, the sins which have come to your remembrance, and their circumstances.*

2. *Consider Who God is against Whom you have sinned, how Great, how Good, how Gracious to you, that He made you, that He gave His Only Son to die for you, that He made you His Child in Baptism, that He has loaded you with blessings and prepared Heaven for you.* Consider how Patient He has been with you—how Long-suffering in calling you and moving you to repent: Say, " O most Loving God, O Infinite Goodness, I repent of having offended Thee, behold me at Thy feet : O my Father, my Creator, my Benefactor, grant me the grace of a true repentance, and the blessing of a free pardon, for Thy dear Son's sake."

3. *Consider the infinite wickedness of sin*: Say, " O my Saviour, I behold Thee on the Cross, torn and wounded. Thy sacred Body streaming with Blood; this is the work of my sin. In Thy Wounds, O my

Saviour, I read the greatness of the guilt and malice of my sins. By the greatness of Thy pains and sorrows, O my loving Redeemer, I measure the hatefulness of my offences."

4. Consider the consequences of one mortal sin: how many souls are now tormented in hell-fire for one single, unrepented, deadly sin; how many have I not committed! O my God, how much do I owe Thee for not cutting me off in the midst of my sins. Before I fell into sin, Heaven was my home, my inheritance, my country, my blessed resting-place; by sin I have given up my title to the glory of the Blessed. For the sake of sin, I have lost the love of Jesus, the sight of Jesus, the communion with the Blessed Saints and with the Angels. O my God would that I had never offended Thee, would that I had never consented to sin. Behold me now in pity at Thy feet, full of sorrow and contrition. I hate sin which is accursed of Thee; I renounce all which would draw me away from Thee; I most bitterly repent my sin and folly, which would have deprived me for ever of Heaven if Thou hadst not mercifully brought me to repentance. I grieve that I have sinned against Thee, O my God, Who art All-Good, All-Bountiful, All-Worthy of love.

EJACULATIONS.

O MY GOD, I cry unto Thee with the prodigal: FATHER, I have sinned against Heaven and before Thee, and am no more worthy to be called Thy son.

I have gone astray like a sheep that is lost. O seek Thy servant, for I do not forget Thy commandments.

Enter not into judgment with Thy servant, O LORD! O spare me for Thy mercy's sake.

Try me, O GOD, and seek the ground of my heart; prove me, and examine my thoughts!

Thou Whose nature and property is ever to have mercy and to forgive, O meet me in pity, embrace me in love, and forgive me all my sin.

I confess my sins unto Thee, O CHRIST, Healer of our souls, O LORD of Life. Heal me, heal me of my spiritual sickness, Thou Who art Long-suffering, and of tender mercy; heal me, O LORD CHRIST.

Accept my supplications, O Thou HOLY SPIRIT, unto Whom all hearts are open, all desires known; and from Whom no secrets are hid, and Who givest life to our souls; hear and answer, O SPIRIT of GOD.

O Heavenly FATHER, Who willest not that any sinner should perish, give me true repentance for this my sin, that I perish not!

To what misery am I come by my own fault! O Merciful GOD, pity and forgive me for JESUS' sake.

Thine eyes, O GOD, are as a flame of fire searching my inmost heart. O be Thou merciful to my sin, for it is great!

Thou, GOD, seest me in all the foulness of my sins! Blessed JESUS, speak for me, plead for me, come between my soul and my offended GOD, that I perish not.

PRAYER BEFORE CONFESSION.

ACCEPT my Confession, O most Loving, most Gracious LORD JESU CHRIST, on Whom alone my soul trusts for salvation. Grant me I beseech Thee contrition of heart, and give tears to mine eyes, that I may sorrow deeply for all my sins with humility and sincerity of heart.

O Good JESU, SAVIOUR of the world, Who gavest Thyself to the death of the Cross to save sinners, look on me, a miserable sinner, who calls upon Thy Name. Spare me, Thou that art my SAVIOUR, and pity my sinful soul; loose its chains, heal its sores. LORD JESU, I desire Thee, I seek Thee, I long for Thee, show me the light of Thy countenance, and I shall be whole. send forth Thy light and Thy truth into my soul, to show me fully all the sins and shortcomings which I must still confess; and to aid and teach me to lay them bare without reserve, and with a contrite heart; O Thou Who livest and reignest with GOD the FATHER, in the Unity of the HOLY GHOST, One GOD for ever and ever. Amen.

FORM OF CONFESSION.

O LORD JESU CHRIST, Very God and Very Man, my Creator and Redeemer; I grieve with my whole heart that I have offended Thee, my LORD and my GOD; Whom I desire to love above all things: I accuse myself of the wrong desires and thoughts which I have indulged, especially. . . . . ; of the unholy words which I have spoken, especially . . . ; of the sinful and ungodly deeds which I have committed, especially . . . . ; I desire earnestly to sin no more, and to shun all occasions of sin. I offer to Thee, in satisfaction for my sins, Thy most sacred Life, Thy Passion, and Thy Death, and the whole price of Thy Blood, which was shed for me. I trust that of Thine infinite goodness and mercy, Thou wilt by the merits of Thy precious Blood, forgive me all my sins ; and that Thou wilt pour on me the riches of Thy grace, whereby I may live holily and serve Thee perfectly to the end ; Who with the FATHER and the HOLY GHOST livest and reignest, GOD, Blessed for ever. Amen.

When you desire to make a Confession to a Priest; call to mind your sins in a certain order, such as may help you to remember them. Enumerate singly, distinctly, and fully all the sins which weigh on your conscience, telling their number and their character. Omit all that is not to the purpose or unnecessary, all that might lead you more to excuse than to accuse yourself. Distinguish what is certain from what is doubtful, grave from venial, deliberate from unpremeditated, purposed from inadvertent, fully consented to from half consented to; also sin from temptation to it.

If it be not your first Confession, mention the time when you last confessed, and say whether you performed the penance that was given you.

FORM FOR SACRAMENTAL CONFESSION.

IN the Name ✠ of the FATHER, and of the SON, and of the HOLY GHOST.

I confess to GOD the FATHER Almighty, to His Only-Begotten SON JESUS CHRIST, and to GOD the HOLY GHOST, before the whole Company of Heaven, and to you my Father, that I have sinned exceedingly in thought, word, and deed, by my fault, by my own fault, by my most grievous fault. Especially I accuse myself that (*since my last Confession which was . . . ago*) I have sinned ;

After your Confession, say:

For these and all my other sins which I cannot now remember, I am heartily sorry, firmly purpose amendment, most humbly ask pardon of GOD; and of you, my Spiritual Father, penance, counsel, and absolution. Wherefore I pray GOD the FATHER Almighty, His Only-Begotten SON JESUS CHRIST, and GOD the HOLY GHOST to have mercy upon me, and you my Father, to pray for me to the LORD our GOD. Amen.

Act of Contrition.

O MY GOD, I am heartily sorry for having sinned thus against Thee, because thereby I have offended Thee, Who art my chief and only Good. I utterly hate my sins, because they displease Thee. From this moment I intend, with Thy help, to flee from all causes, occasions, and danger of sin, and I resolve to take all pain and trouble which may come upon me as a fitting punishment from Thee for my sins. "A broken and contrite heart, O GOD, Thou hast promised not to despise." Amen.

THANKSGIVING AFTER CONFESSION.

O MOST Merciful GOD, Who according to the multitude of Thy mercies dost so put away the sins of those who truly repent that Thou rememberest them no more, look graciously upon me, Thine unworthy Servant, and accept my Confession for Thy mercy's sake: receive my humble thanks, most Loving FATHER, that of Thy great goodness Thou hast given me pardon for all my sins. O may Thy love and pity supply whatsoever has been wanting in the sufficiency of my contrition, and the fulness of my Confession. And do Thou, O LORD, vouchsafe to have me fully and perfectly absolved in Heaven, and grant me the help of Thy grace, that I may diligently amend my life and persevere in Thy service unto the end, through JESUS CHRIST our LORD. Amen.

Psalm ciii. *Benedic, anima mea.*

PRAISE the LORD, O my soul : and all that is within me praise His holy Name.

Praise the LORD, O my soul : and forget not all His benefits ;

Who forgiveth all thy sin : and healeth all thine infirmities.

Who saveth thy life from destruction : and crowneth thee with mercy and loving-kindness ;

Who satisfieth thy mouth with good things : making thee young and lusty as an eagle.

The LORD executeth righteousness and judgement : for all them that are oppressed with wrong.

He shewed His ways unto Moses : His works unto the Children of Israel.

The LORD is full of compassion and mercy : long-suffering, and of great goodness.

He will not alway be chiding : neither keepeth He His anger for ever.

He hath not dealt with us after our sins : nor rewarded us according to our wickednesses.

For look how high the Heaven is in comparison of the earth : so great is His mercy also toward them that fear Him.

Look how wide also the east is from the west : so far hath He set our sins from us.

Yea, like as a father pitieth his own children : even so is the LORD merciful to them that fear Him.

For He knoweth whereof we are made : He remembereth that we are but dust.

The days of man are but as grass : for He flourisheth as a flower of the field.

For as soon as the wind goeth over it, it is gone : and the place thereof shall know it no more.

But the merciful goodness of the LORD endureth for ever and ever upon them that fear Him : and His righteousness upon children's children ;

Even upon such as keep His covenant : and think upon His commandments to do them.

The LORD hath prepared His seat in Heaven : and His Kingdom ruleth over all.

O praise the LORD, ye Angels of His, ye that excel in strength : ye that fulfil His commandment, and hearken unto the voice of His words.

O praise the LORD, all ye His hosts : ye servants of His that do His pleasure. .

O speak good of the LORD, all ye works of His, in all places of His dominion : praise thou the LORD, O my soul.

Glory be to the FATHER.

PRAYER WHEN ABSOLUTION HAS BEEN DEFERRED.

O LORD my GOD, do Thou give me the spirit of true repentance, and take away from me all that separates me from Thee. Assist me, by Thy grace, to gain true sorrow for my sins, and to form a sincere resolution to amend my life. I have wearied Thee, yet turn Thou, O LORD, once more, and seek Thy servant, and I shall live; have mercy on me, and succour me with Thy grace. Create in me a new heart, and renew a right spirit within me; give me grace that I may carefully avoid all occasions of sin, diligently keep all my good resolutions, and obtain from Thee the full pardon of all my offences. Through JESUS CHRIST our LORD. Amen.

PRAYER WHILE WAITING TO MAKE A CONFESSION.

O LORD GOD, Who hast called me from my sins, and of Thy mercy hast not cut me off in the midst of them, give me now, I beseech Thee, time and grace to perfect my repentance according to Thy will. Let the deep of my misery call to the deep of Thy infinite mercy and compassion. Grant to me a humble and teachable mind that I may meekly receive the counsel of Thy Minister. Enable me to fulfil all his godly instruction : melt my heart to true compunction : strengthen me in a hearty determination to renounce all sin for the time to come, that my repentance being at length acceptable in Thy sight, I may, according to Thy gracious promise, obtain the comfort and blessing of Thy free forgiveness, through the merits and mediation of Thy SON, JESUS CHRIST, our LORD. Amen.

PRAYERS FOR PARDON AND AMENDMENT

I.

O MOST Sweet Lord Jesu Christ, I, an unworthy sinner, would call to Thy memory all the holy thoughts which have been Thine from eternity until now; above all, that one by which Thou, O Eternal Word, didst will to become Man.

O most Merciful Lord, I pray Thee from the bottom of my heart, to pardon me all the vain, foul, and evil thoughts which, up to this hour, I have entertained, or in any way have caused others to entertain against or beside Thy will.

Our Father.

II.

O MOST Piteous Lord Jesu Christ, I, a miserable sinner, would call to Thy memory all the good and saving words which Thou ever spakest when on earth.

I humbly pray Thee, O Good Jesu, to forgive me all the words which up to this hour I have uttered or caused others to utter against Thy holy will.

Our Father.

III.

O MOST Sweet Jesu Christ, I, an unworthy sinner, yet redeemed by Thy precious Blood, call to Thy memory all the good works which Thou wroughtest on the earth for our salvation. I beseech Thee, most Piteous Lord, pardon me whatsoever, by my ill deeds, I have at any time knowingly or ignorantly committed, or have caused others to commit, against Thy law, and the glory of Thy Name.

And now, O most gracious Lord, direct and order all my thoughts, words, and works, according to Thy good pleasure, and to the praise of Thy Name; and conform them to the perfect pattern of Thy most holy Life and Conversation. I am Thine, and would be Thine, O Lord, in life and in death. Into Thy hands I commend myself, and all that I have.

Our Father.

PRAYERS
AGAINST
THE SEVEN DEADLY SINS

Against Pride.

O LORD JESU CHRIST, Pattern of humility, Who didst empty Thyself of Thy glory, and take upon Thee the form of a servant : root out of us all pride and swelling of heart, that owning ourselves miserable and guilty sinners, we may willingly bear contempt and reproaches for Thy sake, and glorying in nothing save only in Thee : may esteem ourselves lowly in Thy sight. Not unto us, O LORD, but to Thy Name be the praise, for Thy loving mercy and for Thy truth's sake. Amen.

Against Covetousness.

O LORD JESU CHRIST, Who though Thou wast rich yet for our sakes didst become poor, grant that all over eagerness and covetousness of earthly goods may die in us, and the desire of heavenly things may live and grow in us : keep us from all idle and vain expenses that we may always have to give to him that needeth, and that giving not grudgingly nor of necessity, but cheerfully, we may be loved of Thee, and be made through Thy merits partakers of the riches of Thy heavenly treasure. Amen.

Against Lust.

O LORD JESU CHRIST, Guardian of chaste souls, and lover of purity, Who wast pleased to take our nature, and to be born of a pure Virgin, mercifully look upon my infirmity. Make me a clean heart, C GOD, and renew a right spirit within me ; help me to drive away all evil thoughts, to conquer every sinful desire, and so pierce my flesh with the fear of Thee : that this bosom enemy being overcome, I may serve Thee with a chaste body and please Thee with a pure heart. Amen.

Against Envy.

O MOST Loving JESU, Pattern of charity, Who makest all the commandments of the law to consist in love towards GOD and towards man, grant to us so to love Thee with all our heart, with all our mind, and all our soul, and our neighbour for Thy sake; that the grace of charity and brotherly love may dwell in us, and all envy, harshness, and ill-will may die in us; and fill our hearts with feelings of love, kindness, and compassion, so that by constantly rejoicing in the happiness and good success of others, by sympathizing with them in their sorrows, and putting away all harsh judgments and envious thoughts, we may follow Thee, Who art Thyself the true and perfect Love. Amen.

Against Gluttony.

O LORD JESU CHRIST, Mirror of abstinence, Who to teach us the virtue of abstinence didst fast forty days and forty nights, grant that serving Thee, and not our own appetites, we may live soberly and piously with contentment, without greediness, gluttony, or drunkenness, that Thy will being our meat and drink, we may hunger and thirst after righteousness, and finally obtain of Thee to eat of that Tree of Life which is in the midst of the Paradise of GOD. Amen.

Against Anger.

O MOST Meek JESU, Prince of Peace, Who, when Thou wast reviled, reviled not again, and on the Cross didst pray for Thy murderers: implant in our hearts the virtues of gentleness, and patience, that restraining the fierceness of anger, impatience, and resentment, we may overcome evil with good, for Thy sake love our enemies, and as children of our heavenly Father seek Thy peace and evermore rejoice in Thy love. Amen.

Against Sloth.

O LORD JESU CHRIST, Eternal Love, Who in the Garden didst pray so long and so fervently that Thy Sweat was as it were great drops of blood falling down to the ground, put away from us, we beseech Thee, all sloth and inactivity both of body and mind, kindle within us the fire of Thy love, strengthen our weakness that whatsoever our hand findeth to do we may do it with our might, and that striving heartily to please Thee in this life, Thou mayest hereafter be our exceeding great reward. Amen.

Litany of Repentance.

LORD, have mercy upon us.
CHRIST, *have mercy upon us.*
LORD, have mercy upon us.

O CHRIST, hear us.
O *CHRIST, graciously hear us.*

O GOD the FATHER, of Heaven,
O GOD the SON, Redeemer of the world,
O GOD the HOLY GHOST,
Holy Trinity, One GOD,

Have mercy upon us.

O GOD, Who wouldest not the death of a sinner, but rather that he should be converted and live;
Who sparedst not the Angels that sinned, but didst cast them down to Hell;
Who calledst Adam after his fall, to acknowledgment of his sin and to repentance;
Who didst fearfully punish Pharaoh, feigning repentance, yet hardened in heart;
Who forgavest the sins of Thy disobedient people at the prayer of Moses;
Who sparedst the Ninevites when they fasted and repented in sackcloth and ashes;
Who by the prophet Nathan, broughtest David to acknowledge his sin;
Who didst put away his sin when he humbly confessed it;
Who sparedst Ahab when he humbled himself and repented.
Who camest into the world to save sinners;
Who broughtest salvation to the house of Zaccheus, when he repented and restored fourfold;
Who didst graciously hear the Canaanitish woman when she persevered in prayer;
Who didst receive

Have mercy upon us.

publicans and sinners, and eat with them;

Who freely forgavest the sins of Mary Magdalene because she loved much;

Who didst in mercy look upon Peter when he thrice denied Thee, and didst move him to confess his sins, and to shed tears of penitence;

Who when hanging on the Cross didst promise Paradise to the Penitent Thief;

Who Thyself didst no sin, yet bearest our sins in Thine Own Body on the Tree;

Who wast bruised for our iniquities;

Who wouldest not that any should perish, but that all should come to repentance;

Who camest to seek and to save that which was lost;

Who hast pity on sinners, who turn to Thee, in weeping, fasting, and mourning;

Who after repentance rememberest our sins no more;

Who in putting away our sins, dost renew us unto everlasting life;

} *Have mercy upon us.*

BE merciful to us, and spare us O LORD.

FROM all evil and wickedness;

From a sudden and unprepared death;

By Thy Blood which Thou didst shed for the remission of our sins;

In the time of trouble, in the hour of death, and in the Day of Judgment.

} *Good Lord deliver us.*

WE sinners beseech Thee to hear us.

THAT it may please Thee to bring us to true repentance;

That we may bring forth fruits meet for repentance;

That sin may not reign in our mortal bodies;

That we yield not our members as instruments of unrighteousness;

That being dead to sin, we may live unto righteousness;

That, coming boldly to the Throne of Grace, we may obtain mercy and find grace to help in time of need;

That it may please Thee to chasten and purge us here, and to spare us in Eternity;

} *We beseech Thee to hear us.*

That it may please Thee graciously to hear us.
We beseech Thee to hear us.

O SON of GOD.
We beseech Thee to hear us.

O LAMB of GOD, That takest away the sins of the world.
Spare us, O Lord.

O LAMB of GOD, That takest away the sins of the world.
Graciously hear us, O Lord.

O LAMB of GOD, That takest away the sins of the world.
Have mercy upon us.

O CHRIST, hear us.

O *CHRIST, graciously hear us.*

LORD, have mercy upon us.

CHRIST, have mercy upon us.

LORD, have mercy upon us.

Our FATHER.

Let us pray.

O GOD, Who rejectest not the greatest sinner, but in loving pity art reconciled to him by penitence, mercifully regard our lowly supplications, and give us strength to fulfil Thy commandments.

O GOD, Who justifiest the wicked, and wouldest not the death of a sinner, we humbly beseech Thy Majesty bountifully to protect with Thy heavenly succour, and to preserve, by Thy continual help, us Thy servants, who trust only in Thy mercy; so that we may constantly serve Thee, and that no temptations may separate us from Thee.

O GOD, Who desirest not the death of a sinner, but his repentance, most mercifully regard the weakness of our mortal nature, and by Thy goodness strengthen our endeavours, that of Thine infinite mercy we may obtain pardon for our sins, steadfastness in Thy service, and finally, with joy, the rewards promised to those who persevere unto the end, through our LORD JESUS CHRIST. Amen.

The Penitential Psalms.

Antiphon. Remember not, LORD, our offences, nor the offences of our Forefathers, neither take Thou vengeance of our sins.

Against Anger.

Psalm vi. *Domine, ne in furore.*

O LORD, rebuke me not in Thine indignation : neither chasten me in Thy displeasure.

Have mercy upon me, O LORD, for I am weak : O LORD, heal me, for my bones are vexed.

My soul also is sore troubled : but, LORD, how long wilt Thou punish me?

Turn Thee, O LORD, and deliver my soul : O save me for Thy mercy's sake.

For in death no man remembereth Thee : and who will give Thee thanks in the pit?

I am weary of my groaning ; every night wash I my bed : and water my couch with my tears.

My beauty is gone for very trouble : and worn away because of all mine enemies.

Away from me, all ye that work vanity : for the LORD hath heard the voice of my weeping.

The LORD hath heard my petition : the LORD will receive my prayer.

All mine enemies shall be confounded, and sore vexed : they shall be turned back, and put to shame suddenly.

Glory be to the FATHER.

Against Pride.

Psalm xxxii. *Beati, quorum.*

BLESSED is he whose unrighteousness is forgiven : and whose sin is covered.

Blessed is the man unto whom the LORD imputeth no sin : and in whose spirit there is no guile.

For while I held my tongue : my bones consumed away through my daily complaining.

For Thy hand is heavy upon me day and night : and my moisture is like the drought in summer.

I will acknowledge my sin unto Thee : and mine unrighteousness have I not hid.

I said, I will confess my sins unto the LORD : and so Thou forgavest the wickedness of my sin.

For this shall every one that is godly make his prayer unto thee, in a time when

Thou mayest be found : but in the great water-floods they shall not come nigh him.

Thou art a place to hide me in, Thou shalt preserve me from trouble : Thou shalt compass me about with songs of deliverance.

I will inform thee, and teach thee in the way wherein thou shalt go : and I will guide thee with mine eye.

Be ye not like to horse and mule, which have no understanding : whose mouths must be held with bit and bridle, lest they fall upon thee.

Great plagues remain for the ungodly : but whoso putteth his trust in the LORD, mercy embraceth him on every side.

Be glad, O ye righteous, and rejoice in the LORD : and be joyful, all ye that are true of heart.

Glory be to the FATHER.

Against Gluttony.

Psalm xxxviii. *Domine, ne in furore.*

PUT me not to rebuke, O LORD, in Thine anger : neither chasten me in Thy heavy displeasure.

For Thine arrows stick fast in me : and Thy hand presseth me sore.

There is no health in my flesh, because of Thy displeasure : neither is there any rest in my bones, by reason of my sin.

For my wickednesses are gone over my head : and are like a sore burden, too heavy for me to bear.

My wounds stink, and are corrupt : through my foolishness.

I am brought into so great trouble and misery : that I go mourning all the day long.

For my loins are filled with a sore disease : and there is no whole part in my body.

I am feeble, and sore smitten : I have roared for the very disquietness of my heart.

LORD, Thou knowest all my desire : and my groaning is not hid from Thee.

My heart panteth, my strength hath failed me : and the sight of mine eyes is gone from me.

My lovers and my neighbours did stand looking upon my trouble : and my kinsmen stood afar off.

They also that sought after my life laid snares for me : and they that went about to do me evil talked of wickedness, and imagined deceit all the day long.

As for me, I was like a deaf man, and heard not : and as one that is dumb, who doth not open his mouth.

I became even as a man that heareth not : and in whose mouth are no reproofs.

For in Thee, O LORD, have I put my trust : Thou shalt answer for me, O LORD my GOD.

I have required that they, even mine enemies, should not triumph over me : for when my foot slipped, they rejoiced greatly against me.

And I, truly, am set in the plague and my heaviness is ever in my sight.

For I will confess my wickedness : and be sorry for my sin.

But mine enemies live, and are mighty : and they that hate me wrongfully are many in number.

They also that reward evil for good are against me : because I follow the thing that good is.

Forsake me not, O LORD my GOD : be not Thou far from me.

Haste Thee to help me : O LORD GOD of my salvation.

Glory be to the FATHER.

Against Lust.

Psalm li. *Miserere mei, Deus.*

HAVE mercy upon me, O GOD, after Thy great goodness : according to the multitude of Thy mercies do away mine offences.

Wash me throughly from my wickedness : and cleanse me from my sin.

For I acknowledge my faults : and my sin is ever before me.

Against Thee only have I sinned, and done this evil in Thy sight : that Thou mightest be justified in Thy saying, and clear when Thou art judged.

Behold, I was shapen in wickedness : and in sin hath my mother conceived me.

But lo, Thou requirest truth in the inward parts : and shalt make me to understand wisdom secretly.

Thou shalt purge me with hyssop, and I shall be clean : Thou shalt wash me, and I shall be whiter than snow.

Thou shalt make me hear of joy and gladness : that the bones which Thou hast broken may rejoice.

Turn Thy face from my sins : and put out all my misdeeds.

Make me a clean heart, O GOD : and renew a right spirit within me.

Cast me not away from Thy presence : and take not Thy HOLY SPIRIT from me.

O give me the comfort of Thy help again : and stablish me with Thy free SPIRIT.

Then shall I teach Thy ways unto the wicked : and sinners shall be converted unto Thee.

Deliver me from blood-guiltiness, O GOD, Thou that art the GOD of my health : and my tongue shall sing of Thy righteousness.

Thou shalt open my lips, O LORD : and my mouth shall shew Thy praise.

For Thou desirest no sacrifice, else would I give it Thee : but Thou delightest not in burnt-offerings.

The sacrifice of GOD is a troubled spirit : a broken and contrite heart, O GOD, shalt Thou not despise.

O be favourable and gracious unto Sion : build Thou the walls of Jerusalem.

Then shalt Thou be pleased with the sacrifice of righteousness, with the burnt-offerings and oblations : then shall they offer young bullocks upon Thine altar,

Glory be to the FATHER.

Against Covetousness.

Psalm cii. *Domine, exaudi.*

HEAR my prayer, O LORD : and let my crying come unto Thee.

Hide not Thy face from me in the time of my trouble : incline Thine ear unto me when I call ; O hear me, and that right soon.

For my days are consumed away like smoke : and my bones are burnt up as it were a fire-brand.

My heart is smitten down, and withered like grass : so that I forget to eat my bread.

For the voice of my groaning : my bones will scarce cleave to my flesh.

I am become like a pelican in the wilderness : and like an owl that is in the desert.

I have watched, and am even as it were a sparrow : that sitteth alone upon the house-top.

Mine enemies revile me all the day long : and they that are mad upon me are sworn together against me.

For I have eaten ashes as it were bread : and mingled my drink with weeping ;

And that because of Thine

indignation and wrath : for Thou hast taken me up, and cast me down.

My days are gone like a shadow : and I am withered like grass.

But Thou, O LORD, shalt endure for ever : and Thy remembrance throughout all generations.

Thou shalt arise, and have mercy upon Sion : for it is time that Thou have mercy upon her, yea, the time is come.

And why? Thy servants think upon her stones : and it pitieth them to see her in the dust.

The heathen shall fear Thy Name, O LORD : and all the Kings of the earth Thy Majesty ;

When the LORD shall build up Sion : and when His glory shall appear ;

When He turneth Him unto the prayer of the poor destitute : and despiseth not their desire.

This shall be written for those that come after : and the people which shall be born shall praise the LORD.

For He hath looked down from His sanctuary : out of the Heaven did the LORD behold the earth ;

That He might hear the mournings of such as are in captivity : and deliver the children appointed unto death ;

That they may declare the Name of the LORD in Sion : and His worship at Jerusalem ;

When the people are gathered together : and the kingdoms also, to serve the LORD.

He brought down my strength in my journey : and shortened my days.

But I said, O my GOD, take me not away in the midst of mine age : as for Thy years, they endure throughout all generations.

Thou, LORD, in the beginning hast laid the foundation of the earth : and the heavens are the work of Thy hands,

They shall perish, but Thou shalt endure : they all shall wax old as doth a garment ;

And as a vesture shalt Thou change them, and they shall be changed : but Thou art the Same, and Thy years shall not fail.

The children of Thy servants shall continue : and their seed shall stand fast in Thy sight.

Glory be to the FATHER.

Against Envy.

Psalm cxxx. *De profundis.*

OUT of the deep have I called unto Thee, O LORD: LORD, hear my voice.

O let Thine ears consider well : the voice of my complaint.

If Thou, LORD, wilt be extreme to mark what is done amiss : O LORD, who may abide it?

For there is mercy with Thee : therefore shalt Thou be feared.

I look for the LORD; my soul doth wait for Him : in His word is my trust.

My soul fleeth unto the LORD : before the morning watch, I say, before the morning watch.

O Israel, trust in the LORD, for with the LORD there is mercy : and with Him is plenteous redemption.

And He shall redeem Israel : from all his sins.

Glory be to the FATHER.

Against Sloth.

Psalm cxliii. *Domine, exaudi.*

HEAR my prayer, O LORD, and consider my desire : hearken unto me for Thy truth and righteousness' sake.

And enter not into judgement with Thy servant : for in Thy sight shall no man living be justified.

For the enemy hath persecuted my soul; he hath smitten my life down to the ground : he hath laid me in the darkness, as the men that have been long dead.

Therefore is my spirit vexed within me : and my heart within me is desolate.

Yet do I remember the time past; I muse upon all Thy works : yea, I exercise myself in the works of Thy hands,

I stretch forth my hands unto Thee : my soul gaspeth unto Thee as a thirsty land.

Hear me, O LORD, and that soon, for my spirit waxeth faint : hide not Thy face from me, lest I be like unto them that go down into the pit.

O let me hear Thy lovingkindness betimes in the morning, for in Thee is my trust : shew Thou me the way that I should walk in, for I lift up my soul unto Thee.

Deliver me, O LORD, from mine enemies : for I flee unto Thee to hide me.

Teach me to do the thing that pleaseth Thee, for Thou art my GOD : let Thy loving

Spirit lead me forth into the land of righteousness.

Quicken me, O LORD, for Thy Name's sake : and for Thy righteousness' sake bring my soul out of trouble.

And of Thy goodness slay mine enemies : and destroy all them that vex my soul ; for I am Thy servant.

Glory be to the FATHER.

Antiphon. Remember not, LORD, our offences, nor the offences of our Forefathers ; neither take Thou vengeance of our sins.

Devotions for the Church's Seasons.

ADVENT

Antiphon. The night is far spent, the day is at hand: let us therefore cast off the works of darkness, and let us put on the armour of light.

℣ Come and save us, O Lord God of Hosts.

℟ Shew the light of Thy countenance, and we shall be whole.

O LORD JESUS CHRIST, Who for our sake didst vouchsafe to descend from Thy Throne of glory and from the bosom of the FATHER to this vale of tears and woe; Who wast conceived by the HOLY GHOST, born of the Virgin Mary, and was made Man, make, we beseech Thee, our hearts a fit habitation for Thyself. Beautify and fill them with all spiritual graces, and possess them wholly by Thy power. Give us grace to prepare for Thy Coming with deep humility, to receive Thee with burning love, and to hold Thee fast with a firm faith:. that we may never depart from Thee for ever: through Thy merits. Amen.

O Almighty GOD, the Coming of Whose Only-Begotten SON in time past we believe, and for Whose Second Coming in the Last Day we look and watch; defend us, we beseech Thee, in all our trials and temptations, and keep us free from the defilements of sin. Grant that we may so follow Thy SON JESUS CHRIST in the humility and purity of His First Coming, that we may without terror await His appearing again in His glorious Majesty to judge the world, and that in that great and awful Day our souls, washed in His precious Blood, and clothed in His merits, may be mercifully received by Thee into Heaven, where with all Thy Saints we may praise and bless Thee; through the Same JESUS CHRIST, our LORD, Who liveth and reigneth with Thee in the Unity of the HOLY GHOST, GOD, for ever and ever. Amen.

Ember Week.

O LORD we pray Thee for all those whom Thou hast set over us in Thy Church; that as Thou hast given them authority to exercise their ministry, so Thou wilt give them abundant grace to fulfil the same in innocency of life and purity of doctrine, through JESUS CHRIST our LORD. Amen.

Litany.

LORD, have mercy upon us.

CHRIST, have mercy upon us.

LORD, have mercy upon us.

O GOD the FATHER, Who didst so love the world, as to give Thine Only-Begotten Son, to save us;

O GOD, the SON, Who didst once come in the likeness of sinful flesh to suffer for us, and wilt come again to be our Judge;

O GOD the HOLY GHOST, Who dost mercifully visit the souls of Thine elect, to abide with us for ever;

} *Have mercy upon us.*

HOLY TRINITY, Blessed for evermore,

Be favourable to us, and bless us.

FROM the snares of the world, the flesh, and the devil;

From impenitence, unbelief, and neglect of Thy holy commandments;

From all carelessness, and forgetfulness of Thee;

From Thy wrath, whether in this world, or in the world to come;

From a slumbering conscience, and from an unprepared death;

By the compassion,

} *Good Lord, deliver us.*

and long-suffering of
GOD the FATHER ;
  By Thy first Coming
in lowliness ;
  By Thy Passion, and
most precious Death ;
  By Thy mediatorial
Intercession for us before the FATHER ;
  By Thy second Coming in Thy glorious
majesty.
  By the mercies and
consolations of GOD the
HOLY GHOST ;

} *Good Lord, deliver us.*

I N our day of sorrow, weakness, and tribulation,
  Succour and defend us, O Lord.
  In our last sickness, and in the hour of death,
  Succour and defend us, O Lord.
  In Thy awful Judgment, when the last sentence is pronounced,
  Deliver us, O Holy and Merciful Saviour.

WE beseech Thee, to hear us Good Lord.

THAT Thou wouldest vouchsafe to us
true repentance, and a
pure conscience ;
  That Thou wouldest
enable us to bear all
our trials patiently, and

} *We beseech Thee*

to glorify Thee in our
daily life ;
  That Thou wouldest
defend and govern Thy
Holy Church, especially
in this land ;
  That Thou wouldest vouchsafe to all
our brethren, especially
those most dear to us,
unity, peace, and true
concord ;
  That Thou wouldest
vouchsafe to the afflicted, and suffering in
soul or body, Thy merciful aid and deliverance ;
  That Thou wouldest
vouchsafe to all Thy
faithful departed, perpetual light, and hasten
the consummation of
their bliss ;
  That Thou wouldest
continually exalt our
minds to heavenly desires ;
  That we may be more
and more perfected in
the fruits of the SPIRIT,
and more entirely conformed to Thy most holy
will ;
  That being uncertain
of the hour of our death,
we may study to be
watchful, and prepared
to give an account of
our stewardship ;

} *to hear us, Good Lord.*

O LAMB of God, that takest away the sins of the world;
Hear us, O Lord.

O Lamb of God, that takest away the sins of the world;
Spare us, O Lord.

O Lamb of God, that takest away the sins of the world;
Have mercy upon us.

OUR Father.

Let us pray.

O LORD Jesus Christ, for Whose sudden coming to Judgment Thy Church looks and waits, come now to us in Thy quickening love, and plant Thy holy fear and love within our hearts. Establish us in Thy truth and righteousness, endue us with such boldness to confess Thee before men, that Thou mayest at the last day confess us before Thy Father and all the elect Angels in Heaven, Who liveth and reigneth with the Father, and the Holy Ghost, One God, world without end. Amen.

May the God of peace sanctify us wholly, and may our whole spirit, soul, and body, be preserved blameless unto the Coming of our Lord Jesus Christ. Amen.

CHRISTMAS EVE.

MAY God Almighty, Who by the Incarnation of His Only-Begotten Son drove away the darkness of the world, and by His glorious Birth enlightened this most holy night, drive away from us the darkness of sins, and enlighten our hearts with the light of Christian graces. Amen.

And may He Who willed that the great day of His most holy Birth should be told to the Shepherds by an Angel, pour upon us the refreshing shower of His blessing, and guide us, Himself being our Shepherd, to the pastures of everlasting joy. Amen.

And may He, Who through His Incarnation united earthly things with Heavenly, fill us with the sweetness of inward peace and good will, and make us partakers with the Heavenly Host. Amen.

CHRISTMAS.

Antiphon. Glory to GOD in the Highest, and on earth peace, good will towards men. Alleluia.

℣ Mercy and truth are met together. Alleluia.

℟ Righteousness and peace have kissed each other. Alleluia.

Let us pray.

WE adore Thee, and give thanks to Thee, O SON of the Living GOD, most Gracious JESUS, Who for us wast conceived in the Virgin's Womb, and becamest a tender Infant. Thou didst condescend to be poor and weak, that Thou mightest make us rich. Thou, our GOD, hast become our Brother, that Thou mightest redeem us and bring us to Thy most glorious Kingdom. Behold, we fall down in spirit before Thy holy manger, and adore Thee our LORD, the King of Angels, GOD Blessed for ever. Hail, Holy Child, GOD most High, most Gracious JESUS! Hail! Prince of Peace, Emmanuel, GOD with us, Light of the world, the long-desired SAVIOUR, Desire of all nations, the Hope of all the ends of the earth!

O Gracious SAVIOUR, we beseech Thee, of Thy love and goodness, to remember our manifold infirmities; give us full pardon of our sins, and a new spirit: give us grace that we may always imitate Thy humility, resignation, purity, patience, charity, and all virtues, that we may be well-pleasing to Thee, may become daily more like unto Thee, and may hereafter dwell with Thee for ever. Amen.

O Blessed SPIRIT, cleanse with Thy purifying fire our hearts and bodies; renew us day by day by Thy power, that the fruits of the Incarnation of our LORD may be seen in our lives; fill Thy whole Church and the whole world with the light, joy, and peace of His Nativity, that His Second Coming in glory may be hastened, the elect be gathered in, and the just be perfected in His eternal and everlasting kingdom. Amen.

St. Stephen's Day.

MAY GOD, Who crowned the blessed Stephen His first Martyr, both in his confession of the Faith and in his endurance of martyrdom, encircle us in this present life with the crown of righteousness, and bring us in that which is to come to the crown of glory. Amen.

May He grant us evermore to abound in that love both of GOD and of our neighbour which he held fast even amid the assaults of those who stoned him. Amen.

So that, being strengthened by his example, and also aided by his prayers, we may receive the blessing of Him Whom he saw standing at the Right Hand of GOD. Amen.

St. John the Evangelist's Day.

MAY GOD Almighty, Who through the blessed John, Apostle and Evangelist, willed to reveal to the Church the secret mysteries of His Word, vouchsafe to bless us on this his Festival. Amen.

And may He grant us strength by the gift of the HOLY SPIRIT to receive inwardly in our minds what he, inspired by the gift of the Same Spirit, hath poured into our outward ears. Amen.

That being assured by his teaching of the Divinity of our Redeemer, we may by loving what He taught and by fulfilling what He revealed, attain to the gifts which the Same JESUS CHRIST our LORD hath promised. Amen.

The Holy Innocents' Day.

MAY GOD Almighty, for the adorable Infancy of Whose Only-Begotten troops of innocent children were slain by the cruelty of wicked Herod, bestow on us the precious gifts of His blessing. Amen.

And as He granted to them that they, not by speaking but by dying, should confess His only SON our LORD,

Christmas

so may He grant to us to profess the true Faith not only with our lips but also by a blameless life, and patience even unto death. Amen.

And as He accepted them as the first-fruits of His Holy Church, so may He make us with fruit of good works to attain to the joys of our everlasting Home. Amen.

Litany of the Word Incarnate, our Lord Jesus Christ.

LORD, have mercy upon us.
CHRIST, have mercy upon us.
LORD, have mercy upon us.

O GOD the FATHER, of Heaven,
O GOD the SON, Redeemer of the world,
O GOD the HOLY GHOST,
Holy TRINITY, One GOD,
O Word, made Flesh,
O Word, full of grace and truth,
O Word of the LORD,
GOD by Whom all things were made,
LORD GOD of Israel, Blessed for evermore,
EMMANUEL, GOD with us,
The Only-Begotten SON, Who art in the bosom of the FATHER,
The Beloved SON of GOD, in Whom the FATHER is well-pleased,
To Whom a Name is given which is above every name,
Who upholdest all things by the word of Thy power,
The First-Born of every creature,
The First-Born among many brethren,
The Expectation of the Gentiles,
Wonderful, Counsellor, the Mighty GOD,
Seed of Abraham,
Star risen out of Jacob,
Lion of the tribe of Judah,
Stem of Jesse,
SON of David,
SON of Man,
JESUS of Nazareth,
At whose Name every knee doth bow, of things in Heaven,

Have mercy upon us.

and things in earth, and things under the earth,

In Whom dwelleth all the fulness of the Godhead bodily,

GOD the Prince of Peace,

CHRIST, our Peace, Who hast made both One,

The Brightness of the Everlasting Light,

The Brightness of the Glory and the express Image of the Person of GOD,

The Tree of Life,

The Beginning and the End,

Who art over all GOD blessed for ever,

Have mercy upon us.

BE propitious, spare us, O LORD.

From all evil deliver us, O Lord.

BY Thy eternal Generation from Thy FATHER,

By Thy temporal Nativity from Thy Mother,

By Thy most holy Life and Conversation,

By Thy co-eternal Glory with GOD the FATHER,

Deliver us, O Lord.

WE sinners beseech Thee, to hear us, O Lord.

THAT we may seek first the Kingdom of GOD and His righteousness,

That we may learn of Thee, for Thou art Meek and Lowly of heart,

That we may love our enemies, and do good to them that hate us,

That we may deny ourselves, take up our cross, and follow Thee.

That receiving Thy word into an honest and good heart, we may bring forth much fruit with patience.

That enduring by Thy grace unto the end, we may be saved.

We beseech Thee to hear us, O Lord.

O LAMB of GOD, that takest away the sins of the world,

Have mercy upon us.

O Lamb of GOD, that takest away the sins of the world,

Hearken to us, O Lord.

O Lamb of GOD, that

takest away the sins of the world,
Grant us Thy peace.

OUR FATHER.

Let us Pray.

GRANT, we beseech Thee, O LORD our GOD, that we may alike apprehend both parts of the one Mystery, and adore One CHRIST Very GOD and Very Man, neither divided from our nature nor separate from Thine Essence; through the Same JESUS CHRIST our LORD. Amen.

✠ THE CIRCUMCISION OF CHRIST. (1875)

MAY GOD Almighty, Whose Only-Begotten SON, that He might keep the Law which He came to fulfil, received as on this day the outward Circumcision, cleanse our minds by the inward and spiritual circumcision from all incentives to sin, and pour upon us His abundant blessing. Amen.

And may He Who willed to fulfil in us by His law the righteousness of the law, give us His peace, deliver us from the deadly corruption of sin, and make us to persevere in the new life of virtue. Amen.

That having lived through the six days of this life, we may on the seventh rest among the company of blessed Spirits, and finally, being renewed by His Resurrection on the eighth, we may attain to the joys that shall endure for ever. Amen.

Litany of the Holy Name of Jesus.

LORD, have mercy upon us.
CHRIST, have mercy upon us.
LORD, have mercy upon us.

O JESU, hear us.
O JESU, graciously hear us.

O GOD the FATHER, of Heaven,
Have mercy upon us.

O GOD the SON, Redeemer of the world,

O GOD the HOLY GHOST,

HOLY TRINITY, One GOD,

JESU, SON of the Living GOD,

JESU, Brightness of the FATHER's glory,

JESU, our Everlasting Light,

Have mercy upon us.

Jesu, King of glory,
Jesu, the Sun of Righteousness,
Jesu, Son of the Virgin Mary,
Jesu, Whose Name is Wonderful and Counsellor,
Jesu, the Mighty God, the Everlasting Father, the Prince of Peace,
Jesu, most Mighty.
Jesu, most Patient,
Jesu, most Obedient,
Jesu, Meek and Lowly of heart,
Jesu, Lover of chastity,
Jesu, our Beloved,
Jesu, Author of our life,
Jesu, Pattern of all virtues,
Jesu, Lover of our souls,
Jesu, our Refuge,
Jesu, Father of the poor,
Jesu, Treasure of the faithful,
Jesu, the Good Shepherd,
Jesu, the True Light,
Jesu, Who art eternal Wisdom,
Jesu, Who art infinite Goodness,

} *Have mercy upon us.*

Jesu, the Way, the Truth, and the Life,
Jesu, the Joy of Angels,
Jesu, the Master of Apostles,
Jesu, the Teacher of Evangelists,
Jesu, the Strength of Martyrs,
Jesu, the Light of Confessors,
Jesu, the Purity of Virgins,
Jesu, the Crown and Reward of Saints,

} *Have mercy upon us.*

BE merciful to us, O Jesu.
And spare us, Good Lord.
Be merciful to us, O Jesu.
And graciously hear us.

From all sin,
From Thy Wrath,
From the snares of the devil,
From the sins of the flesh,
From death eternal,
From neglect of Thy inspirations,
By the mystery of Thy holy Incarnation,
By Thy sinless Birth,
By Thy lowly Childhood,
By Thy divine Life and Labours,
By Thine Agony and bloody Sweat,

} *Good Lord, deliver us.*

The Epiphany

By Thy Cross and Passion,
By Thy Pains and Sorrows,
By Thy Death and Burial,
By Thy glorious Resurrection and Ascension,
By Thy Joys and heavenly Glory,
} *Good Lord deliver us.*

O LAMB of GOD, that takest away the sins of the world,
O JESU, spare us.

O LAMB of GOD, that takest away the sins of the world,
O JESU, hear us.

O LAMB of GOD, that takest away the sins of the world,
O JESU, have mercy upon us.

℣ Our help is in the Name of the LORD,
℟ *Who hath made Heaven and earth.*
℣ Our delight shall be daily in Thy Name,
℟ *And in Thy righteousness will we make our boast.*
℣ Blessed be the Name of the LORD,
℟ *From this time forth for evermore.*

OUR FATHER.

Let us pray.

O GOD, Who didst ordain Thine Only-Begotten SON to be the SAVIOUR of mankind, and didst command that His Name should be called JESUS: mercifully grant that as we do love and honour His holy Name on earth, so we may evermore enjoy the Vision of Him in Heaven. Through the Same Thy SON JESUS CHRIST our LORD. Amen.

EVE OF THE EPIPHANY.

GRANT us, we beseech Thee, O LORD, worthily to celebrate that mystery, wherein both the Godhead of our Infant SAVIOUR shines forth in wondrous works, and by His bodily growth His Manhood is plainly shewn. Through the Same JESUS CHRIST our LORD, Who liveth and reigneth with Thee and the HOLY GHOST, One GOD, world without end. Amen.

THE EPIPHANY.

Antiphon. Arise, shine, for thy Light is come, and the Glory of the LORD is risen upon thee. Alleluia.

℣ O LORD, arise, help us:

℟ And deliver us for Thy mercy's sake.

Let us pray.

ALMIGHTY and Everlasting GOD, Who hast made known the Incarnation of Thy SON by the bright shining of a star; which when the Wise Men beheld they presented costly gifts, and adored Thy Majesty: grant that the star of Thy righteousness may always shine in our hearts; and that, as our treasure, we may give ourselves and all we possess to Thy service; through JESUS CHRIST our LORD. Amen.

O GOD, Who through Thine Only-Begotten SON, JESUS CHRIST our LORD, hast endowed the regenerating waters with the grace which halloweth unto eternal salvation; and didst Thyself anoint Him with Thy Spirit, in the descent of the mysterious Dove; grant, we beseech Thee, that there may come upon Thy whole Church a blessing which may keep us all continually safe, unceasingly bless all classes of Thy servants, direct the course of those who follow Thee, and open the door of Thy Heavenly Kingdom to all those who are waiting to enter; through JESUS CHRIST our LORD. Amen.

Litany of the Holy Child Jesus.

LORD, have mercy upon us.

CHRIST, have mercy upon us.

LORD, have mercy upon us.

O CHRIST, hear us.

O CHRIST, graciously hear us.

The Epiphany

O GOD the FATHER, of Heaven,
O GOD the SON, Redeemer of the world,
O GOD the HOLY GHOST,
HOLY TRINITY, One GOD,

O BLESSED JESUS, Very GOD and Very Man,
JESU, Sent into the world by the FATHER,
JESU, Conceived by the HOLY GHOST,
JESU, Who didst take the form of a servant,
JESU, Born of the Virgin Mary,
JESU, Adored by Thy Mother,
JESU, Wrapped in swaddling-clothes,
JESU, Cradled in a manger,
JESU, Worshipped by the Shepherds,
JESU, Fed at a Virgin's breast,
JESU, Adored by the Magi,
JESU, Carried in the arms of S. Joseph,
JESU, Submitting to the law of circumcision,
JESU, Presented in the Temple,
JESU, Taken up into the arms of Simeon,
JESU, Persecuted by Herod,
JESU, Exiled into Egypt,
JESU, Brought up at Nazareth,
JESU, Lost for three days by Thy Blessed Mother and S. Joseph,
JESU, Found in the Temple in the midst of the Doctors,
JESU, Returning to Nazareth at the bidding of S. Mary and S. Joseph,
JESU, Working in the carpenter's shop,
JESU, Subject to S. Mary and S. Joseph,

Have mercy upon us.

BE merciful to us, O JESU.
Spare us, O LORD.

Be merciful to us, O JESU.
Graciously hear us, O LORD.

BY Thy unspeakable Love in making choice of Mary for Thy Mother,
By the ineffable mystery of Thy Incarnation, whereby Thou didst vouchsafe to unite

O Lord deliver us.

Thy Divine Person to our frail nature,

By Thy immaculate Conception, and Thy nine months' abode within the Blessed Virgin's womb,

By Thy holy Nativity in the poor stable at Bethlehem,

By Thy Sobs and Tears,

By Thy Hunger and Cold,

By Thy painful Circumcision,

By the first Shedding of Thy most precious Blood for our sake,

By the Virtue of Thy most blessed Name of JESUS,

By the Adoration of the Magi, whom Thou didst summon to Thyself by a star from the east,

By the mystical Offerings of gold, and frankincense, and myrrh,

By Thy being Redeemed by Thy Virgin Mother with a pair of turtle-doves,

By the Oblation of Thyself to Thy Eternal FATHER in the arms of Simeon,

By Thy Flight into Egypt to escape from Herod's cruelty,

By all Thy Sufferings in Egypt with Thy Mother and S. Joseph,

By Thy Return from Egypt to Nazareth,

By Thy three days' Loss in Jerusalem,

By Thy being Found in the Temple, sitting among the Doctors,

By Thy humble Obedience to Thy parents,

By Thy secret and hidden Life at Nazareth,

By Thy meek and lowly Conversation in the world,

O Lord deliver us.

O LAMB of GOD, Who takest away the sins of the world,
Forgive us, O LORD.

O Lamb of GOD, Who takest away the sins of the world,
Hear us, O LORD.

O Lamb of GOD, Who takest away the sins of the world,
Have mercy upon us, O LORD.

O LORD, hear us.

O LORD, hearken unto us.

OUR FATHER.

Let us pray.

O LORD JESUS, Who didst veil the greatness of Thy Divinity by being born in time, and didst humble Thyself in Thy Humanity by becoming a little Child ; grant that we may acknowledge Infinite Wisdom in childlike simplicity, Power in weakness, Majesty in abasement, so that, adoring Thy humiliation on earth, we may contemplate Thy glories in Heaven, Who with the FATHER and the HOLY GHOST livest and reignest, GOD for ever and ever. Amen.

SEPTUAGESIMA.

MAY GOD Almighty strengthen us with His blessing, and prepare us duly for the approaching Fast of Lent. Amen.

And may the Same most merciful Enlightener, Who by the power of His Godhead restored sight to the blind man upon his coming to Him and entreating Him, clear away also the blindness of our hearts, and graciously enlighten our minds by the rays of His Light. Amen.

That, being cleansed from the defilement of sin, and strengthened by a fervent charity, we may be enabled to attain unharmed to our inheritance in Heaven. Amen.

PRAYERS TO KEEP LENT.

I.

ASSIST, O LORD, by Thy grace, and by Thine infinite goodness, these beginnings of our Fast, and of our humiliations. Accept them, bless them, sustain them, crown them with a courageous perseverance ; give us grace to perfect our holy observances by a pure intention and a sincere conversion, so that our bodily exercises of repentance may be made complete by those of the mind and heart ; and this we beg through the merits of JESUS CHRIST, Thy SON our Adorable SAVIOUR. Amen.

II.

ALMIGHTY GOD, Whose mercies are infinite, we implore Thy pardon, and entreat Thee humbly to shed the grace of Thy blessing upon the penitential exercises which we, with all the faithful, practise at this holy Season, and whilst we chasten and mortify our bodies, do Thou shed upon our souls the joy of a good conscience, and of a sincere and holy devotion, so that subduing all earthly desires and all irregular appetites which attack the purity of our hearts and the innocence of our souls, we may the more easily apply ourselves to things Heavenly; and this we beg, through the merits of JESUS CHRIST Thy SON our LORD. Amen.

III.

PURIFY, O LORD, our intentions and our designs in these our Fasts from all feelings of self-love, and vanity; and from all love of singularity, give us all the strength and all the courage we need, in order to fulfil them worthily unto the end. Mercifully shed upon them Thy abundant blessing, and accompany them with the spirit of penitence, compunction, fervour, and perseverance, and all which may render them more acceptable and more pleasing in Thy sight. Give us grace to wean our flesh from unbecoming delights, and to mortify our senses with a prudent restraint; and this we beg, O LORD JESUS CHRIST, through Thy Merits, Thy Sufferings, and Thy Blood. Amen.

LENT.

Prayers on the Passion

for Daily Use.

DAILY.

Antiphon. Behold now is the accepted time, behold now is the day of salvation.

℣ Turn Thee, O Lord, and deliver my soul:

℟ O save me for Thy mercy's sake.

OUR FATHER.

Act of Contrition.

O LORD JESUS CHRIST, my CREATOR and my SAVIOUR, I offer unto Thee the sacrifice of a troubled spirit. Oh that I had never offended Thee Whom I ought to love above all things. Thou hast bestowed upon me many blessings, and I have returned Thee only evil for Thy good. I acknowledge my transgression, and my sin is ever before me; especially do I lament and grieve that I am yet so carnal and worldly, so unmortified in my passions, so full of the motions of concupiscence; so unwatchful over my outward senses; so often entangled with many vain fancies; so much inclined to outward things; so negligent of things inward and spiritual; so prone to laughter and unbridled mirth, so indisposed to tears and compunction; so prompt to ease and pleasures of the flesh, so dull to strictness of life and zeal; so curious to hear news and to see sights, so slack to embrace what is humble and low; so covetous of abundance; so niggardly in giving, so fast in keeping; so inconsiderate in speech, so reluctant to keep silence; so uncomposed in manner, so fretful in action; so eager about food, so little anxious for the Bread of Life; so hurried to rest, so slow to labour; so wakeful after gossip, so deaf to the Word of GOD; so careless at the Sacred Offices, so hasty to arrive at the end thereof: so inclined to be wandering and inattentive in the prayers, so negligent in preparing to come to GOD'S Altar, so lukewarm at the Celebration of the most Holy Eucharist, and so dry and heartless in the reception of It; so quickly distracted, so seldom wholly gathered into myself; so suddenly moved to anger, so apt to take offence; so ready to judge, so severe to reprove; so joyful in prosperity, so weak in adversity; so often making so many good resolutions, and yet so often bringing them, at last, to so poor an end. But be Thou merciful unto me, O LORD, for I humbly desire to have true sorrow and to confess my sins, to shun all occasions of them, to obtain pardon and forgiveness for them, to receive strength sufficient to fall no more, that cleansed by Thy pity and renewed by Thy grace, I may be strengthened in the love of Thee, and be defended against all temptations of the world, the flesh, and the devil. Amen.

Prayers for Forgiveness.

MAY the Almighty GOD have mercy upon us, ✠ pardon all our sins, and bring us to everlasting life. Amen.

May the Almighty and most Merciful LORD grant to us pardon, absolution, and remission of all our sins. Amen.

SUNDAY.

Jesus Enters into Jerusalem.

ALL hail Sweet JESU : praise, honour, and glory be to Thee, O CHRIST, Who at Thy entry into Jerusalem, didst sit Meek and Lowly upon an ass, and while the multitude who met Thee greeted Thee with songs of praise, didst shed tears, weeping for the destruction of the City, and the loss of ungrateful souls. Grant me an intimate knowledge of myself, that I may know how unworthy a creature I am, and may most deeply humble and despise myself. May I never seek delight in the favour and applause of men, but give myself profitably to tears of penitence and love. May I feel the trials of others, and devoutly mourn for their sins as though they were mine own.

O Good JESU, Gracious JESU ! O my Hope, my Refuge, and my Salvation, have mercy, have mercy on me. I am poor, needy, and weak. I am nothing, I have nothing, I can do nothing of myself. O help Thou me.

O Good JESU, I beseech Thee by Thy sacred Passion and Death, grant to the living pardon and grace, to the faithful departed rest and everlasting life. Amen.

MONDAY.

Jesus Holds Intercourse with Sinners.

ALL hail, sweet JESU : praise, honour, and glory be to Thee, O CHRIST, Who didst not shrink from the company of publicans and sinners, but didst bestow Thy most gracious friendship on Matthew, Zaccheus, Mary Magdalene, on the woman taken in adultery, and on other penitents, and didst give them instant pardon of their sins. Grant that I may manifest a holy fervent love towards all men, readily forgive all who injure me, and perfectly love all who hate me. Give me full pardon for all my sins, sure hope of Thy favour, and an abiding trust in Thee.

O Good JESU, Gracious JESU! O my Hope, my Refuge, and my Salvation, I give myself up wholly to Thee. May Thy most gracious will always be fulfilled in me and by me.

O Good JESU. I beseech Thee by Thy sacred Passion and Death, grant to the living pardon and grace, to the faithful departed rest and everlasting light. Amen.

TUESDAY.

Jesus Begins to be Sorrowful.

ALL hail Sweet JESU: praise, honour, and glory be to Thee, O CHRIST, Who when Thy Passion was at hand didst begin to be sorrowful and very heavy, taking on Thyself the infirmities of Thy children, that Thou mightest comfort and support them in their fears of death. Keep me, I pray Thee, from sinful sadness, and from unseemly mirth. Grant, that every sorrow that I have hitherto had may be to Thy glory, and to the good of my soul. Take from me, of Thy pity, all distrust of Thee, all inordinate faint-heartedness, and strengthen and stablish my whole soul in Thee.

O Good JESU, Gracious JESU. O my Hope, my Refuge, and my Salvation. Give me purity, singleness of purpose, and a thorough knowledge of myself, that I may be a man after Thine Own heart.

O Good JESU, I beseech Thee by Thy sacred Passion and Death, grant to the living pardon and grace, to the faithful departed rest and everlasting light. Amen.

WEDNESDAY.

Jesus Sold for Thirty Pieces of Silver.

ALL hail Sweet JESU: praise, honour, and glory be to Thee, O CHRIST, Who wast sold for paltry money by Thy faithless disciple, when the Jews were persecuting Thee, and conspiring against Thy life. Root out, I pray Thee, from my heart every wrong desire for created things: grant that I may never prefer anything to Thee: grant that I may exhibit sincere affection towards all, and especially to those who bring trouble upon me. Pardon me, O Holy Redeemer, for having so often preferred vain and perishing things to Thee, and turned myself away from Thee for worthless pleasures.

O Good JESU, Gracious JESU! O my Hope, my Refuge, and my Salvation. Give me true humility, patience, charity, the government of my tongue, and control over my senses.

O Good JESU, I beseech Thee, by Thy sacred Passion and Death, grant to the living pardon and grace, to the faithful departed rest and everlasting light. Amen.

THURSDAY.

Jesus Institutes the Holy Eucharist.

ALL hail Sweet JESU: praise, honour, and glory be to Thee, O CHRIST, Who didst institute the Sacrament of the Eucharist out of Thy unspeakable love towards us, and dost give Thyself to us in it with wondrous condescension, to be with us under the form of bread and wine even unto the end of the world. Kindle within me, I beseech Thee, a desire for Thee, and inflame my inmost soul to hunger after Thee in this most Holy Sacrament. Grant that I may receive Thee with pure affection, with deep humility, and entire purity of heart when I approach that Heavenly Feast. May my soul now so thirst for Thee, so faint with love of Thee, that I may hereafter be found meet to enjoy Thy eternal joys in Thy Kingdom, to the glory of Thy Name.

O Good JESU, Gracious JESU! O my Hope, my Refuge, and my Salvation. Grant that all perishing things may be esteemed as worthless by me, and that Thou alone mayest please and delight me. Conform my life to the pattern of Thine.

O Good JESU, I beseech Thee by Thy sacred Passion and Death, grant to the living pardon and grace, to the faithful departed rest and everlasting light. Amen.

FRIDAY.

Jesus Hanging on the Cross.

ALL hail Sweet JESU: praise, honour, and glory be to Thee, O CHRIST, Who didst hang for three whole hours with pierced hands and feet on the Tree of Shame, and didst voluntarily endure unspeakable agony in all Thy holy limbs, with copious shedding of Thy precious Blood. Quicken me, I beseech Thee, by Thy Cross, for my soul cleaveth unto the dust, purge me from the dregs of corrupt affection, and inflame my heart with the love of Thee, and an earnest longing for eternity, and for Heaven. O saving Blood! O life-giving Blood. I desire, O my LORD, I do humbly desire that Thou shouldest straightway heal my soul and purify it washed in that most precious Blood, I would that Thou shouldest offer that precious Blood to GOD the FATHER for the perfect satisfaction of my sins. Grant I pray Thee that my inmost soul may with ardent affection receive and drink the life-giving drops of that same blessed Blood, and truly taste the sweetness of Thy HOLY SPIRIT.

O Good JESU, Gracious JESU! O my Hope, my Refuge, and my Salvation. I give thanks to Thee for Thy adorable Wounds. O hide me in them. Inscribe and impress them deeply on my heart, that I may be wholly inflamed with love of Thee, and suffer with Thee in my inmost soul.

O Good JESU, I beseech Thee, by Thy sacred Passion and Death, grant to the living pardon and grace, to the faithful departed rest and everlasting light. Amen.

SATURDAY.

Jesus Buried.

ALL hail Holy JESU: praise, honour, and glory be to Thee, O CHRIST, Who when Thou wast taken down from the Cross amid the great grief of Thy friends, didst will to be anointed with sweet ointment, to be wrapped in linen, and to be laid in another's tomb. Bury, I beseech Thee, all my senses, and all my powers and affections in Thyself; so that united to Thee by constraining love, I may become dead to all else but Thee, and may know and feel that Thou art the One only Redeemer of my soul, my Chief and Only Good.

O Good JESU, Gracious JESU! O my Hope, my Refuge, and my Salvation. Grant me complete mortification and renunciation of self. Extinguish in me all evil affections and passions.

O Good JESU, I beseech Thee, by Thy sacred Passion and Death, grant to the living pardon and grace, to the faithful departed rest and everlasting light. Amen.

DAILY.

A Prayer to Jesus.

O LORD JESU CHRIST, Maker, Redeemer, Lover, and Benefactor of mankind, Who graciously hearest those who earnestly call upon Thee, have mercy upon me. Cleanse me, I beseech Thee, by Thy most holy Incarnation and Passion from all sin. Cast down in me all haughtiness of pride: destroy all arrogance; break in pieces and utterly crush all hardness of heart and stubbornness. Subdue all bitterness of spirit which is contrary to sincere love. Calm the troubled risings of impatience. Repress and quell the wild impulse and madness of anger; extinguish the wrong desire of vain glory. Root out and destroy the evil motions of wicked lusts. Take from me whatever in me displeases Thee, and give me what is pleasing to Thee. Teach, enlighten, direct, assist, protect, and keep me every hour and moment of my life, that I may do those things which are pleasing to Thee, and rest secure in Thee for ever. Amen.

May GOD Almighty bless me, and of His mercy vouchsafe to defend me from all wickedness. Amen.

Ember Week.

O CHRIST, the true Priest, Whose Priesthood continueth for ever, help, we beseech Thee, Thy servants, our Priests, that they carefully and worthily discharging the holy offices of their priesthood, may through the guidance of Thy HOLY SPIRIT use their talents to Thy service and our need. May they go on, O LORD, from strength to strength; lift them up while they worship Thee; perfect Thy gifts in them, crown them with Thy glory, and fill their hearts with Thy grace, that they may gather into Thy kingdom in Heaven a rich harvest of many souls through the Same JESUS CHRIST our LORD. Amen.

S. Gregory's Prayers on the Passion.

1. I ADORE Thee, O LORD JESU CHRIST! hanging upon the Cross, and wearing on Thy Head the Crown of thorns: I beseech Thee that Thy Cross may deliver me from the destroying Angel. Amen.

Our FATHER.
Glory be to the FATHER.

2. I adore Thee, O LORD JESU CHRIST, wounded on the Cross, and having gall and vinegar given Thee to drink: I beseech Thee that Thy Wounds may be the healing of my soul. Amen.

Our FATHER.
Glory be to the FATHER.

3. I pray Thee, O LORD JESU CHRIST, by that bitterness of Thy Passion, which Thou sufferedst at the hour of Thy death, and then above all when Thy most holy Soul passed forth from Thy blessed Body; pity my soul when it is departing out of my body, and bring it to everlasting life. Amen.

Our FATHER.
Glory be to the FATHER.

4. I adore Thee, O LORD JESU CHRIST, laid in the Sepulchre, embalmed with myrrh and spices: I beseech Thee that Thy Death may be my life. Amen.

Our FATHER.
Glory be to the FATHER.

5. I adore Thee, O LORD JESU CHRIST, descending into Hell and sending forth Thy prisoners: I beseech Thee, suffer me not to enter there. Amen.

Our FATHER.
Glory be to the FATHER.

6. I adore Thee, O LORD JESU CHRIST, rising again from the dead, and ascend-

ing into Heaven, and sitting at the right hand of the FATHER: I beseech Thee that I may be found worthy to follow Thee thither, and dwell in Thy presence. Amen.

Our FATHER.
Glory be to the FATHER.

7. O LORD JESU CHRIST, the Good Shepherd, preserve the righteous, justify sinners, have mercy upon all the faithful, and be gracious to me, a miserable and wretched sinner. Amen.

Our FATHER.
Glory be to the FATHER.

I BESEECH Thee, O LORD JESU CHRIST, that Thy Passion may be unto me virtue, whereby I may be fenced, protected, and defended. Let Thy Wounds be to me meat and drink, by which I may be fed, inebriated, and delighted. Let the sprinkling of Thy Blood be to me the washing away of all my sins. Let Thy death be to me everlasting glory. In these let me find my refreshment, exultation, health, longing, joy, and desire, both of body and soul, now and for ever. Amen.

Prayers of S. Bernardine.

O GOOD JESUS, O Sweet JESUS, O JESUS, SON of the Virgin Mary, full of mercy and truth; have mercy upon me according to Thy great mercy.

O Gracious JESUS, I pray Thee by Thy precious Blood, which Thou didst vouchsafe to shed for us miserable sinners upon the Altar of the Cross, take away from me all mine iniquities, and despise me not who humbly entreat Thee, and call upon Thy most holy Name of JESUS.

Thy Name of JESUS is a sweet Name: Thy name of JESUS is a saving Name. For what does JESUS mean but SAVIOUR.

O Good JESUS, Who didst create me, and with Thy precious Blood didst redeem me, suffer me not to be condemned, whom Thou didst make out of nothing.

O Good JESUS, let not my wickedness destroy me, whom Thine almighty goodness made and formed.

O Good JESUS, acknowledge what is Thine in me, and take away from me all that is not Thine.

O Good JESUS, have mercy upon me whilst it is the time of mercy, and destroy me not in the time of Thy fearful judgment.

O Good JESUS, although I, a miserable sinner, have deserved of Thy strict justice eternal punishment for my most grievous sins, yet I appeal from Thy strict justice to Thine unspeakable mercy; and pray Thee as a loving Father and merciful LORD, to have mercy upon me.

O Good JESUS, what profit is there in my blood, if I go down to the pit? For the dead praise not Thee, O LORD; neither all they that go down into silence.

O most Merciful JESUS, have mercy on me. O most Sweet JESUS, deliver me. O most Loving JESUS, be merciful to me a sinner. O JESUS, admit me, a miserable sinner, into the number of Thine Elect. O JESUS, the Salvation of them that believe in Thee, have mercy upon me.

O JESUS, the sweet remission of all my sins; O JESUS, SON of the Virgin Mary, pour into me Thy grace, wisdom, charity, chastity, and humility, and in all mine adversities, holy patience, that I may be able to love Thee perfectly, and in Thee to make my boast, and to find my chief delight in Thee for ever and ever. Amen.

S. Bridget's Prayers on the Passion.

I.

O JESU CHRIST! Eternal Sweetness of them that love Thee, thrilling joy far surpassing all joy and all desire, the SAVIOUR and Lover of sinners, Who hast testified by becoming Man for man at the end of time, that Thy delight is to be with the sons of men: call to mind that drear foreboding and most inward sorrow, which, as the foreordained time of Thy saving Passion drew near, made Thy human Soul exceeding sorrowful even unto death. Call to mind the sadness and the bitterness that filled Thy Soul, and whereof Thou spakest when at the last supper Thou didst give Thy disciples Thy Own

Body and Blood, didst wash their feet, and sweetly mingle comfort with the announcement of Thy coming Passion. Call to mind all the dread, the anguish, and the grief which Thou didst bear in Thy tender Body before Thy Passion on the Cross, when after Thy thrice repeated prayer and Bloody Sweat Thou wast betrayed by Thy disciple Judas, seized by the chosen people, accused by false witnesses, unjustly judged by three unrighteous judges, and in the elect city, at the Paschal Season, in the prime of manhood, wast condemned, although innocent, stripped of Thine Own garments, and arrayed in strange apparel, wast buffeted and blindfolded, wast bruised with blows, bound to a pillar and scourged, crowned with thorns, smitten with a reed upon Thy Head, and assailed with numberless reproaches.

O LORD GOD, for the memory of these Thy sufferings before Thy Crucifixion, grant me, I entreat Thee, before my death true contrition, full confession, worthy satisfaction, and remission of all my sins. Amen.

Our FATHER.

II.

O JESU! Maker of the world, Whom no measure can mete nor bound contain, Who holdest the earth within the hollow of Thy hand, call to mind the anguish of Thy torment, when the Jews first fastened Thy most holy Hands with blunt nails to the Cross, and added agony on agony to Thy Wounds, when to fit Thy Body for their purpose and drive the nails through Thy tender Feet, they wrenched Thee so upon the Cross's length and breadth, that all Thy Limbs were out of joint.

I implore Thee by the memory of Thy Cross's hallowed and most bitter anguish, make me fear Thee, make me love Thee. Amen.

Our FATHER.

III.

O JESU! Heavenly Physician, call to mind the languor, the bruises, and the pain which, uplifted on the Cross, Thou sufferedst in all Thy rended Limbs: when all were wrenched asunder, and from the sole of the foot even unto the head there was no whole part in Thee, and no sorrow could be found like unto Thy sorrow; and yet, wholly unmindful of all Thy griefs Thou prayedst the FATHER for Thine enemies, and saidst so lovingly "FATHER, forgive them, for they know not what they do."

By this Thy mercy, by the memory of Thy sorrow, grant me that this remembrance of Thy most bitter Passion may be the full remission of all my sins. Amen.

Our FATHER.

IV.

O JESU! Very Glory of Angels! Paradise of delights! call to mind that heaviness and shuddering of Thine when Thy cruel enemies, like ravening wolves, beset Thee, tearing Thy flesh with their sharp nails, and assailing Thee with blows and spitting, and every other untold pain.

By these pains, by all the reproachful gibes, by the cruel tortures which Thy enemies put upon Thee, save me, O LORD JESU, I pray Thee, and set me free from the enemies I see around me: grant me, under the shadow of Thy wings, to come to perfect and everlasting safety. Amen.

Our FATHER.

V.

O JESU! Mirror of everlasting love, call to mind that grief of Thine, when in the mirror of Thy serene Majesty, Thou beheldest the predestination of Thine Elect, whom the merits of Thine Agony should save, and the reprobation of the wicked, who, for their own demerits, should suffer damnation, and by the depth of Thy compassion for us, lost and ruined sinners, which Thou showedst on the Cross, in Thy saying to the robber, "To-day shalt thou be with me in Paradise;" I pray Thee, JESU, deal with me in mercy at the hour of my death. Amen.

Our FATHER.

VI.

O KING most Lovely, and Loving One most dear, call to mind that grief of Thine, when naked and miserable Thou didst hang upon the Cross, and all Thy friends and acquaintances set themselves against Thee;

when Thou foundest none to comfort Thee, save only Thy dear Mother, who still stood by Thee in the bitterness of her soul, and whom Thou commendedst to Thy disciple, saying to her, "Woman, behold Thy Son!"

I pray Thee, most Loving JESU, by that sword of grief which then passed through her soul, have compassion on me in all my distresses and afflictions of soul or body, and give me comfort in the time of trouble, and at the hour of my death. Amen.

Our FATHER.

VII.

O JESU! Unfailing Spring of love, Who from the lowest depth thereof saidst upon the Cross, "I thirst," even for man's salvation: kindle the desires of our hearts, I pray Thee, for every perfect work: allay and staunch in us wholly the thirst of fleshly lust, and all the feverishness of this world's pleasures. Amen.

Our FATHER.

VIII.

O JESU! Very Sweetness to the heart and soul, by the bitterness of the gall and vinegar which for us Thou didst taste, grant us, at the hour of our death, worthily to receive Thy Body and Blood, to the healing and refreshment of our souls. Amen.

Our FATHER.

IX.

O JESU! Royal in Thy might and thrilling in Thy presence in the soul, call to mind that sore distress and agony of Thine, when forlorn and desolate in the bitterness of death, and assailed by the Jews with gibes, Thou criedst with a loud voice to Thy FATHER, "My GOD, My GOD, why hast Thou forsaken Me?"

By this sore distress, I beseech Thee, forsake us not in our distresses, O LORD our GOD. Amen.

Our FATHER.

X.

O JESU! Alpha and Omega, everlasting Life and Strength, call to mind how from the sole of Thy Foot even to Thy Head, Thou wast plunged for us in the flood of Thy Passion.

By Thy Wounds, in their

length and in their breadth, teach me, too deeply plunged in sins, with true charity to keep Thy commandment, which is exceeding broad. Amen.

Our **Father**.

XI.

O JESU! Unfathomed Depth of loving pity, I beseech Thee by the depths of those Thy Wounds, which pierced even to Thy heart and the marrow of Thy bones, raise me out of the floods of my sins, and hide me in Thy Wounds, O LORD, from the face of Thine anger, until Thy wrath pass away. Amen.

Our **Father**.

XII.

O JESU! Mirror of truth, Sign of unity and Bond of charity, call to mind the multitude of Thy countless Wounds which covered Thee from the sole of Thy Foot even unto Thy Head; and how sore a grief Thy Virgin Flesh, red with Thy most holy Blood, endured for us! O Loving JESU, what more couldst Thou have done than that Thou hast!

Impress, I pray Thee, O LORD JESU, all Thy Wounds upon my heart; and in them let me read Thy grief and death, and for ever give Thee thanks even to my life's end. Amen.

Our **Father**.

XIII.

O JESU! Lion of the tribe of Judah, King eternal and invincible, call to mind that grief of Thine when Thy heart strings brake, and all Thy strength gave way, and, bowing Thy Head, Thou saidst, "It is finished."

By this distress and anguish, pity me at my last end, when my course is finished, when my soul is sore amazed, and my spirit is in trouble. Amen.

Our **Father**.

XIV.

O JESU! Only-Begotten of the FATHER most High, Brightness and Image of His Substance, call to mind that strong yearning effort when Thou criedst to the FATHER, "Into Thy hands I commend My Spirit;" when, with a Body torn and a Heart broken, and all the bowels of Thy love exposed for our redemption, with one mighty cry Thou gavest up the ghost. Amen.

By this Thy most precious Death, I pray Thee, King of Saints, give me strength to withstand the Devil, the World, and the Flesh, that being dead to the world I may live to Thee; and in the last hour of my departure hence, receive my soul returning again as an exile and a stranger unto Thee. Amen.

Our FATHER.

XV.

O JESU! True and Fruitful Vine, call to mind the overflowing and abundant streams of Blood, which, Thou as from a rich cluster of grapes didst plentifully shed, when Thou troddest the wine-press on the Cross alone, and from Thy Side, pierced by the soldier's lance, didst so pledge us in water and blood, that no single drop remained within Thee, and Thou hangedst like a bundle of myrrh on high, and Thy flesh was parched, and Thy moisture dried, and the marrow of Thy bones was withered.

By this most bitter Passion and precious Bloodshedding, receive my soul, I pray Thee, O Loving JESU, in the agony of my death. Amen.

Our FATHER.

Seven Thanksgivings
for the
Seven Effusions of our Lord's Blood
AGAINST THE
SEVEN DEADLY SINS.

Pride I.

O MOST Humble Lord and Master, JESU CHRIST, Very GOD and Very MAN, eternal praise and thanksgiving be to Thee, because in Thy tenderest age, on the eighth day of Thy mortal life, Thou didst vouchsafe to shed Thy precious and innocent Blood for us,

Lent

and as a true Son of Abraham to bear the pain of Circumcision.

By this most holy shedding of Thy Blood, I beg of Thee the grace of humility, against all pride and worldly vanity.

Our FATHER.

O SAVIOUR of the world Who by Thy Cross and precious Blood hast redeemed us, save us, and help us we humbly beseech Thee, O LORD.

(Covetousness)

II.

O THOU Whose love is like the pelican's for her young, JESU CHRIST, Very GOD and Very MAN, eternal praise and thanksgiving be to Thee, because in the Garden, out of the exceeding anguish of Thy Heart Thou didst pour forth a Bloody Sweat, and, wholly resigning Thyself to death, didst offer it to Thy FATHER.

By this most holy shedding of Thy Blood, I ask of Thee the grace of liberality against all covetousness and avarice.

Our FATHER.

O SAVIOUR of the world.

(Lust)

III.

O MOST Chaste Spouse, JESU CHRIST, Very GOD and Very MAN, eternal praise and thanksgiving be to Thee, because Thou didst suffer Thyself to be mercilessly bound in Pilate's judgment hall, and Thy virgin Flesh to be cruelly scourged and mangled.

By this most holy shedding of Thy Blood, I implore of Thee the grace of chastity, against all sensuality and lust.

Our FATHER.

O SAVIOUR of the world.

(Anger)

IV.

O MOST Meek Lamb, JESU CHRIST, Very GOD and Very MAN, eternal praise and thanksgiving be to Thee, because Thou didst suffer Thy sacred Head to be crowned with piercing thorns, and struck with a hard reed.

By this most holy shedding of Thy Blood, I pray Thee for the grace of meekness, against all anger and desire of revenge.

Our FATHER.

O SAVIOUR of the world.

(Gluttony)

V.

O MOST Sweet JESU CHRIST, Pattern of temperance and self-denial,

Very GOD and Very MAN, eternal praise and thanksgiving be to Thee, because Thou didst allow Thy garments to be torn from Thy bleeding Body both before and after the carrying of Thy Cross, which opened Thy Wounds again, and caused them to bleed afresh.

By this most holy shedding of Thy Blood, I beseech of Thee the grace of temperance and abstinence, against all greediness and gluttony.

Our FATHER.
O SAVIOUR of the world.

Envy VI.

O GOOD and Faithful Samaritan, JESU CHRIST, Very GOD and Very MAN, eternal praise and thanksgiving be to Thee, because out of Thy burning love for us Thou didst suffer Thy sacred Hands and Feet to be pierced and nailed to the Cross for our redemption.

By this most holy shedding of Thy Blood, I beg of Thee the grace of brotherly love, against all envy and jealousy.

Our FATHER.
O SAVIOUR of the world.

Sloth VII.

O MOST Zealous High Priest, Very GOD and Very MAN, eternal praise and thanksgiving be to Thee, because Thou didst suffer Thy sacred Side to be pierced, opened, and wounded with a spear.

By this most holy shedding of Thy Blood, I earnestly pray Thee for the grace of holy zeal and fervour, against all sloth and weariness in Thy service, and in every religious exercise.

Our FATHER.
O SAVIOUR of the world.

A Devotion

on the

Five Wounds of our Saviour.

I.

O MOST Meek JESU, by the saving Wound of Thy Right Foot, forgive me whatsoever sins of evil thoughts I have committed against Thee; and by its infinite merits make up to me whatever I have lost by the neglect of holy thoughts : so that henceforth I may desire Thee, my chief and only Good, and seek and find Thee alone Whom my soul loveth. Amen.

Our FATHER.

O SAVIOUR of the world, Who by Thy Cross and precious Blood hast redeemed us, save us, and help us, we humbly beseech Thee, O LORD.

II.

O MOST Sweet JESU, by the blessed Wound of Thy Left Foot, forgive me, I pray Thee, all that I have done amiss against Thy divine good-pleasure, by evil imaginations or abuse of my outward senses : and so restrain my thoughts henceforth by Thy holy fear, that becoming dead to the world and all created things, I may feel nothing and desire nothing, save Thee only, my GOD, crucified for me. Amen.

Our FATHER.

O SAVIOUR of the world.

III.

O MOST Sweet JESU, by the sacred Wound of Thy Right Hand, forgive, I most humbly implore Thee, all my bad and sinful deeds; yea, and by its merits supply all that I have by guilty negligence, in whatsoever duty, left undone : and henceforth may I, by Thy grace, trade more profitably with the talents Thou hast given me. Amen.

Our FATHER.

O SAVIOUR of the world.

IV.

O MOST Sweet JESU, by the Wound of Thy Left Hand, forgive my anger and sudden impulses of impatience and wrath, into which I too often rashly and thoughtlessly fall on the least provocation ; and from the rich stores of that heavenly Wound deal out to me the balm of patience in all adversities, that I may be found worthy to inherit the Land of the living which Thou hast promised to the meek. Amen.

Our FATHER.

O SAVIOUR of the world.

V.

O MOST Sweet JESU, by the sacred Wound of Thy pierced Heart, graciously forgive all that my heart has ever offended in through evil intention or perversity of will; engraft my frail heart on Thy most divine Heart, that it may feel nothing, attempt nothing, desire nothing, save what is according to Thine Own Heart; so that by resting constantly on Thy guidance, I may steadfastly persevere in all good even to the end of my life. Amen.

Our FATHER.

O SAVIOUR of the world.

Litany of the Passion.

LORD, have mercy upon us.

CHRIST, *have mercy upon us.*

LORD, have mercy upon us.

O GOD the FATHER, of Heaven,
O GOD the SON, Redeemer of the world,
O GOD the HOLY GHOST,
HOLY TRINITY, One GOD,

Have mercy upon us.

JESU, the Eternal Wisdom,
JESU, conversing with man,
JESU, hated by the world,
JESU, meek King entering Jerusalem,
JESU, zealous for GOD'S house against the buyers and sellers,
JESU, sold for thirty pieces of silver,
JESU, bent to wash Thy disciples' feet,
JESU, Who didst keep the Passover with Thy disciples,
JESU, Who gavest us Thy Body for food, Thy Blood for drink,
JESU, prostrated in prayer,
JESU, in Agony, bathed in bloody sweat,
JESU, strengthened by an Angel,
JESU, betrayed by Judas with a kiss,
JESU, bound roughly by the servants,
JESU, forsaken by Thy disciples,
JESU, taken before Annas and Caiaphas,
JESU, accused by false witnesses,
JESU, judged worthy of death,

Have mercy upon us.

Lent

Jesu, blindfolded, buffeted, and spit upon,

Jesu, Who gavest Thy Body to the smiters, Thy cheeks to them that plucked off the hair,

Jesu, thrice denied by Peter,

Jesu, delivered bound to Pilate,

Jesu, mocked and set at nought by Herod,

Jesu, rejected for Barabbas,

Jesu, cruelly torn with scourging,

Jesu, bruised for our iniquities,

Jesu, clad in a purple robe,

Jesu, crowned with thorns,

Jesu, mocked with a reed for a sceptre,

Jesu, condemned to a most ignominious death,

Jesu, delivered to the will of Thine enemies,

Jesu, burdened with the weight of Thy Cross,

Jesu, led as a sheep to the slaughter,

Jesu, offered wine mingled with myrrh,

Have mercy upon us.

Jesu, stripped of Thy garments,

Jesu, nailed naked to the Cross,

Jesu, Who lovedst us and washedst us from our sins in Thine Own Blood,

Jesu, Who for the joy set before Thee, endured the Cross, despising the shame,

Jesu, Who givest Thyself for us as an offering and a sacrifice to God for a sweet-smelling savour,

Jesu, reckoned among transgressors,

Jesu, crucified between two thieves,

Jesu, distinguished by Pilate with a royal superscription on the Cross,

Jesu, Intercessor with the Father for Thine enemies,

Jesu, made a scorn of men,

Jesu, blasphemed and scoffed at by the passers-by,

Jesu, derided by the Jews,

Jesu, mocked on the Cross by the soldiers,

Jesu, reviled by the robber,

Have mercy upon us.

Jesu, Promiser of Paradise to the penitent thief,
Jesu, Who didst commend S. John to Thy Mother for a Son,
Jesu, Who saidst, "Why hast Thou forsaken me?"
Jesu, presented with vinegar in Thy thirst,
Jesu, Who declaredst that all things written of Thee were accomplished on the Cross,
Jesu, Who in dying didst commend Thy Spirit to Thy Father,
Jesu, made obedient even to the death of the Cross,
Jesu, pierced by the lance,
Jesu, from Whose Side came out Blood and Water,
Jesu, Who didst bear our sins in Thine Own Body on the Tree,
Jesu, by Whose stripes we are healed,
Jesu, made a Propitiation for us,
Jesu, taken down from the Cross,
Jesu, wrapped in clean linen,

⎫
⎬ *Have mercy upon us.*
⎭

Jesu, laid in the new sepulchre,
Jesu, Who after death descended into Hell,
Jesu, Who didst die for our sins, and rise again for our justification,
Jesu, exalted into Heaven,
Jesu, placed with the Father at His Right Hand,
Jesu, crowned with glory and honour,
Jesu, King of Kings, and Lord of Lords,
Jesu, Who hast prepared for us a place in Thy Father's House,
Jesu, our Advocate with the Father,
Jesu, Who pouredst the Holy Ghost, the Comforter, on the disciples,
Jesu, Who shalt judge the quick and dead,
Jesu, Who shalt drive the wicked into everlasting fire,
Jesu, Who shalt bestow on the elect the Kingdom prepared for them,

⎫
⎬ *Have mercy upon us.*
⎭

BE gracious, spare us
JESU.

FROM all evil,
From sudden and unprepared death,
From the snares of the devil,
From anger, hatred, and all ill-will,
From everlasting death,
By the mystery of Thy holy Incarnation,
By Thine Advent,
By Thy Nativity,
By Thy Circumcision,
By the giving of Thy all-holy Name,
By Thy Baptism and holy Fasting,
By Thy Labours and Watchings,
By Thine Agony and Bloody Sweat,
By Thy Buffeting and Stripes,
By Thy Crown of Thorns,
By Thy Cross and Passion,
By Thy Thirst, Tears, and Nakedness,
By Thy five most sacred Wounds,
By Thy Death and Burial,
By Thy holy Resurrection,
By Thy wondrous Ascension,
By the Sending of the HOLY GHOST, the Comforter,
In the Hour of Death,
In the Day of Judgment,

} *Deliver us, JESU.*

WE sinners do beseech Thee to hear us, O LORD JESUS.

THAT being dead to sin, we may live unto righteousness,
That we delight not in glorying, save in the Cross of our LORD JESUS CHRIST,
That for love of Thee the world may be crucified unto us, and we unto the world,
That we continually bear about in the body the dying of the LORD JESUS,
That we study to crucify the flesh with its affections and lusts,
That as Thou hast suffered for us in the flesh, we may be armed likewise with the same mind,
That we may be able

} *We beseech Thee JESU, hear us.*

to take up our cross daily, and follow Thee,

That what is gain to us we may count as loss for Thee,

That we strive above all things to know JESUS crucified,

That Thy Blood may cleanse us from dead works to serve the living GOD,

That being bought at a great price, we may glorify GOD in our body,

That, being dead unto sin, and buried with Thee, we may walk henceforth with Thee in newness of life ;

That once cleansed from dead works, we beware lest we crucify Thee, the SON of GOD, afresh, and put Thee to an open shame.

That ever looking to the ensample left us by Thee, we may follow Thy steps,

That as we are partakers of the suffering, we may be also of the consolation,

We beseech Thee JESU, hear us.

O LAMB of GOD, that takest away the sins of the world.
Spare us, JESU.

O LAMB of GOD, That takest away the sins of the world.
Hear us, JESU.

O LAMB of GOD, That takest away the sins of the world.
Have mercy on us, JESU.

OUR FATHER.

Let us pray.

O GOD, Who to redeem the world didst condescend to be born and to be circumcised, to labour with Thine Hands, to suffer hunger, thirst, and weariness, to fast, and to be tempted, to teach, and to work miracles, to be rejected by the Jews, betrayed by a kiss from Judas, and forsaken of all Thy friends; to be bound, led like a lamb to the slaughter, falsely accused, beaten with rods, blindfolded, crowned with thorns, mocked, and spit upon : to be nailed to a Cross in company with malefactors, to suffer bitter agony, to die, to be pierced with a lance, and to be laid in the grave : O LORD, by all these sacred sorrows, by Thy most holy Cross and Death, deliver us, we beseech Thee, from eternal woe, and conduct us to the Paradise of bliss.   Amen.

HOLY WEEK.

Readings for the Hours of the Passion.

MAUNDY THURSDAY.

The Last Passover.

S. Matt. xxvi. 17-20.
S. Mark xiv. 12-17.
S. Luke xxii. 7-18.
S. John xiii. 1-17.

The Institution of the Blessed Sacrament.

S. Matt. xxvi. 21-29.
S. Mark xiv. 18-25.
S. Luke xxii. 19-23.
S. John xiii. 18-38.
1 Cor. xi. 23-25.

Discourses in the Upper Chamber.

S. Luke xxii. 24-38.
S. John xiv. xv. xvi. xvii.

Jesus Goes to Gethsemane.

S. Matt. xxvi. 30-35.
S. Mark xiv. 26-31.
S. Luke xxii. 39.
S. John xviii. 1.

The Agony.

S. Matt. xxvi. 36-46.
S. Mark xiv. 32-42.
S. Luke xxii. 40-46.
S. John xviii. 1.

GOOD FRIDAY.

The Betrayal.

S. Matt. xxvi. 47-56.
S. Mark xiv. 43-52.
S. Luke xxii. 47-53.
S. John xviii. 2-11.

Jesus before the High Priest and the Council.

S. Matt. xxvi. 57-68.
S. Mark xiv. 53-65.
S. Luke xxii. 54, 55, 63-71.
S. John xviii. 12-16, 19-24.

Jesus Denied by S. Peter.
Three o'Clock a.m.

S. Matt. xxvi. 69-75.
S. Mark xiv. 66-72.
S. Luke xxii. 56-62.
S. John xviii. 17, 18, 25-27.

Jesus before Pilate.

S. Matt. xxvii. 1-10.
S. Mark xv. 1.
S. Luke xxiii. 1.
S. John xviii. 28; xix. 1-14.

Jesus before Herod.

S. Luke xxiii. 7-12.

Pilate on the Judgment-Seat.

Six o'Clock a.m.

S. Matt. xxvii. 11-26.
S. Mark xv. 2-15.
S. Luke xxiii. 2-6, 13-25.
S. John xix. 14-16.

Jesus Delivered to be Crucified.

S. Matt. xxvii. 27-31.
S. Mark xv. 16-20.
S. Luke xxiii. 26.
S. John xix. 16.

Jesus Led to Calvary.

S. Matt. xxvii. 31-34.
S. Mark xv. 20-23.
S. Luke xxiii. 26-33.
S. John xix. 16, 17.

Jesus Nailed to the Cross.

Nine o'Clock a.m.

S. Matt. xxvii. 35-44.
S. Mark xv. 24-32.
S. Luke xxiii. 33-43.
S. John xix. 18-27.

Jesus on the Cross.

Noon.

S. Matt. xxvii. 45.
S. Mark xv. 33
S. Luke xxiii. 44, 45.

Jesus Dies.

Three o'Clock p.m.

S. Matt. xxvii. 46-56.
S. Mark xv. 34-41.
S. Luke xxiii. 45-49.
S. John xix. 28-30.

Jesus' Side Pierced.

S. John xix. 31-37.

Jesus Taken down from the Cross.

S. Matt. xxvii. 57-58.
S. Mark xv. 42-45.
S. Luke xxiii. 50-52.
S. John xix. 38, 39.

Jesus Laid in the Grave.

S. Matt. xxvii. 59-61.
S. Mark xv. 46, 47.
S. Luke xxiii. 53-56.
S. John xix. 40-42.

A PRAYER

After reading any part of the Passion.

O LORD JESU CHRIST, SON of the Living GOD, place Thy Passion,

Cross, and Death between Thy judgment and my soul now and at the hour of my death. Vouchsafe to give me grace and mercy, pardon to the living, rest to the departed, peace to Thy Church, and everlasting life and glory to all sinners: Who livest and reignest with the FATHER and the HOLY GHOST, One GOD, world without end. Amen.

☩ The glorious Passion of our LORD JESUS CHRIST deliver us from sorrowful heaviness, and bring us to the joys of Paradise. Amen.

The Way of the Cross.

Prayer in Preparation.

O JESUS, my Adorable SAVIOUR, behold me prostrate at Thy feet, imploring Thy mercy. Vouchsafe to apply to my soul the infinite merits of Thy Passion, on which I am now about to meditate. Grant that while I follow Thee along this Way of Sorrows, my heart may be so touched with true contrition, that I may be willing to accept cheerfully for Thy sake all the sufferings and humiliations of this my pilgrimage on earth. Amen.

℣ O LORD, open Thou our lips.

℟ And our mouth shall shew forth Thy praise.

℣ O GOD, make speed to save us.

℟ O LORD, make haste to help us.

℣ Glory be to the FATHER.

℟ As it was in the beginning.

FIRST STATION.

JESUS CONDEMNED TO DEATH.

℣ We adore Thee, O CHRIST, and we bless Thee,

℟ Because by Thy Cross, and precious Blood Thou hast redeemed the world.

JESUS after leaving the house of Caiaphas, where He had been blasphemed, and the palace of Herod, where He had been mocked, is dragged before Pilate; His back is torn with scourges; His head is crowned with thorns, and He Who on the last day will judge the living and the dead, is condemned to a shameful death.

Prayer.

O INNOCENT JESUS, Who with wonderful submission wast for our sakes condemned to die. Grant that we may bear in mind that our sins were the false-witnesses; our blasphemies, backbitings, and evil speakings were the cause of Thy accepting with gladness the sentence of the impious Judge. Oh may this thought touch our hearts and make us hate those sins which caused Thy Death. Amen.

Act of Contrition.

O GOD of infinite mercy! I grieve for love of Thee, and am heartily sorry that I have ever sinned against Thee. I love Thee with my whole heart, may I never again offend Thee. O may I love Thee without ceasing, and delight in all things to do Thy holy will.
Our FATHER.
℣ Glory be to the FATHER.
℟ As it was in the begining.

LORD have mercy upon us.
CHRIST have mercy upon us.
LORD have mercy upon us.

From pain to pain, from woe to woe,
With loving heart and foot-steps slow,
To Calvary with CHRIST we go.
See how His precious Blood
  At every Station pours;
Was ever grief like His?
  Was ever sin like ours?

SECOND STATION.

JESUS RECEIVES HIS CROSS.

℣ We adore Thee, O CHRIST, and we bless Thee.
℟ Because by Thy Cross and precious Blood Thou hast redeemed the world.

A heavy cross is laid upon the bruised shoulders of JESUS. He receives it with meekness, nay with a secret joy, for it is the instrument with which He will redeem the world.

Prayer.

O BLESSED JESUS, grant us by virtue of

Thy Cross and bitter Passion, cheerfully to submit to and willingly to embrace all the trials and difficulties of this our earthly pilgrimage, and may we be always ready to take up our cross daily and follow Thee. Amen.

Act of Contrition.

O GOD of infinite mercy! I grieve for love of Thee, and am heartily sorry that I have ever sinned against Thee. I love Thee with my whole heart, may I never again offend Thee. O may I love Thee without ceasing, and delight in all things to do Thy holy will.

Our FATHER.

℣ Glory be to the FATHER.

℟ As it was in the beginning.

LORD, have mercy upon us.

CHRIST, have mercy upon us.

LORD, have mercy upon us.

From pain to pain, from woe to woe,
With loving heart and footsteps slow,
To Calvary with CHRIST we go.

See how His precious Blood
At every Station pours;
Was ever grief like His?
Was ever sin like ours?

THIRD STATION.

JESUS FALLS UNDER THE WEIGHT OF THE CROSS.

℣ We adore Thee, O CHRIST, and we bless Thee,

℟ Because by Thy Cross and precious Blood Thou hast redeemed the world.

JESUS bowed down under the weight of the Cross, slowly sets forth on the way to Calvary, amidst the mockings and insults of the crowd. His Agony in the Garden has exhausted His Body: He is sore with blows and wounds, His strength fails Him, He falls to the ground under the weight of the Cross.

Prayer.

O JESUS, Who for our sins didst bear the heavy burden of the Cross and didst fall under its weight, may the thought of Thy sufferings make us watchful against temptation, and do Thou stretch out Thy sacred

Hand to help us lest we fall into any grievous sin. Amen.

Act of Contrition.

O GOD of infinite mercy! I grieve for love of Thee, and am heartily sorry that I have ever sinned against Thee. I love Thee with my whole heart, may I never again offend Thee. O may I love Thee without ceasing, and delight in all things to do Thy holy will.
Our FATHER.

℣ Glory be to the FATHER.
℟ As it was in the beginning.

LORD, have mercy upon us.
CHRIST, have mercy upon us.
LORD, have mercy upon us.

From pain to pain, from woe to woe,
With loving heart and footsteps slow,
To Calvary with CHRIST we go.
  See how His precious Blood
    At every Station pours;
  Was ever grief like His?
  Was ever sin like ours?

FOURTH STATION.

THE CROSS IS LAID UPON SIMON OF CYRENE.

℣ We adore Thee, O CHRIST, and we bless Thee,
℟ Because by Thy Cross and precious Blood Thou hast redeemed the world.

The strength of JESUS fails Him, and He is unable to proceed; the executioners seize, and compel Simon of Cyrene to bear His Cross.

Prayer.

O JESUS! I thank Thee, that Thou hast permitted me to suffer with Thee, may it be my privilege to bear my cross, may I glory in nothing else; by it may the world be crucified unto me, and I unto the world, may I never shrink from suffering, but rather rejoice, if I be counted worthy to suffer for Thy Name's sake. Amen.

Act of Contrition.

O GOD of infinite mercy! I grieve for love of Thee, and am heartily sorry that I have ever sinned against Thee. I love Thee with my whole heart, may I never again offend Thee. O may I love Thee without ceasing, and delight in all things to do Thy holy will. Amen.

Our FATHER.

℣ Glory be to the FATHER.

℟ As it was in the beginning.

LORD, have mercy upon us.

CHRIST, have mercy upon us.

LORD, have mercy upon us.

From pain to pain, from woe
  to woe,
With loving heart and foot
  steps slow,
To Calvary with CHRIST we
  go.
    See how His precious
      Blood
    At every Station pours;
Was ever grief like His?
Was ever sin like ours?

FIFTH STATION.

JESUS SPEAKS TO THE WOMEN OF JERUSALEM.

℣ We adore Thee, O CHRIST, and we bless Thee,

℟ Because by Thy Cross and precious Blood Thou hast redeemed the world.

Some holy women in the crowd were so touched with sympathy at the sight of the sufferings of JESUS, that they openly bewailed and lamented Him.

JESUS, knowing the things that were to come to pass upon Jerusalem, because of their rejection of Him, turned to them and said, "Daughters of Jerusalem, weep not for Me, but weep for yourselves and for your children."

Prayer.

O LORD JESUS, we mourn and will mourn both for Thee and for ourselves; for Thy sufferings, and for our sins which caused them. Oh, teach us so to mourn, that we may be comforted, and escape those dreadful judgments prepared for all those who reject or neglect Thee. Amen.

Act of Contrition.

O GOD of infinite mercy! I grieve for love of Thee, and am heartily sorry that I have ever sinned against Thee. I love Thee with my whole heart, may I never again offend Thee. O may I love Thee without ceasing, and delight in all things to do Thy holy will. Amen.

Our FATHER.

℣ Glory be to the FATHER.

℟ As it was in the beginning.

LORD, have mercy upon us.

CHRIST, have mercy upon us.

LORD, have mercy upon us.

From pain to pain, from woe to woe,
With loving heart and footsteps slow,
To Calvary with CHRIST we go.
 See how His precious Blood
 At every Station pours;
Was ever grief like His?
Was ever sin like ours?

SIXTH STATION.

JESUS IS STRIPPED OF HIS GARMENTS.

℣ We adore Thee, O CHRIST, and we bless Thee,
℟ Because by Thy Cross and precious Blood Thou hast redeemed the world.

JESUS having arrived at last at the place of sacrifice, His murderers prepare to crucify Him. His garments are torn from His bleeding Body, and He the Holy of Holies stands exposed to the vulgar gaze of the rude and scoffing multitude.

Prayer.

O LORD JESUS! Thou didst suffer shame for our most shameful deeds. Take from us, we beseech Thee, all false shame, conceit, and pride, and make us so to humble ourselves in this life, that we may escape everlasting shame in the life to come. Amen.

Act of Contrition.

O GOD of infinite mercy! I grieve for love of Thee, and am heartily sorry that I have ever sinned against Thee. I love Thee with my whole heart; may I never again offend Thee. O may I love Thee without ceasing, and delight in all things to do Thy holy will. Amen.

Our FATHER.

℣ Glory be to the FATHER.

℞ As it was in the beginning.

Lord, have mercy upon us.

Christ, have mercy upon us.

Lord, have mercy upon us.

From pain to pain, from woe to woe,
With loving heart and footsteps slow,
To Calvary with Christ we go.
  See how His precious Blood
At every Station pours;
Was ever grief like His?
Was ever sin like ours?

SEVENTH STATION.

JESUS IS NAILED TO THE CROSS.

℣ We adore Thee, O Christ, and we bless Thee,

℞ Because by Thy Cross and precious Blood Thou hast redeemed the world.

The Cross is laid upon the ground, and Jesus is stretched upon His bed of death. At one and the same time He offers His bruised Limbs to His Heavenly Father, in behalf of sinful man, and to His fierce executioners to be nailed by them to the Tree of Shame. The blows are struck; the blood gushes forth.

Prayer.

O JESUS! Crucified for me, subdue my heart with Thy holy fear and love, and since my sins were the cruel nails that pierced Thee, grant that in sorrow for my past life I may pierce and nail to Thy Cross all that offends Thee. Amen.

Act of Contrition.

O GOD of infinite mercy! I grieve for love of Thee, and am heartily sorry that I have ever sinned against Thee. I love Thee with my whole heart; may I never again offend Thee. O may I love Thee without ceasing, and delight in all things to do Thy holy will. Amen.

Our Father.

℣ Glory be to the Father.

℞ As it was in the beginning.

Lord, have mercy upon us.

Christ, have mercy upon us.

Lord, have mercy upon us.
From pain to pain, from woe to woe,
With loving heart and footsteps slow,
To Calvary with Christ we go.
See how His precious Blood
At every Station pours;
Was ever grief like His?
Was ever sin like ours?

EIGHTH STATION.

JESUS DIES UPON THE CROSS.

℣ We adore Thee, O Christ, and we bless Thee,
℟ Because by Thy Cross and precious Blood Thou hast redeemed the world.

Jesus has hung from the third until the ninth hour upon the Cross; the weight of His Body is borne by His pierced Hands. His Blood has run in streams down His Body, and bedewed the ground; in the midst of excruciating sufferings He has pardoned His murderers, promised the bliss of Paradise to the penitent thief, and committed His Blessed Mother and beloved disciple to each other's care. All is now consummated, and meekly bowing down His Head, He gives up the Ghost.

Prayer.

O JESUS! we devoutly embrace that honoured Cross, where Thou didst love us even unto death. In Thy Death is all our hope. Henceforth let us live only unto Thee, so that whether we live or die we may be Thine. Amen.

Act of Contrition.

O GOD of infinite mercy! I grieve for love of Thee, and am heartily sorry that I have ever sinned against Thee. I love Thee with my whole heart; may I never again offend Thee. O may I love Thee without ceasing, and delight in all things to do Thy holy will. Amen.

Our Father.

℣ Glory be to the Father.
℟ As it was in the beginning.

Lord, have mercy upon us.
Christ, have mercy upon us.

Lord, have mercy upon us.

From pain to pain, from woe to woe,
With loving heart and footsteps slow,
To Calvary with Christ we go.
   See how His precious Blood
   At every Station pours;
   Was ever grief like His?
   Was ever sin like ours?

NINTH STATION.

JESUS IS TAKEN DOWN FROM THE CROSS.

℣ We adore Thee, O Christ, and we bless Thee,
℟ Because by Thy Cross and precious Blood Thou hast redeemed the world.

Joseph of Arimathæa goes to Pilate, and begs the Body of Jesus; Pilate commands the Body to be delivered to him: it is anointed and wrapped in linen clothes by Joseph and Nicodemus, and prepared for burial.

Prayer.

O LORD Jesu, grant that we may never refuse to bear that Cross, which Thou hast laid upon us: Who willed not to be taken down from the Cross, until Thou hadst accomplished the work which Thou camest to do. Amen.

Act of Contrition.

O GOD of infinite mercy! I grieve for love of Thee, and am heartily sorry that I have ever sinned against Thee. I love Thee with my whole heart; may I never again offend Thee. O may I love Thee without ceasing, and delight in all things to do Thy holy will. Amen.

Our Father.

℣ Glory be to the Father.
℟ As it was in the beginning.

Lord, have mercy upon us.
Christ, have mercy upon us.
Lord, have mercy upon us.

From pain to pain, from woe to woe,
With loving heart and footsteps slow,
To Calvary with Christ we go.

See how His precious Blood
  At every Station pours?
Was ever grief like His?
Was ever sin like ours?

TENTH STATION.

JESUS IS LAID IN THE SEPULCHRE.

℣ We adore Thee, O CHRIST, and we bless Thee,

℟ Because by Thy Cross and precious Blood Thou hast redeemed the world.

The Body of JESUS is laid by His disciples in the tomb. The tomb is closed, and there the lifeless Body remains until the hour of Its glorious Resurrection.

Prayer.

O JESU, most Compassionate LORD, we adore Thee dead and enclosed in the Holy Sepulchre. We desire to enclose Thee within our hearts, that, united to Thee, we may rise to newness of life, and by the gift of final perseverance die in Thy grace. Amen.

Act of Contrition.

O GOD of infinite mercy! I grieve for love of Thee, and am heartily sorry that I have ever sinned against Thee. I love Thee with my whole heart; may I never again offend Thee. O may I love Thee without ceasing, and delight in all things to do Thy holy will. Amen.

Our FATHER.

℣ Glory be to the FATHER.

℟ As it was in the beginning.

LORD, have mercy upon us.

CHRIST, have mercy upon us.

LORD, have mercy upon us.

From pain to pain, from woe to woe,
With loving heart and footsteps slow,
To Calvary with CHRIST we go.
  See how His precious Blood
    At every Station pours.
Was ever grief like His?
Was ever sin like ours?

Prayer in Conclusion.

Antiphon. CHRIST became obedient unto death, even the death of the Cross.

ALMIGHTY GOD, we beseech Thee graciously to behold this Thy family, for which our LORD JESUS CHRIST was contented to be betrayed, and given up into the hands of wicked men, and to suffer death upon the Cross, Who now liveth and reigneth with Thee and the HOLY GHOST, ever One GOD, world without end. Amen.

Benediction. May our LORD JESUS CHRIST, Who for our sakes was scourged, made to bear His Cross, and crucified, bless us, and keep us from all sin. Amen.

Seven Words from the Cross.

A DEVOTION ON OUR BLESSED LORD'S LAST SAYINGS ON THE CROSS.

℣ O GOD, make speed to save us.

℟ O LORD, make haste to help us.

Glory be to the FATHER. As it was in the beginning.

THE FIRST WORD.

"*Father, forgive them, for they know not what they do.*"

℣ We adore Thee, O CHRIST, and we bless Thee,

℟ Because by Thy Cross and precious Blood Thou hast redeemed the world.

O MOST Beloved LORD JESU CHRIST, Who for love of me didst suffer agonies on the Cross, that Thou mightest by Thy sufferings pay the debt of my sins; and even in that hour of Thy Passion didst pray for my pardon from GOD's eternal justice, have mercy on all Christians in the hour of death, and on me in my last agony. Through the merits of Thy most precious Blood, shed for our salvation, give me a true and deep sorrow for my sins, and grant that at the hour of my death I may in peace and confidence breathe out my soul into the bosom of Thine Infinite Mercy. Amen.

Our FATHER.

Glory be to the FATHER.

℣ Have mercy on us, O LORD.

℟ Have mercy on us.

O my GOD, I believe in Thee, I hope in Thee, I love Thee, and I grieve that I have so often wounded Thee by my sins.

THE SECOND WORD.

"To-day shalt thou be with me in Paradise."

℣ We adore Thee, O CHRIST, and we bless Thee,

℟ Because by Thy Cross and precious Blood Thou hast redeemed the world.

O MOST Beloved LORD JESU CHRIST, Who for love of me didst suffer agonies on the Cross, and Who with such readiness and lovingkindness didst reward the faith of the Penitent Thief, when in the midst of Thy humiliation he acknowledged Thee to be the SON of GOD. O Thou Who hadst mercy on him, and didst promise him to be with Thee in Paradise, have mercy on all Christians at their death, and on me in my last agony. Through the merits of Thy most precious Blood give me such firm and unwavering faith in Thee that my faith may not be shaken by any suggestion of the Devil, and that I may attain to dwell with Thee in Paradise. Amen.

Our FATHER.

Glory be to the FATHER.

℣ Have mercy on us, O LORD.

℟ Have mercy on us.

O my GOD, I believe in Thee, I hope in Thee, I love Thee, and I grieve that I have so often wounded Thee by my sins.

THE THIRD WORD.

"He saith unto His Mother, Woman, behold Thy Son! Then saith He to the disciple, Behold Thy Mother."

℣ We adore Thee, O CHRIST, and we bless Thee,

℟ Because by Thy Cross and precious Blood Thou hast redeemed the world.

O MOST Beloved LORD JESU CHRIST, Who for love of me didst suffer agonies on the Cross, and forgetful of Thine Own sufferings in Thy care for Thy Blessed Mother didst commend her to the love of Thy beloved disciple, and thus leave us such an example of Thy love, have mercy on all Christians at their death, and on me in my last agony. Preserve ever in my heart a firm hope in the infinite merits of Thy most precious Blood, that I may be a partaker of Thy Love, and through Thee may be saved from the eternal misery which my sins have deserved. Amen.

Our FATHER.
Glory be to the FATHER.
℣ Have mercy on us, LORD.
℟ Have mercy on us.

O my GOD, I believe in Thee, I hope in Thee, I love Thee, and I grieve that I have so often wounded Thee by my sins.

THE FOURTH WORD.

"*My God, My God, why hast Thou forsaken Me?*"

℣ We adore Thee, O CHRIST, and we bless Thee,
℟ Because by Thy Cross and precious Blood Thou hast redeemed the world.

O MOST Beloved LORD JESU CHRIST, Who for love of me didst suffer agonies on the Cross, and adding suffering to suffering, didst endure with infinite patience not only Thy many bodily tortures, but the most heavy affliction of Spirit through being forsaken by Thy Eternal FATHER, have mercy on all Christians at their death, and on me in my last agony. Through the merits of Thy most precious Blood give me grace to bear with true patience all the sufferings of my last agony, that so uniting them with Thine, I may be a partaker of Thy glory hereafter. Amen.

Our FATHER.
Glory be to the FATHER.
℣ Have mercy on us, O LORD.
℟ Have mercy on us.

O my GOD, I believe in Thee, I hope in Thee, I love Thee; and I grieve that I have so often wounded Thee by my sins.

THE FIFTH WORD.

"*I thirst.*"

℣ We adore Thee, O CHRIST, and we bless Thee,
℟ Because by Thy Cross and precious Blood Thou hast redeemed the world.

O MOST Beloved LORD JESUS CHRIST, Who for love of me didst suffer agonies on the Cross, and Who, to all Thy shame, and all Thy sufferings, wouldest if needful willingly have added yet more, so that all men might be saved: since all the torments of Thy Passion did not allay the thirst of Thy tender Heart, have pity on all Christians at their death, and on me in my last agony. Through the merits of Thy most precious Blood enkindle in my heart such a fire of Thy love, that I may thirst for Thy glory here, and with earnest longings desire to be united to Thee hereafter throughout the ages of eternity. Amen.

Our FATHER.

Glory be to the FATHER.

℣ Have mercy on us, LORD.

℟ Have mercy on us.

O my GOD, I believe in Thee, I hope in Thee, I love Thee, and I grieve that I have so often wounded Thee by my sins.

THE SIXTH WORD.

"It is finished."

℣ We adore Thee, O CHRIST, and we bless Thee,

℟ Because by Thy Cross and precious Blood Thou hast redeemed the world.

O MOST Beloved LORD JESU CHRIST, Who for love of me didst suffer agonies on the Cross, and from that Throne of Truth didst announce the completion of the work of our Redemption, through which from being children of wrath we have become children of GOD and heirs of eternal life, have pity upon all Christians at their death, and on me in my last agony. Through the merits of Thy most precious Blood detach me entirely from love of the world, and from love of self, and from all creatures, and at the moment of my death enable me to offer to Thee the sacrifice of my life, and to seek from Thee the pardon of all my sins. Amen.

Our FATHER.

Glory be to the FATHER,

℣ Have mercy on us, O LORD.

℟ Have mercy on us.

O my GOD, I believe in Thee, I hope in Thee, I love Thee, and I grieve that I have so often wounded Thee by my sins.

THE SEVENTH WORD.

"Father, into Thy hands I commend My Spirit."

℣ We adore Thee, O CHRIST, and we bless Thee,

℟ Because by Thy Cross and precious Blood Thou hast redeemed the world.

O MOST Beloved JESU CHRIST, Who for love of me didst suffer agonies on the Cross, and Who, to complete so great a Sacrifice, didst accept the will of Thy FATHER, by resigning Thy Spirit into His Hands, and bowing Thy Head and dying; have mercy on all Christians at their death, and on me in my last agony. Through the merits of Thy most precious Blood give me in my last moments an entire conformity to Thy Divine Will, so that I may be ready to live or die, as it shall best please Thee, desiring nothing but that Thy holy will should be done in and by me. Amen.

Our FATHER.
Glory be to the FATHER.

℣ Have mercy on us, O LORD.

℟ Have mercy on us.

O my GOD, I believe in Thee, I hope in Thee, I love Thee, and I grieve that I have so often wounded Thee by my sins.

A Prayer.

O LORD JESU CHRIST, SON of the Living GOD, place Thy Passion, Cross, and Death between Thy Judgment and my soul, now and at the hour of my death.

Vouchsafe to give me grace and mercy, pardon to the living, eternal rest to the dead, peace to Thy Church, and to all sinners everlasting life and glory: Who with the FATHER and the HOLY SPIRIT livest and reignest, One GOD, world without end. Amen.

EASTER EVE.

MAY GOD Almighty bless us, and of His mercy vouchsafe to defend us from all wickedness. Amen.

And may He Who willed to enlighten this most holy night by the Resurrection of our Redeemer, cleanse our minds from the darkness of our sins, and make them glisten with abundant virtues. Amen.

To the end that, striving to imitate the innocence of the newly-baptized, we may be enabled like the Wise Virgins to enter with the shining lights of good works into the chamber of that Bridegroom, Whose Resurrection we are about to celebrate. Amen.

EASTER DAY.

HE liveth unto GOD. Alleluia.

℣ Open me the gates of righteousness. Alleluia.

℟ That I may go into them and give thanks unto the LORD. Alleluia.

Let us pray.

WE adore Thee, O CHRIST, SON of the living GOD, Who didst rise in great triumph from the grave, and didst bear in Thy pierced Hands the keys of hell and death. We rejoice, O LORD our GOD, in Thy Almighty power and glory. Raise Thou us up with Thee, O Blessed SAVIOUR, above all earthly desires. Inspire us with thoughts of joy; of hope, and love. Enter Thou within the chamber of our hearts, and say unto us, "Peace be unto you." Give us the grace to see Thee, Blessed SAVIOUR, the eyes of our understanding being enlightened, that we may know Thee walking by our side, in this our earthly pilgrimage. Come unto us, O our LORD, and dwell within us. Abide with us through our night of weeping. Make Thyself known to us in the Breaking of Bread. Teach us, O Blessed LORD GOD most High, to look and see Thee beyond this dark tempestuous sea, standing on the everlasting shore of peace; and suffer us to come unto Thee through the waters. Give us grace, O LORD our GOD, to arise with Thee, to leave all for Thee, that we may be made like unto Thee, that we may follow Thee, O Thou Blessed Lamb of GOD, whithersoever Thou goest. Amen.

We adore Thee and give thanks to Thee, most Gracious JESU, SON of the living GOD, Who for us didst arise from the dead. Have mercy upon us, O LORD our GOD, and grant that we, rising above all the evils of this sinful world, may walk before Thee in newness of life, and being daily renewed by Thy HOLY SPIRIT, may serve Thee with a pure and steadfast heart, until we come to Thy Heavenly Kingdon, Who livest and reignest with the FATHER, in the Unity of the HOLY GHOST, GOD, for ever and ever. Amen.

Litany of the Resurrection.

LORD have mercy upon us.
CHRIST have mercy upon us.
LORD, have mercy upon us.

O CHRIST, hear us.
O CHRIST, graciously hear us.

O GOD the FATHER, of Heaven,
O GOD the SON, Redeemer of the world,
O GOD the HOLY GHOST, the Comforter,
HOLY TRINITY, Three Persons, and One GOD,

} *Have mercy upon us.*

JESUS, our Paschal Lamb, Who wast offered for us, and hast taken away the sins of the world,
JESUS, Who by Thy Death hast destroyed death, and by Thy Rising to life again hast restored to us everlasting life,
JESUS, the First Fruits of them that slept, over Whom death hath no more dominion,

JESUS, the Second Adam, by Whom came the Resurrection from the dead,
JESUS, Who art Thyself the Resurrection and the Life,
JESUS, Who didst lay down Thy Life for Thy sheep,
JESUS, Who broughtest life and immortality to light,
JESUS, declared to be the SON of GOD with power,
JESUS, the First-Begotten of the Dead, and the Prince of the Kings of the earth,
JESUS, the First and the Last, that livest and wast dead, and art alive for evermore,
JESUS, the Lamb that wast slain, and hast redeemed us to GOD by Thy Blood,
JESUS, Who didst rise very early in the morning on the first day of the week,
JESUS, Who didst appear to Mary Magdalene while it was yet dark,
JESUS, Who didst

} *Have mercy upon us.*

send Thy Angels to tell the women that Thou wast risen, as Thou hast said,

JESUS, Who didst suffer Thyself to be seen of the Women, and to be worshipped by them,

JESUS, Who didst appear unto the two Disciples on the way to Emmaus, and wast known of them in the Breaking of Bread,

JESUS, Who didst appear to the Eleven, saying, "Peace be unto you," and didst open their understanding that they might understand the Scripture,

JESUS, Who didst breathe upon Thine Apostles, that they might receive the HOLY GHOST,

JESUS, Who didst confirm the faith of Thomas by shewing unto him Thy Hands and Thy Feet,

JESUS, Who didst show Thyself again to Thy disciples at the Sea of Tiberias, and Who restoring Peter after his fall, didst commission him to feed

} *Have mercy upon us.*

Thy lambs and Thy sheep,

JESUS, Who didst converse with Thy Disciples upon a mountain in Galilee,

JESUS, Who wast seen of above five hundred Brethren at once,

JESUS, Who by many infallible proofs didst shew Thyself alive after Thy Passion,

JESUS, Who didst converse with Thine Apostles, eating and drinking with Thee after Thou didst rise from the dead, to whom Thou spakest of the things pertaining to the Kingdom of GOD,

JESUS, Who didst commission Thine Apostles to teach all nations, to baptize and to absolve, to celebrate the Holy Eucharist, and to preach the Gospel to every creature,

} *Have mercy upon us.*

BY Thy glorious Resurrection,
  Good LORD, deliver us.

By Thy Victory over death,
  Good LORD, deliver us.

By the glorious Majesty of Thy Risen Body,
  Good LORD, deliver us.

WE sinners do beseech Thee to hear us, O LORD JESUS.

THAT we, who in Baptism were buried and rose again with Thee, may put off the old man with his deeds, and die no more in sin,

That we may put on the new man, which after God is created in righteousness and true holiness,

That like as Thou wast raised up from the dead by the glory of the FATHER, even so we also should walk in newness of life,

That we may reckon ourselves to be dead indeed unto sin, but alive unto GOD, through Thee, Who art our LORD,

That we may not henceforth live unto ourselves, but unto Thee, Who diedst for us, and didst rise again,

That we may walk in the Spirit, and may crucify the flesh, with its affections and lusts,

That we may walk in love as Thou lovedst us, Who gavest Thyself for us, an Offering and a Sacrifice to GOD for a sweet-smelling Savour,

That, being risen with Thee, we may seek those things which are above, where Thou sittest at the Right Hand of GOD,

That we may set our affections on things above, not on things on the earth,

That, earnestly believing in Thy Resurrection and triumph over death, we may not fear to die when Thou shalt call us,

That when we are absent from the body we may be present in Paradise with Thee,

That we, with all Thy faithful departed, may speedily have our perfect consummation and bliss, both in body and soul,

That we, in the Last Day, being set at Thy Right Hand, may behold Thy Face with joy,

That we may hear those words of joy: " Come, ye blessed of My FATHER, inherit the Kingdom prepared for

Grant us, Good LORD.

you from the foundation of the world,"

That Thou wouldest change our vile body, that it may be fashioned like unto Thy glorious Body,

That, according as Thou prayedst, we may be for ever with Thee where Thou art, and may behold Thy glory which GOD hath given Thee,

That we, seeing Thee as Thou art, may be made like Thee, and equal unto the Angels, as Thou didst promise,

That we may dwell with Thee for ever in the new Heaven and Earth, in Thy Holy City, the New Jerusalem,

Grant us, Good LORD.

O LAMB of GOD, that takest away the sins of the world,
O JESU, spare us.

O Lamb of GOD, that takest away the sins of the world,
O JESU, hear us.

O Lamb of GOD, that takest away the sins of the world,
O JESU, have mercy upon us.

O JESU, hear us.
O JESU, graciously hear us.

OUR FATHER.

Let us pray.

O GOD, Who makest us glad by the yearly Festival of the Resurrection of the LORD : mercifully grant that we, who now do celebrate these joyous Holy Days on earth, may attain hereafter to eternal joys in Heaven. Through the Same, Thy SON JESUS CHRIST our LORD. Amen.

Rogation Days.

MAY the LORD Almighty mercifully regard our devotion, and bestow upon us the gifts of His blessing.. Amen.

May He forgive us all the evils which we have done, and grant us the pardon which we entreat from Him. Amen.

And may He so accept our fasting and our prayers,

as to turn away from us all the evils which we deserve in punishment for our sins, and may He pour down upon us the gift of the HOLY GHOST, the Comforter. Amen.

For the Crops.

ALMIGHTY and Everlasting GOD, Ruler of the universe, Who governest the world which hangeth upon nothing, and Who hast commanded us to till the land with our labour for the support of mankind and the sustenance of the body; we humbly beseech Thy mercy that Thou wouldest graciously look upon whatsoever good seed is sown or planted in the fields; give temperate weather, keep it from all weeds and thorns, make the crops plentiful, and grant that they may arrive at full perfection, that we, Thy servants, thankfully receiving the abundant fruit of Thy gifts, may pay due and acceptable praise to Thy Name; Through JESUS CHRIST our LORD. Amen.

ASCENSION EVE.

GRANT, we beseech Thee, Almighty GOD, that the thoughts of our hearts may thither tend whither Thine Only-Begotten SON, in Whose honour we celebrate the coming Festival, hath entered in : so that as we ascend thither by faith, our whole conversation may be in Heaven; through the Same, JESUS CHRIST our LORD. Amen.

ASCENSION DAY.

Antiphon. GOD is gone up with a merry noise, and the LORD with the sound of the trump. Alleluia.

℣ O sing praises, sing praises unto our GOD. Alleluia.

℟ O sing praises, sing praises unto our King. Alleluia.

O LORD JESU CHRIST, Who art ascended into Heaven, there to intercede for us Thy servants, to bring the kingdoms of the earth beneath the sceptre of Thy righteousness, and to draw up Thine Elect in blessed union with Thee their Head, Who art gone before; Grant us firm faith in Thine Almighty power, CHRIST our GOD. Strengthen our hope in Thee, Who art for ever offering Thyself, in Thy risen and glorified Body, in the most Holy Place, O CHRIST, our Advocate! Quicken our love towards Thee, O JESU King most Wonderful, Who didst lead captivity captive, and give gifts unto men, especially the most unspeakable gift of Thy HOLY SPIRIT, uniting us to Thee in bonds of Heavenly love. Hear us, O Thou Who hast triumphed gloriously, Bridegroom of Thy Holy Church, and only Mediator between GOD and man! and grant that we may so follow Thee now in patient toil and suffering, that when Thou comest again to judge the world we may be counted worthy to sit with Thee in Heavenly places, through Thy merits, O LORD and only SAVIOUR, Who with the FATHER and the HOLY GHOST, livest and reignest ever One GOD, world without end. Amen.

Litany of the Ascension.

O LORD, have mercy upon us.

O CHRIST, have mercy upon us.

O LORD, have mercy upon us.

O CHRIST, hear us.
O CHRIST, graciously hear us.

O GOD, the FATHER, of Heaven,
Have mercy upon us.

O GOD the SON, Redeemer of the world,

O GOD the HOLY GHOST, the Comforter,

HOLY TRINITY, Three Persons, and One GOD,

} *Have mercy upon us.*

JESUS, King of glory, Who, leading out Thy disciples as far as to Bethany, didst, in their sight, ascend up into Heaven,

Jesus, Lord and Christ,

Jesus, Prince and Saviour,

Jesus, the King of Kings and Lord of Lords,

Jesus, Who didst ascend up far above all Heavens, that Thou mightest fill all things, and be Head over all things to Thy Church,

Jesus, Who didst ascend up unto Thy Father and our Father, unto Thy God and our God,

Jesus, Who leddest captivity captive, and gavest gifts unto men,

Jesus, Who art by the Right Hand of God exalted far above all principality and power, and every name that is named,

Jesus, at Whose Name every knee must bow,

Jesus, Who art seated in glory at the Right Hand of the Father,

Jesus, unto Whom all power is given in Heaven and in Earth,

Jesus, Who in Thy sacred Manhood art crowned with glory and honour at the Right Hand of the Majesty on High,

Jesus, Who must reign until Thou hast put all enemies under Thy Feet, and of Whose Kingdom there shall be no end,

Jesus, Who art adored by all the Angels of God,

Jesus, Who art anointed with the oil of gladness above Thy fellows,

Jesus, Who art the happiness of the Blessed, and Whose Presence is Life,

Jesus, Who hast opened the Kingdom of Heaven to all believers,

Jesus, our High Priest for ever, the Mediator of the New Covenant, Who hast entered into the true Holy of Holies, even Heaven itself, for us,

Jesus, the Lamb slain from the foundation of the world, Who art the One Propitiation for our sins for ever,

Jesus, who ever livest to make intercession for us, pleading evermore Thy Precious Body

Have mercy upon us.

and Blood before the FATHER for us, both openly on the one Altar in Heaven, and mystically on the many altars on earth,

JESUS, Who art able to save to the uttermost those that come unto GOD by Thee,

JESUS, Who didst send down Thy HOLY GHOST on Thy disciples, and dost promise that whatsoever we ask in Thy Name, Thou wilt do it,

JESUS, Who art gone up into Heaven, and yet, by the power of the HOLY GHOST, art supernaturally present with us in the Sacrament of the Altar,

JESUS, Who art gone to prepare a place for us,

JESUS, Who wilt come again in glory to judge the world,

JESUS, Who wilt receive Thine Own unto Thyself, that they may be with Thee where Thou art, to behold Thy glory,

} *Have mercy upon us.*

BY Thy glorious Resurrection and Ascension,
By Thine all powerful Intercession,
By Thy triumphant Majesty and Power,

} *Good LORD, deliver us.*

WE sinners, do beseech Thee to hear us, O LORD JESUS, that we who are risen with Thee may set our affections on things above, not on things on earth,

That we, whom Thou hast blessed with all spiritual blessings in heavenly places, may be holy and without blame before Thee in love,

That now, when the world seeth Thee no more, we may see Thee by faith, and live through Thee,

That keeping Thy commandments, we may abide in Thy love,

That through the power of the Comforter Thou wouldest abide with us, and manifest Thyself to us,

That the Spirit of Truth may testify of Thee, and may take of

} *Hear us, Good LORD.*

Ascension Tide

Thine and shew it unto us,

That in Thy spiritual presence with us our heart may rejoice with the joy that no man taketh from us,

That in Thee we may have peace,

That in our tribulations which we have in the world we may be of good cheer, knowing that Thou hast overcome the world,

That, whilst we are in the world the Eternal FATHER may, through Thy intercession, preserve us from the evil, and sanctify us through His Word of Truth,

That, as Thou and the FATHER art One, so all Thy people may inwardly and outwardly be one in Thee,

That the world may believe that the FATHER sent Thee, and may know Thee and Thine Almighty love,

That Thou wouldest draw all men unto Thee,

That Thou wouldest pour down plenteously Thy HOLY GHOST upon Thy Church,

⎬ *Hear us, Good LORD.*

That Thou wouldest quicken the whole Body of Thy Church by the power of Thy HOLY GHOST,

That Thou wouldest especially endue the Clergy with the Spirit of power, and love, and of a sound mind, and wouldest give them the graces of courage and faithfulness and of fervent zeal,

That Thou wouldest increase the number of Thy Ministers, and wouldest stir up all Thy people to love and to good works,

That Thou wouldest preserve Thy Church from the powers of the world, and from all her enemies,

That Thou wouldest give to Thy Church purity, unity, liberty, and peace, and every needful means to do her proper work,

That Thou wouldest shortly accomplish the number of Thine Elect and hasten Thy Kingdom,

⎬ *Hear us, Good LORD.*

O LAMB of God, that takest away the sins of the world,
O JESUS, spare us.

O Lamb of God, that takest away the sins of the world,
O JESUS, hear us.

O Lamb of God, that takest away the sins of the world,
O JESUS, have mercy upon us.

℣ God is gone up with a merry noise. Alleluia !

℟ *And the LORD with the sound of the trump. Alleluia.*

OUR FATHER.

Let us pray.

ASSIST us mercifully, O Lord, in these our supplications : and grant, that like as we do believe the Saviour of mankind to be seated with Thee in Thy Majesty, so we may feel that He abideth with us, according to His promise, even unto the end of the world; Through the Same Thy Son Jesus Christ our Lord, Who liveth and reigneth with Thee, in the Unity of the Holy Ghost, ever One God, world without end. Amen.

WHITSUN EVE.

MAY God Almighty bless us, Who in honour of the Coming of the Holy Ghost the Comforter are dutifully preparing our minds by fasting, and observing this present day with solemn praises. Amen.

May we, after the example of the infants now born again, preserve such innocence, that, of His good gift, we may be able to be a Temple of the Holy Ghost. Amen.

And may the Same Holy Ghost make us this day so worthy of His indwelling, that He may to-morrow pour Himself into our minds to dwell therein for ever, and after the course of this present life is over, may lead us unto His heavenly gifts. Amen.

WHITSUN DAY.

Antiphon. The SPIRIT of the LORD filleth the world; and that which containeth all things hath knowledge of the Voice. Alleluia.

℣ As many as are led by the SPIRIT of GOD. Alleluia.

℟ They are the Sons of GOD. Alleluia.

O HOLY SPIRIT, GOD of Love, Who proceedest from the Almighty FATHER and His most Blessed Son, All-powerful Advocate, Blessed and Only Comforter; infuse Thy manifold gifts into our hearts; enlighten our darkened souls with the fulness of Thy glorious presence, dwell within us, and make us to drink of Thy spiritual pleasures as out of a river; let Thy heavenly Sweetness so chasten and purify our tastes, as to leave no desire or relish for mere worldly delights. Teach us to do the thing that pleaseth Thee; for Thou art our GOD. Thou dwellest in the High and Holy Place, and with them also that are of a humble and contrite spirit. And where Thou dwellest, there also the FATHER and the SON do make their abode. Oh, blessed are they in whom so divine a Life, so glorious a Presence dwells. O that it may please Thee to come to us, Thou kindest Comforter of mourning souls, Thou mighty Defence in distresses, and ready Help in time of need. O come, Thou Purger of all inward pollutions, Thou Healer of spiritual diseases. Come, Thou Strength of the feeble, and Helper of them that fall; Thou Hope of the poor, and Refreshment of them that languish and faint; Thou Glory and Crown of the living and only Safeguard of the dying, come. Come, Thou HOLY SPIRIT, in much mercy come; make us fit to receive Thee, and condescend to our infirmities, that our meanness may not be disdained by Thy Greatness, nor our weakness by Thy Strength; all which we beg for the sake of JESUS CHRIST our SAVIOUR, Who in the Unity of Thee, O HOLY SPIRIT, liveth and reigneth with the FATHER, One GOD, world without end. Amen.

Ember Week.

O GOD, Who hast sent Thy servants to preach Thy word, and to labour for the salvation of others, grant unto them spotless purity of life, and ardent zeal for the salvation of souls, that in all good works and steadfast faith they may preach Thee, and through Thy mercy at length come unto Thee, Who art the Author and Giver of all blessedness; through JESUS CHRIST our LORD. Amen.

Litany of the Holy Ghost.

LORD, have mercy upon us.
CHRIST, have mercy upon us.
LORD, have mercy upon us.

O GOD the FATHER, of Heaven,
O GOD the SON, Redeemer of the world,
O GOD the HOLY GHOST, the Comforter,
HOLY TRINITY, Three Persons, and One GOD,
} *Have mercy upon us.*

O HOLY SPIRIT most merciful and long suffering, Who, amid all his wanderings, hast ever striven with Thy creature man;
O HOLY SPIRIT, by Whose quickening power the Blessed Virgin did conceive and bear a SON,
O HOLY GHOST, through Whom the Holy Child JESUS waxed strong in Spirit, and was filled with wisdom,
O HOLY GHOST, Who descending upon JESUS at His Baptism, wast given unto Him without measure,
O HOLY GHOST, in Whose power, JESUS, after His Baptism, fulfilled His earthly ministry, teaching and working miracles, and
} *Have mercy upon us.*

Whitsun Tide

preaching the Kingdom of GOD,

O Eternal SPIRIT, through Whom JESUS, our Priest and Victim, offered Himself without spot to GOD,

O Comforter, proceeding from the FATHER, and promised by the LORD to His disciples in their hour of sorrow,

O HOLY GHOST, given to the Apostles by the breath of CHRIST,

O HOLY GHOST, Who on the Day of Pentecost didst descend upon the Apostles in the likeness of fiery tongues,

O HOLY GHOST, Who didst endue the Apostles with wisdom and with power to preach the Gospel, to found the Church, and to ordain successors for its perpetual government and extension,

O HOLY GHOST, Who didst inspire the Apostles and Evangelists to write the Holy Books of the New Testament for the comfort and edification of the Church,

O HOLY GHOST, the

Have mercy upon us.

LORD and Life-Giver of the new as of the old Creation, Who by Thy Divine Power dost quicken the whole Body of CHRIST,

O HOLY GHOST, Who by Thy supernatural agency givest power and efficacy to all the ordinances of grace,

O HOLY GHOST, Who in all ages hast comforted and strengthened Martyrs and Confessors, and enlightened with heavenly wisdom the holy Doctors of the Church,

O most Blessed Paraclete, Who hast ever been the sustaining Comfort and sweet Refreshment of the sorrowful and the suffering,

O HOLY GHOST, Who sheddest abroad love, joy, and peace, in the hearts of the faithful and obedient followers of CHRIST,

O most Gracious and Long-Suffering SPIRIT, Who, of Thine unspeakable mercy, seekest evermore to recall us from our backslidings, and to bring us back in penitence to God,

Have mercy upon us.

By Thy Life-giving Power and Might,
By Thine all powerful Grace and Strength,
By Thy continual abiding in the Church,

Good LORD, deliver us.

WE sinners beseech Thee to hear us, O HOLY GHOST.

THAT we, who of GOD's mercy have been made members of CHRIST, may be filled with all the fulness of Thy gifts of grace,

That we may never resist Thy godly motions, but by Thy holy inspiration may think those things that be good, and by Thy merciful guiding may perform the same,

That through Thee we may always enjoy the full blessing of CHRIST'S Sacramental Gifts,

That being led by the SPIRIT, we may live and walk in the SPIRIT, rightly using the liberty wherewith CHRIST hath made us free,

That as there is One Body and One Spirit, so the Church may be enabled to keep the Unity of the SPIRIT in the bond of peace,

That Thou wouldest illuminate all the Ministers and Stewards of Thy mysteries with true knowledge and understanding of Thy Holy Word,

That Thou wouldest vouchsafe unto all Thy people a right apprehension of Christian Truth, and a brotherly love and affection one towards another,

That Thou wouldest take away from us all hatred and prejudice and whatsoever else doth hinder us from godly union and concord,

That Thou wouldest give unto us the grace of perseverance, that, being faithful unto death, we may hereafter be glorified with CHRIST,

That Thou wouldest vouchsafe so to quicken the Church, that growing to the full measure of the stature of CHRIST,

Hear us, Good LORD.

it may speedily be manifested in glory, in the general Resurrection at the final consummation of all things, } *Hear us, Good LORD.*

O LAMB of GOD, that takest away the sins of the world,
Pour forth Thy HOLY SPIRIT upon us.

O Lamb of GOD, that takest away the sins of the world,
Send forth on us the promised SPIRIT of the FATHER.

O Lamb of GOD, that takest away the sins of the world,
Give unto us the Spirit of Peace.

OUR FATHER.

Let us pray.

GRANT, we beseech Thee, Almighty and Merciful GOD, that the HOLY GHOST may come upon us, and by His gracious in-dwelling, may make us a temple of His glory; through JESUS CHRIST our LORD. Amen.

TRINITY.

Devotions to the Blessed Trinity.

Antiphon. O Holy, Blessed, and Glorious Trinity, Three Persons and One GOD: have mercy upon us now and ever, and to ages of ages. Alleluia.

℣ Blessed be the Name of the LORD. Alleluia.

℟ From this time forth for evermore. Alleluia.

Let us pray.

BLESSED and Glorious Trinity, FATHER, SON, and HOLY SPIRIT, thanks be to Thee, Very and One Trinity, One and Perfect Deity, Holy and Simple Unity, Thee, the FATHER Unbegotten, Thee the Only-Begotten SON, Thee the HOLY SPIRIT, the Paraclete, Holy and Undivided Trinity, Thee with our whole heart and our mouth do we confess and praise and bless: to Thee be glory for ever and ever. Alleluia.

O LORD GOD, FATHER Almighty, bless and protect Thy servants who are obedient to Thy Majesty, through Thine Only SON, in the power of the HOLY SPIRIT, that being secure in every danger, we may continually rejoice in praising Thee.

O LORD JESUS CHRIST, pour forth upon us the promised SPIRIT of the FATHER, to give us life and to teach us the fulness of truth in the mystery of the Blessed and Undivided TRINITY, that our salvation may be accomplished through His gift, in which the perfection of all virtue consists.

O HOLY SPIRIT, the Comforter, Who with the FATHER and the SON, abidest One GOD in TRINITY, descend this day into our hearts, that while Thou dost intercede for us with the FATHER, we may call upon Him with steadfast faith.

May the Infinite and Ineffable Trinity, the FATHER, the SON, and the HOLY GHOST, direct our lives in all good works, and after our earthly pilgrimage vouchsafe to us eternal life with the Saints. Grant this, O Almighty and everlasting GOD. Amen.

ADORATION OF THE BLESSED TRINITY.

O MOST Holy, Merciful, and Gracious Trinity, FATHER, SON, and HOLY GHOST, One GOD; teach, direct, and help me who place my hopes on Thee. O GOD the FATHER, by Thine incomprehensible power, establish my mind in Thee, and fill it with holy and heavenly thoughts. O GOD the SON, by Thine infinite wisdom, enlighten my understanding, and fill it with the knowledge of the highest truth, and my own vileness.

O HOLY SPIRIT, Who art the love of the FATHER and the SON, by Thy incomprehensible goodness, transform my will into Thine and inflame it with an inextinguishable ardour of love. O Adorable TRINITY, I would that I could love and praise Thee as perfectly as all the Saints and Angels praise Thee! Behold, O LORD, I magnify Thy Almighty wisdom and goodness: I bless Thy omnipotent and gracious wisdom: I glorify Thy wise and gracious power. But since I cannot worthily praise Thee, do Thou deign most perfectly to praise Thyself in me: Had I the love of all Thy creatures, I would willingly give it to Thee alone. Amen.

Ember Week.

O GOD, Who employest men to plant and water Thy Vineyard, whilst Thou alone dost give the increase: grant Thy grace unto Thy fellow-workers, that going on unto perfection in holiness and good works, they may not only save themselves, but those to whom they minister; through JESUS CHRIST our LORD. Amen.

Litany to the most Holy Trinity.

LORD, have mercy upon us,
CHRIST have mercy upon us.
LORD, have mercy upon us.

O GOD the FATHER, of Heaven,
O GOD the SON, Redeemer of the world,
O GOD the HOLY GHOST,
HOLY TRINITY, One GOD,

O GOD from Whom, by Whom, and in Whom are all things,
GOD in Whom we live and move and have our being,

} *Have mercy upon us.*

Who only hast immortality, and dwellest in the light which no man can approach unto,
Whose Majesty filleth the whole earth,
Whom the Heaven, and the Heaven of Heavens cannot contain,
Wonderful in Thy doing towards the children of men,
Who worketh all things after the counsel of Thine Own will,
In Whose Hand is the soul of every living thing, and the breath of all mankind,
Who openest Thine Hand, and fillest all things living with plenteousness,

} *Have mercy upon us.*

Who hast power to cast body and soul into Hell,

Who doest great things, and unsearchable, marvellous things without number,

Whose Eyes are brighter than the sun, beholding all the ways of men,

Who searchest the heart, and triest the reins,

Who givest food to all flesh,

Who hast made all things for Thyself,

Who livest for ever and ever,

Who art a FATHER of the fatherless, and defendest the cause of the widow,

GOD, full of compassion and mercy, long-suffering, plenteous in goodness and truth,

GOD our Shield, and our exceeding great Reward,

One GOD and FATHER of all, Who art above all, and through all, and in us all,

} *Have mercy upon us.*

BE propitious, spare us, *O HOLY TRINITY.*

Be propitious, hear us, *O HOLY TRINITY.*

From all evil, deliver us, *O HOLY TRINITY.*

FROM all pride and vain glory,

From gluttony, surfeiting, and greediness,

From anger, envy, and all ill-will,

From all luxury and uncleanness,

From all sloth and undue sadness,

By the Immensity of Thy Power,

By the Infinity of Thy Wisdom,

By the Abundance of Thy Goodness,

By the Eternity of Thy Glory and Thy Majesty,

By the Depth of Thy Knowledge and Thy Providence,

By the unspeakable Greatness of Thy Love and Pity,

By the unfathomable Depths of Thy Justice and Judgment,

In the Day of Judgment,

} *Deliver us, O HOLY TRINITY.*

WE sinners beseech Thee, to hear us, O HOLY TRINITY.

THAT we may love Thee, our GOD, with all our heart, with all our soul, and with all our strength,

That we may serve Thee in holiness and righteousness all our days,

That we may worship Thee, the LORD our GOD, and serve Thee only,

That we may never take Thy holy Name in vain,

That we may keep holy the Fasts and Festivals of the Church, by religious worship and deeds of mercy,

That we may pay all due honour, reverence, and obedience to our Parents, Bishops, Superiors, and all who stand to us in the place of parents,

That we may never, from anger, hatred, or envy, hurt the life, good name, or reputation of any man,

That we may love Thee above all things, and our neighbour, for Thy sake, as ourselves,

That we may never do to another what we would they should not do unto us,

That we covet not the goods of our neighbour,

That we may keep our hearts from all carnal desires and impure affections,

That Thou wouldest make all grace abound in us,

That we may present our bodies a living sacrifice, holy, acceptable unto GOD,

That Thou wouldest vouchsafe to bring us to the Kingdom Thou hast prepared for us from the foundation of the world,

We beseech Thee to hear us.

O LAMB of GOD, that takest away the sins of the world,
Intercede for us with the FATHER.

O Lamb of GOD, that takest away the sins of the world,
Be propitious to us, sinners.

O Lamb of GOD, that takest away the sins of the world,
Bestow upon us Thy HOLY SPIRIT.

O BLESSED TRINITY, hear us.

O Adorable TRINITY, *hearken unto us.*

LORD, have mercy upon us.
CHRIST, *have mercy upon us.*
LORD, have mercy upon us.

OUR FATHER.

℣ Blessed art Thou, O LORD GOD of our Fathers.
℟ *Greatly to be praised and glorified for ever.*
℣ Blessed art Thou, O LORD, in the firmament of Heaven.
℟ *Greatly to be praised, and glorified, and highly exalted for ever.*
℣ Let all Thy Angels and Saints praise Thee.
℟ *Praise Thee and glorify Thee for ever.*

℣ Let us bless the FATHER, and the SON, and the HOLY GHOST.
℟ *Let us praise and exalt Him for ever.*
℣ LORD, hear our prayer.
℟ *And let our cry come unto Thee.*

Let us pray.

ALMIGHTY and Everlasting GOD, Who hast given unto us, Thy servants, grace by the confession of a true faith to acknowledge the glory of the Eternal TRINITY, and in the power of the Divine Majesty to worship the Unity; We beseech Thee, that Thou wouldest keep us steadfast in this faith, and evermore defend us from all adversities, Who livest and reignest, One GOD, world without end. Amen.

Devotions to God the Father.

OBLATION TO GOD THE FATHER.

O MOST Merciful FATHER, and GOD of all Comfort! I Thine unworthy creature and unprofitable servant, do humbly present myself before Thee my most Gracious LORD and Creator.

To Thee, O most Gracious FATHER! Who art the giver and the preserver of all, I offer my whole self and all that I have for a most ready service and obedience unto Thee: and this I do in union with the Oblation which Thy most Beloved SON, our LORD JESUS CHRIST made, when He offered and commended Himself unto Thee, first in His Infancy in the Temple, then when praying in the Garden, and lastly when dying on the Altar of the Cross.

O most Merciful GOD, be gracious to me, a most miserable sinner; despise me not, the work of Thine Own hands; but vouchsafe, of Thy infinite goodness and mercy, favourably to accept this my unworthy service to the greater glory of Thy Name, and the salvation of my soul. Amen.

Litany to God the Father.

LORD, have mercy upon us.

CHRIST have mercy upon us.

LORD, have mercy upon us.

HOLY FATHER, hear us.

Righteous FATHER hearken unto us.

O GOD the FATHER, of Heaven,
O GOD the SON, Redeemer of the world,
O GOD the HOLY GHOST,
HOLY TRINITY, One GOD,
Our FATHER, Which art in Heaven,
The Blessed GOD and FATHER of our LORD JESUS CHRIST,
FATHER of mercies and GOD of all comfort,
Who comfortest us in all our tribulation,
The FATHER Everlasting,
The FATHER, of Whom are all things,
The FATHER of glory, and LORD of Heaven and earth,
Who hast sent Thine Only-Begotten SON into the world that we may live through Him,
The FATHER of our LORD JESUS CHRIST, of Whom the whole family in Heaven and earth is named,
Who hast predestinated us unto the adoption of children by JESUS CHRIST,
Who hast blessed us with all spiritual blessings in heavenly places,

Have mercy upon us.

Who forgivest us our trespasses,

Who givest the HOLY SPIRIT to them that ask Thee,

The FATHER of Lights, from Whom every good gift and every perfect gift cometh down,

The FATHER Who seest in secret,

Who makest Thy Sun to rise on the evil and on the good,

Who sendest rain on the just and on the unjust,

Who dost number all the hairs of our head,

Who sparedst not Thine Own SON, but hast delivered Him up for us all,

Who hast called us into the fellowship of Thy SON,

Who hast translated us into the Kingdom of the SON of Thy love,

Who hast made us meet to be partakers of the Saints in light,

Who didst so love the world, that Thou gavest Thine Only-Begotten SON,

Who hast bestowed such love upon us, that we should be called and be the Sons of GOD,

Who wouldest have us to be conformed to the Image of Thy SON,

Who hast prepared a Kingdom for Thine Elect from the foundation of the world,

In Whose House are many mansions.

Have mercy upon us.

BE propitious, spare us, O LORD.

Be propitious, hearken to us, O LORD.

Be propitious, deliver us, O LORD.

FROM all evil,

From the power of Satan,

From anger, hatred, and all ill-will,

From the imminent peril of sin,

From eternal death,

By Thy deep Knowledge, whereby Thou fathomest the unfathomable,

By Thy immeasurable Power, whereby Thou hast created all things out of nothing,

By Thy tender Providence, whereby Thou rulest all things,

Deliver us, O LORD.

By Thine eternal Love, wherewith Thou hast loved the world,

By Thine infinite Goodness, wherewith Thou fillest all things,

In the Day of Judgment,

Deliver us, O LORD.

WE sinners beseech Thee to hear us, O GOD.

THAT Thy Name may be always and in all places hallowed,

That it may please Thee that Thy Kingdom come to us,

That Thy Will may be ever done in us, as in Heaven so in earth,

That Thou wouldst vouchsafe to give us our daily Bread,

That Thou wouldst vouchsafe mercifully to forgive us our trespasses,

That Thou wouldst vouchsafe to defend us under the shadow of Thy wings, and deliver us from all temptations,

That Thou wouldst vouchsafe to deliver us from all evil,

That Thou wouldst vouchsafe to give Thy HOLY SPIRIT to them that ask Thee,

That what we ask faithfully we may obtain effectually,

That Thou wouldst grant us, according to the riches of Thy glory, to be strengthened with might by Thy SPIRIT in the inner man,

O FATHER, in the Name of Thy SON,

We sinners beseech Thee to hear us.

O LAMB of GOD, that takest away the sins of the world,

Have mercy upon us.

O Lamb of GOD, that takest away the sins of the world,

Hearken to us, O LORD.

O Lamb of GOD, that takest away the sins of the world,

Grant us Thy peace.

℣ Regard us, O GOD, our Protector,

℟ *And look upon the Face of Thine Anointed.*

℣ Remember us in Thy good pleasure, O LORD,

℟ *Visit us with Thy Salvation.*

℣ O LORD, show Thy mercy upon us,

℟ *And grant us Thy Salvation.*

℣ Turn us, O Lord God of Hosts,
℟ *Shew the light of Thy countenance, and we shall be whole.*
℣ O Lord, hear our prayer,
℟ *And let our cry come unto Thee.*

Let us pray.

O ALMIGHTY Everlasting God, order our doings in Thy good pleasure, that in the Name of Thy Beloved Son, we may obtain grace to abound in all good works.

O God, the High Tower of the lowly, and the Strength of the upright, Who by Thine Only-Begotten Son hast so vouchsafed to teach the world, that all His actions should be for our instruction; stir up in us the fervour of Thy Spirit, that the things which He by word or deed taught to our soul's health, we may have strength firmly to imitate.

O God, from Whom all good things do come, grant to us, Thy humble servants, that by Thy holy inspiration we may think those things that be good, and by Thy merciful guiding may perform the same, through Christ our Lord. Amen.

Devotions to God the Son.

OBLATION TO GOD THE SON.

O LORD Jesus Christ, most Gracious to my soul, Saviour of the world! I an unworthy sinner, yet redeemed by Thy precious Blood, flee unto Thee my God and Saviour in lowliness of mind and with deepest affection of my heart. And because Thou didst offer Thy whole Self to God the Father on the Altar of the Cross as the price of my redemption; I too, O most Loving Jesu, do offer my whole self, whatever I am, whatever I shall be, unto Thee, with all that I have or ever shall have. Take, O Lord, I pray Thee, into the hands of Thy unspeakable pity both my soul and body, my senses, words, and actions; vouchsafe in all things so to direct and govern me, that I may ever flee every occasion of sin, that I may never fall into the snare of the evil spirit, but may so constantly cleave to Thee, my GOD and my Redeemer, and to Thy commandments, that neither life nor death, nor anything which may befall me, may separate me from Thee.

I pray Thee, O most Loving JESU, by that love which for our salvation drew Thee from the bosom of the Supreme FATHER into the womb of the Virgin, fill up the imperfect measures of my actions; for small, indeed, is their value and worth, unless their defect be supplied out of Thy fulness. Unite, I implore Thee, my most unworthy service with all that Thou hast done and suffered out of Thy most perfect and ineffable love and obedience; vouchsafe to offer it to Thine Eternal FATHER together with the riches of the merits and satisfactions of Thy love, so that out of Thy abundance my poverty may be enriched, and the grace which of myself I in no wise deserve, I may through Thy mediation obtain.

I implore Thee also, O most Sweet JESU, by Thy holy Incarnation, Passion, and Death, and by all that Thou hast done for our salvation, have mercy upon my Parents, Brothers, Sisters, Friends, and Benefactors, whether living or departed; communicate unto them the merits of Thy precious Blood, and of Thy Passion, that by the help of Thy grace they may so live here, as finally to receive the rewards of eternal life in Heaven. Amen.

THIRTY-THREE ASPIRATIONS

In honour of the years of the Life of our Lord Jesus Christ, in Commemoration of His principal Titles and Attributes.

ARRANGED FROM HOLY SCRIPTURE.

JESUS, VERY GOD.

O JESU! Very GOD of VERY GOD; be Thou my Strong Rock, and House of Defence, that Thou mayest save me.

O JESU! Word of the Everlasting FATHER, Who hath in these last days spoken unto us by His SON: O that I might hear what the LORD sayeth unto me.

O JESU! Wisdom of the FATHER, grant that I may seek those things which are above, that I may taste and see how gracious the Lord is.

JESUS, VERY MAN.

O JESU! First-born among many brethren, grant me, as Thou hast promised, a place in the Kingdom of Thy FATHER, that where Thou art, I may be also.

O JESU! the Word made Flesh, Who being in the form of GOD, didst empty Thyself, and tookest upon Thee the form of a servant. Let me not feel it hard to be humbled for Thee.

O JESU! Son of Man, made in the likeness of man, and found in fashion as a man: make me by grace partaker of the Divine Nature.

JESUS, OUR CREATOR.

O JESU! my Creator. Make me a clean heart, and renew a right spirit within me.

O JESU! my Maker. Remember that Thou hast made me as the clay. O may I be a vessel of honour, and not of dishonour in Thy House.

O JESU! Author of my life; may my soul live to Thee: for to me to live is CHRIST, and to die is gain.

JESUS, OUR LORD.

O JESU! my LORD and my GOD; I am Thy servant. Do Thou and none but Thou possess me.

O JESU! my King! rule me, and I shall lack nothing in the green pastures, where Thou hast set me.

O JESU! my FATHER. I am not worthy to be called Thy son, yet cast me not away from Thy Presence.

JESUS, OUR TEACHER.

O JESU! Who art a Teacher come from GOD to us, teach me goodness, discipline, and knowledge.

O JESU! Instructor, Who didst begin to do and to teach: teach me to do Thy will, that I may learn of Thee, for Thou art meek and lowly of heart.

O JESU! Light of the world, the Way, the Truth, and the Life, lighten mine eyes, and lead me in the way of Thy commandments, for therein is my desire.

JESUS, OUR SHEPHERD.

O Jesu! the Good Shepherd, Who didst lay down Thy life for Thy sheep; lead me forth and feed me for Thy Name's sake.

O Jesu! Bread of Life, lo my soul waiteth for Thee; send me not away fasting, lest I faint by the way.

O Jesu! Fountain of Life: my soul thirsteth after Thee; O let me draw water with joy out of the wells of salvation.

JESUS, OUR ADVOCATE.

O Jesu! our Advocate with God the Father; cause Him to turn away His anger from us.

O Jesu! Mediator between God and Man: may Thy Blood cry not for vengeance upon us, but for our pardon.

O Jesu! Saviour, Thou that camest to seek, and to save that which was lost, save us.

JESUS, OUR SPOUSE.

O Jesu! Husband of blood, espouse me to Thyself in mercies and loving-kindnesses.

O Jesu! Beloved, fairer than the children of men, draw me after Thee with the cords of Thy love.

O Jesu! Lover of souls, Whose delight is to be with the sons of men! may I love Thee, and nothing else except for Thy sake.

JESUS, OUR PHYSICIAN.

O Jesu! Physician, Who by Thy stripes didst heal our sicknesses. Heal my soul, for I have sinned against Thee.

O Jesu! Innocent Lamb led to the slaughter. Take away the sins of the world: take away mine, the chief of sinners.

O Jesu! Good Samaritan, pour into my wounds the wine of penitence, and the oil of loving-kindness.

JESUS, OUR JUDGE.

O Jesu! Who shalt come to judge the quick and the dead, enter not into judgment with Thy servant.

O Jesu! merciful Judge, Who camest not to destroy any, spare me and answer for me.

O Jesu! Judge of awful majesty, set me with Thy sheep, and Thine elect, nor let me be afraid of any evil tidings.

JESUS, OUR REWARD.

O Jesu! Lot of mine inheritance, and my Portion in the Land of the living, restore to me mine inheritance.

O Jesu! our Glory, our Crown, and exceeding great Reward, admit me to those good things which Thou hast prepared for them that love Thee.

O Jesu! our Life, our Health, and Resurrection: I desire to be dissolved, and be with Thee. Nothing shall ever separate me from Thee. It is a good thing for me to cleave to Thee. For what have I in Heaven but Thee? and there is nothing upon earth that I desire in comparison of Thee.

Collect.

O GOD, Who hast made that most glorious Name of Thy Son Jesus Christ our Lord, ineffably sweet and full of deepest love unto Thy faithful ones, and to evil spirits full of fearful terror and amazement; mercifully grant that all who devoutly venerate this Name of Jesus upon earth, may reap the sweetness of holy consolation in this life, and in the world to come joyful exultation and endless bliss in Heaven: through the Same Jesus Christ our Lord. Amen.

Litany to God the Son.

LORD, have mercy upon us.

CHRIST, *have mercy upon us.*

LORD, have mercy upon us.

O GOD the Father, of Heaven, } *Have*

O GOD the Son, Redeemer of the world,

O GOD the Holy Ghost,

Holy Trinity, One God,

O Word of the Lord,

The Only-Begotten Son of God,

The Beloved Son of God,

} *mercy upon us.*

Trinity

Our SAVIOUR, CHRIST the LORD,
First-born SON of Mary,
JESUS, Son of Joseph of Nazareth,
Truth, that hath flourished out of the earth,
In Whom are hid all the treasures of wisdom and knowledge,
By Whom all things were made, and without Whom was not anything made,
In Whom dwelleth all the Fulness of the Godhead bodily,
High Priest for ever after the order of Melchizedec,
High Priest of good things to come,
High Priest, holy, harmless, undefiled, separate from sinners, and made higher than the Heavens,
A High Priest, Who art passed into the Heavens,
Head of the body, the Church,
Head of all principality and power,
Messiah, the Desire of all nations,
Anointed by the

} *Have mercy upon us.*

LORD with the HOLY GHOST and with power,
Anointed by GOD with the oil of gladness above Thy fellows,
Fairer than the children of men,
The great King upon all the earth,
The Way, the Truth, and the Life,
The true Vine whereof we are the branches,
The Door of the Sheep,
The Hidden Manna,
The Living and True Bread, Which came down from Heaven,
The Bread that strengtheneth man's heart,
Who hast loved us, and washed us from our sins in Thine Own Blood,
Upon Whom GOD hath laid the iniquity of us all,
Who hast purchased a Church with Thine Own Blood,
To Whom all power is given in Heaven and in earth,
Who didst ascend up far above all Heavens,
Who sittest at the

} *Have mercy upon us.*

Right Hand of the Majesty on High,

By Whom we have access unto the FATHER,

Who livest for ever and ever,

CHRIST our Peace, Who hast made both One,

Have mercy upon us.

BE propitious, spare us, O LORD.

From all evil deliver us, O LORD.

BY Thy most holy Life and Conversation,

By Thy most bitter Death and Passion,

By Thy glorious Resurrection and Ascension,

By Thy Coming to Judgment,

Deliver us, O LORD.

WE sinners beseech Thee, to hear us,

THAT our light may so shine before men that they may see our good works, and glorify our FATHER which is in Heaven,

That we fear not them that kill the body, but Him which is able to destroy both soul and body in Hell,

That we lay not up for ourselves treasure upon the earth, but in Heaven,

That we may never judge our neighbours rashly,

That when we ask the FATHER in Thy Name, we may, according to Thy promise, have grace to be heard,

That all things whatsoever we would that men should do unto us, we may do to them,

That we take heed to ourselves, lest at any time our hearts be overcharged with surfeiting, and drunkenness, and cares of this life,

That leaving the broad way that leadeth to destruction, we may all strive to enter in at the strait gate which leadeth unto life,

That we may gladly and willingly take upon us, Thy easy yoke and Thy light burden,

That we may carefully put out to interest the talents we have received from Thee,

We sinners beseech Thee to hear us, O LORD.

That being uncertain of the hour of our death, and of Thy Coming, we may ever study to be watchful and prepared,

That we may seriously prepare ourselves to give an account of our stewardship,

We sinners beseech Thee to hear us, O LORD.

O LAMB of GOD, that takest away the sins of the world,
Have mercy upon us.

O Lamb of GOD, that takest away the sins of the world,
Hearken to us, O LORD.

O Lamb of GOD that takest away the sins of the world,
Grant us Thy peace.

OUR FATHER.

Let us pray.

O GOD, Who by Thy co-eternal Wisdom didst create man when as yet he was not, and didst mercifully create him anew when he was lost, grant, we beseech Thee, that by the inspiration of the same Wisdom, we may love Thee with all our mind, and seek Thee with all our heart, through the Same JESUS CHRIST our LORD, Who liveth and reigneth with Thee in the Unity of the HOLY GHOST now and ever. Amen.

Devotions to God the Holy Ghost.

OBLATION TO GOD THE HOLY GHOST.

O HOLY GHOST, One and True GOD with the FATHER and the SON, without Thee man hath nothing. Regenerated by water and the HOLY SPIRIT, we are Members of CHRIST JESUS, and Children of His Church; which Thou dost rule, protect, make fruitful and sanctify by Thy grace and goodness. To Thee, therefore, I offer my heart and my whole self; I humbly devote and consecrate to Thee, all I have and all I do. Purify, I pray Thee, by the infusion of Thy gifts and grace, my senses and my heart, that I may ever serve Thee with a chaste body, and please Thee with a pure mind. And because without Thy help we cannot think any good thought, much less carry it into act, may Thy grace, I beseech Thee, always prevent and follow me, and make me ever to be given to all good works; and forasmuch as my deeds cannot of themselves please Thee, mercifully accept them, I pray Thee, in union with the most holy works and merits of CHRIST JESUS our LORD, that as He was conceived by Thy overshadowing a most pure Virgin, and became unto us a SAVIOUR, so out of His grace, charity, and infinite merits, our wants and infirmities may be supplied. Amen.

PRAYERS FOR THE SEVEN GIFTS OF THE HOLY SPIRIT.

Spirit of Wisdom.

COME, O Blessed Spirit of Wisdom, and reveal to my soul the mysteries of Heavenly things, their exceeding greatness, and power, and beauty. Teach me to love them above and beyond all the passing joys and satisfactions of earth. Show me the way by which I may be able to attain to them, and possess them, and hold them hereafter, mine own for ever. Amen.

Spirit of Understanding.

COME, O Blessed Spirit of Understanding, enlighten my mind, that I may perceive and embrace all the mysteries of the deep things of GOD; that in the end I may be meet in Thy light clearly to see the Eternal Light, and may come unto a perfect knowledge of Thee, and of the FATHER, and of the SON. Amen.

Spirit of Counsel.

COME, O Blessed Spirit of Counsel, help and guide me in all my ways, that I may ever do Thy holy will. Incline my heart to that which is good, turn it away from all that is evil, and direct me by the straight path of Thy commandments to that goal of eternal life for which I long. Amen.

Spirit of Ghostly Strength.

COME, O Blessed Spirit of Might, uphold my soul in every time of trouble or adversity. Sustain all my efforts after holiness; strengthen my weakness, give me courage against all the assaults of my enemies, that I may never be overcome, and separated from Thee, my GOD, my chiefest Good. Amen.

Spirit of Knowledge.

COME, O Blessed Spirit of Knowledge, grant that I may perceive and know the will of the FATHER, shew me the nothingness of earthly things, that I may know their vanity, and use them only for Thy glory, and my own salvation, looking ever beyond them to Thee, and Thy eternal great rewards. Amen.

Spirit of Godliness.

COME, O Blessed Spirit of Godliness, possess my heart, incline it to a true faith in Thee, to a holy love of Thee my GOD, that with my whole soul I may seek Thee, and find Thee my best, my truest Joy. Amen.

Spirit of Holy Fear.

COME, O Blessed Spirit of Holy Fear, penetrate my heart with Thy fear, that I may set Thee, my LORD and GOD, before my face for ever; and shun all things that can offend Thee, so that I may be made meet to appear before the pure eyes of Thy Divine Majesty in the Heaven of Heavens, where Thou livest and reignest in the Unity of the Ever-blessed TRINITY, God for ever and ever. Amen.

PRAYER TO THE HOLY SPIRIT.

O HOLY SPIRIT, Love of GOD; Who proceedest from the Almighty FATHER, and His most Blessed SON, infuse Thy grace most plentifully into my heart. Come Thou and dwell in this soul that longs to be Thy holy Temple. Heal the lurking distempers of my heart; pierce me through with the dart of Thy love, kindle in me such a holy fire, that it may flame out in a bright and devout zeal, and burning up all the dross of sensual affections, may possess and purify my whole spirit, soul, and body; grant this, O Blessed SPIRIT, for the sake of JESUS CHRIST our only LORD and SAVIOUR. Amen.

PRAYER FOR THE TWELVE FRUITS OF THE HOLY GHOST.

O HOLY SPIRIT, Eternal Love of the FATHER and of the SON, grant me to taste the sweetness of Thy loving-kindness: the Fruit of Love, that I may love Thee above all things, and my neighbour as myself; the Fruit of Joy that I may be filled with holy consolation; the Fruit of Peace, that I may be at peace with Thee, my neighbour, and myself; the Fruit of Longsuffering, that I may humbly submit to everything that is opposed to my own desires; the Fruit of Gentleness, that I may be kind and considerate to all men; the Fruit of Goodness, that I may be ever ready to do good to all; the Fruit of Faith, that nothing may be impossible to me; the Fruit of Meekness, that I may subdue every rising of angry temper, and so far from offering the least injury may never return the greatest; the Fruit of Patience, that I may not be discouraged by delay, but may persevere in prayer; the Fruit of Modesty, that I may be holy in my thoughts, watchful in my words, and discreet in all my behaviour; the Fruit of Temperance, that using Thy creatures to Thy glory I may keep my body in subjection; the Fruit of Chastity, that with a pure body and a clean heart, I may adore and please Thee to my life's end; so that having served Thee faithfully here on earth I may attain in CHRIST JESUS to praise Thee eternally in Heaven, with the FATHER and the SON, Three Persons, One Glorious and Eternal GOD, to Whom be glory now and for ever. Amen.

Litany to God the Holy Ghost.

LORD, have mercy upon us.
CHRIST, *have mercy upon us.*
LORD, have mercy upon us.

O GOD the FATHER, of Heaven,
O GOD the SON, Redeemer of the world,
O GOD the HOLY GHOST,
Holy TRINITY, One GOD,

} *Have mercy upon us.*

O HOLY GHOST, proceeding from the FATHER and the SON,
O HOLY GHOST, co-equal with the FATHER and the SON,
SPIRIT, that testifieth of CHRIST,
SPIRIT of Truth, that teachest us all things,
SPIRIT, that guidest into all truth,
SPIRIT by Whose marvellous power the Incarnation of the LORD was effected in the Virgin's Womb,

SPIRIT of the LORD, that fillest the world,
SPIRIT of GOD, that dwellest in us,
SPIRIT of Wisdom and Understanding,
SPIRIT of Counsel and Might,
SPIRIT of Knowledge and Piety,
SPIRIT of the Fear of the LORD,
SPIRIT of Compunction and Repentance,
SPIRIT of Grace and of Prayer,
SPIRIT of Charity, Peace, and Joy,
SPIRIT of Patience, Longsuffering, and Goodness,
SPIRIT of Mildness, Gentleness, and Faith,
SPIRIT of Modesty, Purity, and Chastity,
SPIRIT of manifold Grace,
SPIRIT of the LORD, Who at the beginning of creation moving upon the face of the waters, didst brood over them, and make them fruitful,
SPIRIT, by Whose

} *Have mercy upon us.*

inspiration holy men of God did speak,
Spirit, Whose unction teacheth us of all things,
Spirit, Who searchest all things, even the deep things of God,
Spirit, Who intercedest for us with groanings which cannot be uttered,
Spirit by Whom we are born again,
Spirit of Adoption of the sons of God,
Spirit, that helpest our infirmities,
Spirit, Who convincest the world of sin, of righteousness, and of judgment,
Spirit, Who purifiest our hearts by faith,
Spirit, Who quickenest us,
Spirit, Who dividest to every man severally as Thou wilt,
Spirit, the Discerner of the thoughts and intents of the heart,
Spirit Paraclete, Who abidest with us for ever,
} *Have mercy upon us.*

From all evil, deliver us,
O Holy Spirit.

Be propitious, spare us,
O Holy Spirit.

Be propitious, hearken unto us,
O Holy Spirit.

From all sin,
From the temptations and snares of the devil,
From all presumption, and despair,
From questioning acknowledged truth,
From envying brotherly love,
From all obstinacy and impenitence,
From all uncleanness of mind and body,
From the spirit of anger, strife, and dissension,
From every evil spirit,
By Thine Eternal Procession from the Father and the Son,
By the miraculous Conception of the Son of God, by Thy co-operation,
By Thy Descent on Christ at His Baptism,
By Thy Appearance
} *Deliver us, O Holy Spirit.*

at the Transfiguration,
By Thy Coming upon the Disciples of CHRIST,

IN the Day of Judgment, we sinners beseech Thee to hear us.

That Thou mayest spare us.

THAT as we live in the SPIRIT, we may also walk in the SPIRIT,
That by the SPIRIT we may mortify the deeds of the body,
That we grieve not the HOLY SPIRIT of GOD,
That we be careful to keep the unity of the SPIRIT in the bond of peace,
That walking in the SPIRIT, we fulfil not the lusts of the flesh,
That Thou wouldest vouchsafe to create in us hunger and thirst after true righteousness,
That Thou wouldest vouchsafe to pour into us sincere affections of love and mercy,

That we may patiently and constantly endure persecution for righteousness' sake,
That Thou wouldest grant to us to persevere unto the end in faith, hope, and charity,

We beseech Thee to hear us.

O LAMB of GOD, that takest away the sins of the world,
Pour on us the HOLY SPIRIT.

O Lamb of GOD, that takest away the sins of the world,
Send forth on us the promised SPIRIT of the FATHER.

O Lamb of GOD, that takest away the sins of the world,
Give unto us the Spirit of Peace.

OUR FATHER.

℣ Make me a clean heart, O GOD,
℟ *And renew a right spirit within me.*

℣ Cast me not away from Thy presence,

℟ *And take not Thy* HOLY SPIRIT *from me.*

℣ *O give me the comfort of Thy help again,*

℟ *And stablish me with Thy free* SPIRIT.

℣ *May the grace of Thy* HOLY SPIRIT,

℟ *Enlighten our senses and our hearts.*

℣ O LORD, hear our prayer,

℟ *And let our cry come unto Thee.*

Let us pray.

GRANT, we beseech Thee, Almighty GOD, that Thy HOLY SPIRIT may remove all carnal affections from our minds, and mightily pour into us His spiritual gifts; through JESUS CHRIST our LORD. Amen.

DEVOTIONS FOR SAINTS' DAYS.

MEMORIALS.

Of the Saints.

Antiphon. These are they which came out of great tribulation, and have washed their robes, and made them white in the Blood of the Lamb : therefore are they before the throne of GOD, and serve Him day and night in His Temple.

℣ The Souls of the Righteous are in the Hand of GOD :

℟ *And there shall no torment touch them.*

Let us pray.

BLESSED, praised, and hallowed be Thy Name, O LORD, for all Thy Saints, (especially N., whom we commemorate this day,) after whose example we commend ourselves and one another, and our whole life, unto CHRIST our GOD; and pray that we, with all who from the beginning have pleased Thee, may be made partakers of Thine eternal and incorruptible benefits. Amen.

Of the Blessed Virgin.

Antiphon. The HOLY GHOST shall come upon thee, and the power of the Highest shall overshadow Thee : therefore also that holy thing which shall be born of thee shall be called the SON of GOD.

℣ Blessed art thou among women :

℞ And blessed is the Fruit of thy womb.

Let us pray.

O GOD, Who in the overshadowing of the HOLY GHOST wast conceived in the womb of a human mother, still a Virgin, who gave Thee birth and nurtured Thee ; and Who, laid in her bosom, wert presented in the Temple to the FATHER, an Offering and Sacrifice for us ; grant, we beseech Thee, that we, sharing Thy nature, one flesh and one spirit with Thee, a new creation in Thyself, may be made like unto Thee in all things ; and, living according to Thy holy Will, may be presented a living sacrifice, holy, acceptable to GOD through Thy merits and perpetual intercession ; to Whom be glory for ever. Amen.

O LORD JESUS CHRIST, born of the Virgin Mary ; teach me to reverence Thy Holy Mother, according to Thy will. Thou didst send Thy Angel to salute her as highly favoured, and blessed among women, meet to be the mother of GOD by the operation of the HOLY GHOST. Thou wast subject unto her, and didst commit her to Thy beloved disciple, saying, " Behold thy mother." With Thy Angel, I would give her praise ; with Thyself love her ; with Thine Apostle honour her. Howsoever Thy Saints have profited through her intercessions, may I in like manner profit ; through Thee, Who with the FATHER and the HOLY GHOST, livest and reignest, One GOD, world without end. Amen.

Of an Apostle or Evangelist.

Antiphon. Ye are my friends if ye do whatsoever I command you.

℣ Their sound is gone out into all lands,

℟ And their words into the ends of the world.

Let us pray.

ALMIGHTY, Everlasting GOD, Who in the hearts of Thy Saints lightest up the flame of Thy love: grant unto our souls the same strength of faith and charity which Thou gavest them; that as we rejoice in their triumphs, so we may also profit by their examples; through JESUS CHRIST our LORD. Amen.

Of a Martyr.

Antiphon. Theirs is the Kingdom of Heaven who have despised the life of this world, to gain a reward hereafter, and have washed their robes in the Blood of the Lamb. Alleluia.

℣ O GOD, Wonderful art Thou in Thy Saints.

℟ And glorious in Thy Majesty.

Let us pray.

GRANT, we beseech Thee, Almighty GOD, that the example of Thy blessed servant, Saint N., may incite us to a better life: that as we solemnly celebrate his Festival, so we may also imitate his actions, and by despising the things of earth, may attain to everlasting joys in Héaven; through JESUS CHRIST our LORD. Amen.

Of a Confessor and Bishop.

Antiphon. Well done thou good and faithful servant; thou hast been faithful over a few things, I will make thee ruler over many things: enter thou into the joy of thy LORD. Alleluia.

Saints' Days

℣ The Righteous shall grow as the lily.

℟ He shall flourish for ever before the LORD.

Let us pray.

O ALMIGHTY and Everlasting GOD, Who makest us glad this day with the Festival of Thy Bishop and Confessor, Saint N.: we humbly beseech Thy mercy that we may be aided by the holy prayers of him whose solemnity we reverently keep, and may finally attain to the joys of everlasting life; through JESUS CHRIST our LORD. Amen.

Of a Doctor.

Antiphon. Light eternal shall shine on Thy Saints, O LORD, and length of days. Alleluia.

℣ Rejoice in the LORD, O ye Righteous.

℟ For it becometh well the just to be thankful. Alleluia.

Let us pray.

O GOD, Who willedst Thy blessed servant, Saint N., to be an illustrious Teacher for the instruction and edification of Thy Holy Church: grant, we beseech Thee, that as on earth he taught us the way of life, so now he may plead and pray for us in Heaven; through JESUS CHRIST our LORD. Amen.

Of a Virgin and Martyr.

Antiphon. When the Bridegroom came, they that were ready went in with Him to the marriage. Alleluia.

℣ The virgins that be her fellows,

℟ Shall bear her company.

Let us pray.

ALMIGHTY and Everlasting GOD, Who choosest the weak things of the world to confound the wise: mercifully grant that we, who celebrate the Festival of Thy holy servant, Saint M., Virgin (and Martyr), may also enjoy the advantage of her prayers in our behalf before Thee; through JESUS CHRIST our LORD. Amen.

Of S. Michael and all Angels.

Antiphon. The Angel of the LORD tarrieth round about them that fear Him; and delivereth them.

℣ He maketh His Angels spirits,

℞ And His ministers a flaming fire.

Let us pray.

O GOD, Who of Thine unspeakable Providence vouchsafest to send Thy holy Angels to have a charge over us: grant that we, Thy humble servants, may both be evermore defended by their protection, and also rejoice in their eternal companionship hereafter; through JESUS CHRIST our LORD. Amen.

The Golden Litany
of the
Life and Passion of our Lord Jesus Christ.

LORD, have mercy upon us.

CHRIST, *have mercy upon us: and grant us strength of soul, inward and outward, that we may serve Thee according to the pleasure of Thy will.*

O LORD GOD, FATHER of Heaven,
By Thy Heavenly power have mercy upon us.

O SON of GOD, Redeemer of the world,

O HOLY GHOST, One GOD, with the FATHER and the SON,

} *Have mercy upon us.*

O LORD GOD, by Thine uncreate and undivided TRINITY,

By Thy divine Being and Nature,

By Thine infinite Glory and Beauty,

By Thy Self, and all Goodness that Thou beholdest in Thy Self,

By Thy Creation of Heaven and earth, and all things that are in them,

By Thy Goodness in the creation of Man in Thine Own Image and Likeness,

By that great Love,

} *Have mercy upon us.*

whereby Thou didst elect to restore man when he fell,

By that ineffable Love, whereby Thou chosest Mary most pure Virgin to be Thy Mother,

By that meek Affection and Love which drew Thee from the bosom of the FATHER unto the womb of the Virgin,

By the Humility of Thy high and awful Majesty, which disdained not to descend into the womb of the Virgin,

For that Thou didst not loathe to take upon Thee the Frailty of man for our sins,

For Thy holy Nativity, wherein Thou didst vouchsafe to be born of a woman,

By that cold Manger which Thou layest in, wrapped in poor clothes, and fed with maiden's milk,.

By the great Joy of the Shepherds, who worshipped Thee lying in a manger,

For Thy painful Circumcision, and Shedding of Thy precious Blood, and by the Virtue of Thy holy Name JESUS, and all Thy blessed Names,

For the blessed Oblation of Thyself to Thy FATHER in the Temple,

For Thy Flight into Egypt, and all that Thou didst suffer there,

For Thy coming again from Egypt to Nazareth, and thy Obedience to Thy Father and Mother,

For Thy lowly and meek Conversation, for three and thirty years on earth,

For Thy most holy Meditations, Words, and Works of mercy,

For Thy holy Baptism, and the glorious Manifestation of the HOLY TRINITY,

For Thy holy Fasting, Meditation, and Temptation,

For the Thirst, Hunger, Cold, and Heat which Thou didst suffer,

For Thy Heaviness, Labour, and Weariness,

For the Detraction and evil Words wherewith Thine enemies reviled Thee,

Have mercy upon us.

For Thy Watching and Prayers,

For Thy wholesome Doctrine, and Thy mighty Resistance, whereby Thou gavest no place to Thine enemies,

For the wonderful Signs and Miracles which Thou wroughtest,

For Thy holy Tears and lowly Entrance into Jerusalem on Palm Sunday,

By that fervent and charitable Desire, that Thou hadst to redeem us,

By that great Lowliness which Thou showedst in washing the feet of Thy disciples, and of Judas who betrayed Thee,

For Thy most noble and worthy Institution of the Sacrament of Thy most precious Body and Blood,

For that profound Love, whereby Thou didst permit S. John the Evangelist to rest upon Thy breast at Thy Supper,

For the Peace which Thou gavest to Thy disciples,

Have mercy upon us.

For Thy holy Words and Sermons,

For the great inward Heaviness which Thou hadst when Thou prayedst to Thy FATHER in the Garden,

By the virtue of Thy holy Prayer which Thou prayedst there three times,

For Thy fearful Dread of Thy death,

For that Agony wherein Thou offeredst Thyself willingly to death in obedience to Thy Almighty FATHER, and for Thy Bloody Sweat,

By that great Meekness whereby Thou didst will to be comforted by an Angel, so comfort me in every time of trouble, and

By Thy mighty and victorious Courage, wherewith Thou wentest to meet them that sought to kill Thee,

By Thy fearful Taking, when the Jews laid their hands violently upon Thee,

For Thy great Goodness, in that Thou refusedst not the kiss of Judas, Thy betrayer,

Have mercy upon us.

and didst heal the ear of Malchus that Peter smote off,

For those holy Bonds wherewith Thou wast bound, and led as a prisoner: and the opprobrious Words that Thou didst suffer all that night,

For the Blow Thou didst endure in the presence of the High Priest Annas, and other shame done to Thee,

For that Love and Charity that Thou hadst when Thou wert brought bound before Caiaphas the High Priest,

By the false Witnesses, and Thine unrighteous Condemnation,

By the Spitting upon Thee, and the Scorning of Thee,

By the Buffetings and sore Strokes given to Thee,

By the Binding and Blindfolding of Thine holy eyes, by all the Shame and Reproof that Thou didst suffer all that night,

For that merciful Look wherewith Thou beheldest Peter, and for all that Labour and Torment, secret and unknown, which Thou didst suffer all that night,

By Thy Presentation before Pilate, and the Accusations that the Jews made against Thee,

For the Contempt and Mockery that Thou didst suffer when Herod arrayed Thee in a gorgeous robe, and sent Thee again to Pilate,

For all the Shame, Labour, Upbraiding, and Reproof which Thou didst suffer going from one Judge to another,

For Thy great Patience and Stillness,

For the shameful Stripping of Thy clothes, and the Binding of Thy most holy Body to a pillar,

For Thy Scourgings, and cruel Beatings,

For Thine innumerable Wounds, and the plenteous Shedding of Thy blood,

For all Thy Pain, Sorrow, Cold, and Shivering,

For the purple Garment, and the Crown of

Have mercy upon us.

Have mercy upon us.

thorns violently pressed upon Thy head,

For the great Pain that Thou didst suffer in Thy Head, when it was smitten on the crown of thorns,

By the scornful Worshipping of the Jews and their Salutation, when they said, "Hail King of the Jews,"

By the Spitting on Thy divine Face, and the cruel Beatings,

For that Heaviness of Heart which Thou hadst when Pilate brought Thee forth before the multitude of the people, wearing the crown of thorns and the purple robe, and said to them, "Behold the Man,"

For that fearful Sentence of death and shameful Leading to the Mount of Calvary,

For Thy great Love shewed to us when Thou barest Thy heavy Cross upon Thy shoulders, to the place where Thou sufferedst Thy most painful Passion; and the Labour, Anguish, Slanders, and

Beatings Thou didst suffer by the way,

For all Thy bloody Steps, as Thou didst go to Thy death,

By the great Weariness that Thou hadst in Thy shoulders, bearing the Cross until Thou fellest down,

By the great Compassion of Thy Heart, when bearing the Cross, Thou didst meet the Holy Women sorrowing and making lamentation,

By Thy Heaviness of soul, and the Going up to the Mount of Calvary, where Thou wast crucified,

By the Stripping of Thy Clothes to Thy great shame in the sight of all the people,

By that cold Sitting that Thou satest, piteously full of wounds, so abiding until Thy Cross was ready,

For those sore and painful Steps that Thou madest going to Thy Cross,

For Thy great Anguish, Mournings, and Weepings,

For the great Stretch-

Have mercy upon us.

Have mercy upon us.

The Golden Litany

ing of Thy sinews, and veins, and all Thy members,

By the Nailing of Thy Right Hand, and Shedding of Thy precious Blood, clear us LORD from all sin, and

By the Nailing of Thy Left Hand, and Thy most holy Wound, and precious Blood, save us, and

For the Nailing of Thy most Holy Feet, and by the precious Blood flowing out of them, purge us, enlighten us, and reconcile us to GOD the FATHER, and

For the Lifting up of Thy most holy Body on the Cross, and the sore Bruising thereof that gave to all parts of Thy Body an incredible pain,

For the Heaviness of Thy Heart, and all the powers of Thy Soul, save us, deliver us, and

For the Parting of Thy Garments, and the Casting lots upon Thy seamless coat,

For Thy great Love whereby Thou didst

Have mercy upon us.

hang alive upon the Cross three hours,

For those opprobrious and scornful Words, which, hanging on the Cross, Thou heardest spoken unto Thee,

For the Blasphemy, Sorrow, and Confusion that Thou didst suffer on the Cross,

For all the Pain that, being strained upon the Cross, Thou didst suffer in Thy Hands and Feet and all Thy Members,

For that wonderful Charity when Thou prayedst Thine Almighty FATHER for Thine enemies,

For Thy tender Mercy in that Thou didst promise Paradise to the Penitent Thief,

For the tender Care which Thou hadst for Thy Mother in Thy torments, commending her to Thy well-beloved disciple S. John,

For that great and piteous Cry which Thou madest to Thy FATHER,

For those holy Tears, which Thou sheddest on the Cross, and in all Thy Life-time,

Have mercy upon us.

For Thy Thirst and Tasting of Gall and Vinegar, grant us to taste the Sweetness of Thy Spirit, and

For all those holy Words that Thou spakest on the Cross, and in all Thy Life,

For that piteous Cry in the which Thou commendedst Thy Soul to Thy FATHER, may our souls be commended to Thee, and

By the Departing of Thy holy Soul from Thy blessed Body,

By the Resting of Thy most blessed Head upon Thy Breast, incline most Sweet JESU to us, and

By the Bitterness of Thy Death, and the intolerable pains wherewith Thy Heart brake,

By the Opening of Thy Side with a spear, and the flowing out of Thy most precious Blood, smite through, Good LORD, my heart, with the spear of Thy divine love, and

By that precious Blood and Water that ran out of Thy most holy Heart, wash and cleanse us in the same most holy Water and Blood from all our sins, and

For that great Mercy which Thou shewedst to the Centurion beneath Thy Cross, and all Thy mercies which Thou hast ever shown unto men,

By the Descent of Thy holy Soul to Hell,

For the Taking down of Thy most holy Body from the Cross, and the Solemn Burial thereof and the great Lamentation of Thy Blessed Mother, and Mary Magdalene, and others, Thy friends,

For all Thy painful Labours, Weariness, Sorrow, and Heaviness, which Thou didst suffer from the day of Thy Nativity unto the hour that Thy Soul departed from Thy Body,

For Thy glorious Resurrection in body and in soul,

For that special Grace, when Thou didst appear in a glorious Body, after Thy Resurrection, to Mary Magdalene, to the other

Have mercy upon us.

Have mercy upon us.

Mysteries of the Incarnation

women, and to Thy disciples,

For Thy wonderful and glorious Ascension, comfort us, Good LORD, in all necessities, and,

For Thy divine Sending of the HOLY GHOST the Comforter to Thy disciples, comfort us, sanctify us, and strengthen us in faith, hope, and charity, and,

For Thy glory and the divine Majesty and Virtues of Thy holy Name, save us and govern us, now and ever, and,

For the Love that dwelt both in Thy Manhood and Thy Godhead,

For that Joy whereby Thou hast fruition in Thyself,

For Thyself and all Goodness and Merits that Thou beholdest in Thyself,

} Have mercy upon us.

Let us pray.

SUCCOUR us, most Sweet JESU, in that fearful day of Thy most strict Judgment, and grant us in this transitory life all things necessary to the health of our bodies and our souls, and that this life ended we may live with Thee in joy everlasting: Who livest and reignest God for ever and ever. Amen.

℣ LORD, hear our prayer,
℟ *And let our cry come unto Thee.*

Mysteries of the Incarnation,

OR

THE FIVE JOYFUL MYSTERIES.

To be used especially on the Sundays from Advent to Lent.

IN the Name ✠ of the FATHER, and of the SON, and of the HOLY GHOST. Amen.

℣ O LORD, open Thou our lips:

℟ And our mouth shall show forth Thy praise.

℣ O GOD, make speed to save us:

℟ O LORD, make haste to help us.

I.

THE ANNUNCIATION OF THE B. V. MARY.

LET us meditate on the message of the Angel Gabriel to the Blessed Virgin announcing to her the Incarnation of our LORD and SAVIOUR JESUS CHRIST.
S. Luke i. 26-38.
Our FATHER.
Glory be to the FATHER.

Let us pray.

WE beseech Thee, O LORD, pour Thy grace into our hearts; that, as we have known the Incarnation of Thy SON JESUS CHRIST by the message of an Angel, so by His Cross and Passion we may be brought unto the glory of His Resurrection; through the Same JESUS CHRIST our LORD. Amen.

II.

THE VISITATION OF THE B. V. MARY.

LET us meditate on the Blessed Virgin going to visit her cousin, S. Elizabeth, when she heard from the Angel that she had also conceived a son.
S. Luke i. 39-56.
Our FATHER.
Glory be to the FATHER.

Let us pray.

O ALMIGHTY GOD, Who didst move the Mother of Thy SON, JESUS CHRIST, to visit her cousin Elizabeth; grant that our hearts may be so visited by Thy most Holy SON, that being freed from all sin, we may evermore give praise and thanks to Him, Who with Thee and the HOLY GHOST liveth and reigneth ever One GOD, world without end. Amen.

III.

THE BIRTH OF OUR B. LORD.

LET us meditate on the Blessed Virgin's bringing forth her First-born Son, JESUS CHRIST, and laying him in a manger.
S. Luke ii. 1-20.
Our FATHER.
Glory be to the FATHER.

Let us pray.

ALMIGHTY GOD, Who hast given us Thy Only-Begotten SON to take our nature upon Him, and to be born of a pure Virgin; grant that we being regenerate, and made Thy children by adoption and grace, may daily be renewed by Thy HOLY SPIRIT; through the Same our LORD JESUS CHRIST, Who liveth and reigneth with Thee and the Same SPIRIT, ever One GOD, world without end. Amen.

IV.

THE PRESENTATION OF CHRIST IN THE TEMPLE.

LET us meditate on the Blessed Virgin, when the days of her Purification were accomplished, presenting the Child JESUS in the Temple to the LORD.
S. Luke ii. 22-40.
Our FATHER.
Glory be to the FATHER.

Let us pray.

ALMIGHTY and Everliving GOD, we humbly beseech Thy Majesty, that, as Thy Only-Begotten SON was presented in the Temple in substance of our flesh, so we may be presented unto Thee with pure and clean hearts, by the Same Thy SON JESUS CHRIST our LORD. Amen.

V.

THE FINDING OF THE CHILD JESUS IN THE TEMPLE.

LET us meditate on the Blessed Virgin and S. Joseph's losing our Blessed LORD, and finding Him after the space of three days in the Temple, sitting in the midst of the doctors.
S. Luke ii. 41-51.
Our FATHER.
Glory be to the FATHER.

Let us pray.

O LORD, we beseech Thee mercifully to receive the prayers of Thy people which call upon Thee; and grant that they may both perceive and know what things they ought to do, and also may have grace and power faithfully to fulfil the same; through JESUS CHRIST our LORD. Amen.

Mysteries of the Redemption,

OR

THE FIVE SORROWFUL MYSTERIES.

To be used especially on the Sundays in Lent.

I.

THE BLOODY SWEAT OF JESUS IN THE GARDEN.

LET us meditate on our SAVIOUR'S Agony of mind, when His sweat was as it were great drops of blood falling down to the ground.

S. Luke xxii. 44.
Our FATHER.
Glory be to the FATHER.

Let us pray.

O LORD JESU CHRIST, the Good Shepherd, Who dost feed and purify Thy sheep with Thy Own most precious Blood, may this my meditation on Thine Agony and Bloody Sweat move me to sincere repentance for all my sins, and may the thought of Thy Passion be for comfort and salvation to me and to all Thy faithful people; and this I pray for Thy most tender mercy's sake. Amen.

II.

THE SCOURGING OF JESUS.

LET us meditate on the Sufferings of JESUS in being bound to a pillar and cruelly scourged by the Roman soldiers.

S. John xix. 1.
Our FATHER.
Glory be to the FATHER.

Let us pray.

O MOST Chaste Spouse, JESU CHRIST, Very GOD and Very Man, Who wast stripped of Thy garments, bound to a pillar, and most cruelly scourged, we implore Thee by these most grievous pains, and by all the other torments of Thy Passion, to enable us to bear patiently whatsoever chastisements Thou mayest think fit to lay upon us, and to remember that whom the LORD loveth He chasteneth, and scourgeth every son whom He receiveth. Amen.

III.

THE CROWNING WITH THORNS.

LET us meditate on our Saviour's sufferings when the Crown of thorns was pressed down on His sacred Head.
S. John xix. 2, 3.
Our FATHER.
Glory be to the FATHER.

Let us pray.

O LORD JESU CHRIST, Who wast crowned with thorns, blindfolded, buffeted, struck with a reed, clothed in derision with a purple garment, mocked and reviled; have mercy on us, and pierce us so throughly with the thorns of penitence, that we may find pardon in this life, and may hereafter be found meet to be crowned by Thee with glory in Heaven. Amen.

IV.

THE BEARING THE CROSS.

LET us meditate on our Saviour's sufferings when He bore the Cross on which He was to be crucified.
S. John xix. 17.
Our FATHER.
Glory be to the FATHER.

Let us pray.

O LORD JESU CHRIST, Who didst bear Thy Cross along the road to Calvary, grant that we may glory in nothing save only in the Cross, that by it the world may be crucified unto us, and we unto the world; give us strength to bear our Cross after Thee, and to follow in Thy footsteps, that we may not shrink from suffering with Thee, but rather rejoice that we are counted worthy to suffer for Thy Name's sake. Amen.

V.

THE CRUCIFIXION.

LET us meditate on the sufferings of our LORD, when His sacred Hands and Feet were nailed to the Cross.
S. John xix. 18-31.
Our FATHER.
Glory be to the FATHER.

Let us pray.

ALMIGHTY GOD, we beseech Thee graciously to behold this Thy family, for which our LORD JESUS

CHRIST was contented to be betrayed, and given up into the hands of wicked men, and to suffer death upon the Cross, Who now liveth and reigneth with Thee and the HOLY GHOST, ever One GOD, world without end. Amen.

Mysteries of the Resurrection,

OR

THE FIVE GLORIOUS MYSTERIES.

To be used especially on the Sundays from Easter to Advent.

I.
THE RESURRECTION OF OUR B. LORD.

LET us meditate on our Blessed LORD's triumphing over death and rising from the grave.
S. Matt. xxviii. 1-9.
Our FATHER.
Glory be to the FATHER.

Let us pray.

ALMIGHTY GOD, Who through Thy Only-Begotten SON JESUS CHRIST hast overcome death, and opened unto us the gate of everlasting life; we humbly beseech Thee, that, as by Thy special grace preventing us Thou dost put into our minds good desires, so by Thy continual help we may bring the same to good effect; through JESUS CHRIST our LORD, Who liveth and reigneth with Thee and the HOLY GHOST, ever One GOD, world without end. Amen.

II.
THE ASCENSION OF OUR B. LORD.

LET us meditate on our Blessed LORD's Ascension into Heaven in the presence of the Apostles and Angels.
Acts i. 9-12.
Our FATHER.
Glory be to the FATHER.

Let us pray.

GRANT, we beseech Thee, Almighty GOD, that like as we do believe Thy Only-Begotten SON our LORD JESUS CHRIST to have ascended into the Heavens;

so we may also in heart and mind thither ascend, and with Him continually dwell, Who liveth and reigneth with Thee and the HOLY GHOST, One GOD, world without end. Amen.

III.

THE DESCENT OF THE HOLY GHOST.

LET us meditate on our Blessed LORD sending down the HOLY GHOST on the Apostles as He had promised.
  Acts ii. 1-5.
  Our FATHER.
  Glory be to the FATHER.

Let us pray.

GOD, Who didst teach the hearts of Thy faithful people, by the sending to them the light of Thy HOLY SPIRIT; Grant us by the Same SPIRIT to have a right judgment in all things, and evermore to rejoice in His holy comfort; through the merits of CHRIST JESUS our SAVIOUR, Who liveth and reigneth with Thee, in the Unity of the Same Spirit, One GOD, world without end. Amen.

IV.

THE TRIUMPH OF THE CHURCH IN THE SAINTS.

LET us contemplate the worship which the Saints and Angels in Heaven pay to our Blessed LORD.
  Revelation vii. 2-13.
  Our FATHER.
  Glory be to the FATHER.

Let us pray.

O ALMIGHTY GOD, Who hast knit together Thine elect in one communion and fellowship, in the mystical Body of Thy SON CHRIST our LORD; grant us grace so to follow Thy blessed Saints in all virtuous and godly living, that we may come to those unspeakable joys, which Thou hast prepared for them that unfeignedly love Thee; through JESUS CHRIST our LORD. Amen.

V.

THE BEATIFIC VISION.

LET us contemplate the unspeakable bliss of dwelling for ever in the presence of GOD.
  Revelation iv. 1-11.
  Our FATHER.
  Glory be to the FATHER.

Let us pray.

ALMIGHTY and Everlasting GOD, Who hast given unto us Thy servants grace by the confession of a true faith to acknowledge the glory of the Eternal TRINITY, and in the power of the Divine Majesty to worship the Unity; We beseech Thee, that Thou wouldest keep us steadfast in this faith, and evermore defend us from all adversities, Who livest and reignest, One GOD, world without end. Amen.

Final Prayer.

O ALMIGHTY GOD, Whose Only-Begotten SON, by His Life, Death, and Resurrection, hath purchased for us the gifts of everlasting life, grant we beseech Thee, that through devout meditation on these mysteries of His joys, His sorrows, and His glory, we may imitate what they teach, and receive what they promise; through the Same CHRIST our LORD. Amen.

Litany for the Church.

LORD, have mercy upon us.
CHRIST, have mercy upon us.
LORD, have mercy upon us.

O JESUS, hear us.
O JESUS, graciously hear us.

O GOD the FATHER, of Heaven,
O GOD the SON, Redeemer of the world,
O GOD the HOLY GHOST,
O HOLY TRINITY, One GOD,
} *Have mercy*

O GOD, Eternal FATHER, Who didst choose the Church of Thine Elect before the foundation of the world,

O GOD, Who on the fall of man, didst promise redemption through Thine Only-Begotten SON, in Whose Incarnation Thou hast knit all things in Heaven and earth in one,

O GOD, Who after the flood didst renew Thy covenant with Noah, and afterwards didst call Thy servant
} *upon Thy people, Thy chosen.*

Litany for the Church

Abraham to be the Father of the faithful,

O GOD, Who broughtest Israel out of Egypt by a mighty hand and by a stretched out arm,

O GOD, Who leddest Thy people like sheep by the hand of Moses and Aaron,

O GOD, Who, smiting down their enemies before them, didst bring Thy people into the promised land by the hand of Joshua their captain,

O GOD, Who, casting out the heathen before them, didst make the tribes of Israel to dwell in their tents,

O GOD, Who in mercy didst chasten Thy people when they fell away from Thee,

O GOD, Who in mercy didst always hear and deliver them when they cried unto Thee in their affliction,

O GOD, Who didst think upon Thy covenant, and didst pity them, according to the multitude of Thy mercies,

O GOD, Who unto

Thy servant David didst promise that Thou wouldest stablish his kingdom for ever, and that Thy mercy should not depart from him,

O GOD, Who when the house of Israel had become idolatrous didst raise up Thy servant Elijah, to revive Thy true religion,

O GOD, Who in the most evil times didst evermore preserve unto Thyself a faithful remnant,

O GOD, Who didst comfort and enlighten Thy people by the mouth of Thy servants the prophets,

O GOD, Who in the days of Hezekiah, and at other times, didst miraculously deliver Jerusalem from the hands of her enemies,

O GOD, Who in the days of their captivity didst comfort Judah with the promise of restoration,

O GOD, Who didst so order the affairs of this world as to bring about the return of Thy people that they might

Have mercy upon Thy people, Thy chosen.

rebuild Thy holy Temple,

O GOD, Who in the fulness of time didst send Thy SON to be the anointed Prophet, Priest, and King of Thy people Israel,

O GOD, Who by the Cross didst bring both Jew and Gentile into Thy One Holy Catholic and Apostolic Church,

} *Have mercy upon Thy people, Thy chosen.*

O JESUS, Who building Thy Church on the foundation of Thy holy Apostles and Prophets in the glorious confession of Thy true Godhead, hast promised that the gates of hell shall never prevail against it,

O JESUS, Who by the mouth of Paul vouchsafest to call Thy Church Thy Bride, bone of Thy bone, and flesh of Thy flesh,

O JESUS, Who vouchsafest to call Thy Church Thine Own Body, the fulness of Thee Who fillest all in all,

O JESUS, Who lovedst Thy Church and gavest Thyself for it, that Thou mightest present it unto Thyself a glorious Church,

O JESUS, Who didst promise to be with us always, even unto the end of the world,

O JESUS, our great High Priest, Who ever livest to make intercession for us,

O JESUS, our King, to Whom is given all power in Heaven and in earth, Who rulest in all the kingdoms of the world, King of Kings, and Lord of Lords,

O JESUS, Whom blessed John saw in vision as Thou walkedst in the midst of the seven golden candlesticks, guiding and ruling the Churches of Thy Saints,

O JESUS, Who in the last great manifestation of Thyself wilt come to deliver Thy Church from the malice of her enemies, and to receive her unto Thyself for Thy Bride at the Marriage Supper of the Lamb,

O JESUS, Who in the prophetic revelation of

} *Have mercy upon Thy Holy Church.*

} *Have mercy upon Thy Holy Church.*

Litany for the Church

the Holy City, the New Jerusalem, hast comforted us with the prospect of the promised glories of the Church Triumphant,
} *Have mercy upon Thy Holy Church.*

BY Thine Ascension into Heaven, and enthronement at the Right Hand of GOD,

By Thine Almighty Intercession,

By Thy tender love, and multitude of Thy mercies,
} *Good LORD, deliver Thy Church.*

WE sinners do beseech Thee to hear us, O LORD JESUS, that as Thou hast promised to avenge Thine Own Elect, Thou wilt mercifully hear us when we call upon Thee,

That Thou wouldest pour down plenteously Thy HOLY GHOST upon Thy Church,

That Thou wouldest quicken the whole Body of Thy Church by the power of Thy HOLY GHOST, leading all unto fuller knowledge of the truth and more perfect holiness of life,

That Thou wouldest especially endue the clergy with the spirit of power and love and of a sound mind, and wouldest give them more abundantly the graces of courage and faithfulness and of fervent zeal,

That Thou wouldest inspire all the Ministers of Thy Word and Sacraments with a true knowledge and love of Thee and of Thy truth, an earnest desire of unity both in faith and discipline, and a devoted zeal for the propagation of the Gospel,

That Thou wouldest vouchsafe unto all Thy people a right apprehension of Christian truth, and a brotherly love and affection one toward another,

That Thou wouldest take away all hatred and prejudice, and whatsoever else doth hinder us from godly union and concord; and wouldest teach us all to love the truth and peace,

That as in all controversies concerning the faith Thou hast in the end made Thy truth
} *We beseech Thee, Good LORD.*

to triumph, so Thou wouldest bring all present controversies to like happy issue, for the glory of Thy Name,

That Thou wouldest continually raise up mighty teachers in Thy Church, that the false doctrine of heretics and unbelievers may be confuted, and their hearts brought back to Thee, to the establishment of Thy truth, and the salvation of their souls,

That Thou wouldest evermore give unto us all the spirit of perfect charity and love in all our strivings for the faith, that we may so contend only through sincere desire for Thy glory, and out of love for the souls of men,

That Thou wouldest give unto all Christians, especially in this land, a right understanding and a reverent estimation of the grace of the Apostolic Ministry, and of the blessed efficacy of Thy Sacraments,

That Thou wouldest bring back all separatists to the One Communion of Thy Holy Church, that we may glorify Thee with one mind and one mouth, and Thy united Church may be the more strengthened for her work of converting the world,

That Thou wouldest richly bless the divided portions of Catholic Christendom, and removing all hindrances to a perfect reunion, enable them to serve Thee as at the beginning with one mind and one heart,

That Thou wouldest preserve the Church, more especially in this land, from the power of the world, granting to her inward union and peace, and liberty to fulfil her mission to the glory of Thy Name,

That Thou wouldest increase the number of her Ministers, and enlarge in them the gifts of sanctity and spiritual knowledge, and stir up all her children to love and to good works,

That Thou wouldest help her speedily to set in order the things that

We beseech Thee, Good LORD.

We beseech Thee, Good LORD.

are wanting, and, removing all hindrances, wouldest enable her to bring this great nation to the acknowledgment and love of Thy truth,

That Thou wouldest vouchsafe unto her the long-desired restoration of her godly discipline, and the rightful freedom of her governing and deliberative councils,

That Thou wouldest especially bless her endeavours for the propagation of the Gospel among the heathen and the unconverted,

That Thou wouldest so guide and prepare her by the gifts of Thy grace, that she may do whatever in her lies towards her reunion with the rest of Thy Holy Church throughout the world,

} *We beseech Thee, Good LORD.*

O LAMB of GOD, that takest away the sins of the world,
Have mercy upon Thy Holy Church.

O Lamb of GOD, that takest away the sins of the world,
Deliver us out of all our troubles.

O Lamb of GOD, that takest away the sins of the world,
Let us not be confounded, for our trust is in Thee.

O JESUS, hear us,
O JESUS, graciously hear us.

LORD, have mercy upon us.
CHRIST, have mercy upon us.
LORD, have mercy upon us.

OUR FATHER.

℣ Hearken unto our voice, O LORD, when we cry unto Thee,
℟ *Have mercy upon us and hear us.*
℣ Show Thy servants the light of Thy countenance,
℟ *And save us for Thy mercy's sake.*
℣ Forsake us not, O LORD, our GOD,
℟ *Be not Thou far from us.*
℣ O LORD, arise and help us,
℟ *Awake, and be not absent from us for ever.*

℣ O be Thou our help in trouble,
℟ *For vain is the help of man.*

℣ Arise, O GOD, maintain Thine Own cause,
℟ *And forget not the congregation of the poor for ever.*

℣ Help us, O GOD of our salvation, for the glory of Thy Name,
℟ *O deliver us, and be merciful unto our sins, for Thy Name's sake.*

℣ Turn Thee again, O LORD, at the last,
℟ *And be gracious unto Thy servants.*

℣ Let Thy priests be clothed with righteousness,
℟ *And let Thy Saints sing with joyfulness.*

℣ O LORD, hear our prayer,
℟ *And let our crying come unto Thee.*

Let us pray.

ALMIGHTY and Everlasting GOD, Who in CHRIST hast manifested forth Thy glory unto all nations: preserve that which Thy mercy has wrought, and grant that Thy Church, being spread throughout the world, may persevere with steadfast faith in the confession of Thy Name, through the Same Thy SON JESUS CHRIST our LORD. Amen.

Meditation

OR

MENTAL PRAYER.

THERE are two sorts of Prayer Mental and Vocal. The first is called Meditation, which may be defined to be a conversation or intercourse of the mind and heart with GOD. Vocal Prayer may be defined to be the use of words to make our requests known to GOD, Meditation may also be viewed as the application of the three powers of the soul to religious truth, for when the memory has recalled a revealed truth, and the understanding seeks to penetrate it, and the will to submit, cling to, and love the same, then we may be said to be engaged in meditation. It may be divided into four parts : 1. The Preparation. 2. The Considerations, or Exercise of the Understanding. 3. The Affections and Resolutions, or Exercise of the Will. 4. The Conclusion.

THE PREPARATION.

THIS is of two sorts, the one Habitual, the other Immediate.

I. The Habitual Preparation consists in ;

(*a.*) Purifying one's self from all sin, at least from all deadly sin.

(*b.*) Keeping the mind as free and detached as possible from all worldly and dissipating thoughts.

(*c.*) Having always some good end in view, such as to glorify GOD, to praise Him, to thank Him ; to get rid of our defects, to animate and encourage ourselves in the service of GOD ; to overcome weariness, distaste to our duty, and other temptations which may assault us; to love GOD better, to acquire the graces we stand in need of, etc.

II. The Immediate Preparation consists in ;
- (*a.*) Choosing a particular time, which should, if possible, be not too soon after a meal for fear of weariness and injury to our health. The early part of the day is generally the best.
- (*b.*) Reading over the subject of the meditation and dividing it into two or three parts: which may be done the night before; and determining on the subject of the meditation, its purpose, the affections which we wish to cherish, and the habit of life we wish to form.
- (*c.*) Kneeling or prostrating one's self at the commencement and conclusion of the meditation; during the meditation, the posture of either sitting, standing, kneeling, or walking may be chosen, as may best ensure the ease and freedom of mind which is so desirable in meditating.

The following are Four Methods of practising recollection, or applying all the powers of our mind, the imagination, understanding, memory, and will to the work we have in hand.

1. Reflect on the Omnipresence of GOD. "O my Soul of a truth GOD is here," or think of Him, intimately present within you, sustaining and quickening your soul. "In Him, we live, and move, and have our being," or :
2. Think of the SON of GOD, in His Human Nature, looking from His throne upon the children of men, especially watching Christians who are His Own elect, and above all those who are engaged in prayer. Remember that this is no mere imagination, but a simple fact, for though we see Him not, as S. Stephen did, His eyes are fixed on us : or, think of Him as present in the room in which you are, as though He were before you.
3. Call upon GOD. Knowing that as you are in the presence of GOD you should be penetrated with awe and veneration, and remember that you are absolutely unworthy to be in His sacred presence. But know-

ing that GOD wills it, ask of Him grace to glorify Him in your meditation. Say, "Cast me not away from Thy presence, take not Thy HOLY SPIRIT from me," or something of the kind. Then say the "Veni Creator."

4. Place the mystery on which you intend to meditate clearly before the mind by the exercise of your imagination. For instance, if you are going to meditate on the Death of our LORD, picture to yourself all the surrounding circumstances; the various persons, what they say or do, and the Form of our LORD on the Cross; contemplate and study this scene diligently and attentively.

THE CONSIDERATIONS.

APPLY your understanding to such considerations as are calculated to move the will towards GOD, for whilst mere knowledge is the end of ordinary study, the love of GOD and the practice of virtue is the end of meditation. Consider then the subject with all your mind, and if you find that any one point of it supplies you with sufficient material, stop and pause on it. But if you do not seem to derive profit from one point, pass on to another, only without impatience and haste.

THE AFFECTIONS AND RESOLUTIONS.

THEN let your affections fasten on the particular mystery or truth, until you are resolved to act upon its teaching. Speak to our LORD in the simple language of your heart. Do not let your resolutions be merely general; for instance, the First Word of our LORD on the Cross will produce in your soul the desire to imitate Him, by pardoning those who have offended you; but do not rest content with this general desire; go on to make a particular resolution. "I will forgive those unkind words which I have to suffer from this or that person, I will overlook this or that slight, I will say such and such a thing to sweeten his or her temper, or engage his or her heart."

THE CONCLUSION.

1. THANK God for His mercy in allowing you to come into His presence, in spite of your extreme unworthiness, and in visiting you with good thoughts and affections, and enabling you to form good resolutions.

2. Offer Him all the glory which can accrue to Him from this His mercy: and present to Him yourself together with your resolutions and affections, in union with all the virtues of His Son, and the merits of His Death.

3. Pray for grace to fulfil the resolutions you have made.

4. Take with you one or two thoughts which have impressed themselves upon you in your meditation, to be with you during the rest of the day.

A Meditation on Our Sins.

Considerations.

1. CONSIDER how early you began to sin, how you have multiplied your sins from day to day, against God, yourself, and your neighbour, by thought, word, deed.

2. Consider your evil inclinations and the eagerness you have shown in following them; these two sights will convince you that your sins are more in number than the hairs of your head, or the sand of the sea.

3. Lay great stress on your ingratitude towards God, for that is a sin which spreads itself over all the others, and infinitely increases their enormity; count up, if you can, all the blessings received from Him, which your malice has turned against Him to His dishonour, all the inspirations you have slighted, all the blessed movements of grace you have rendered useless, and all your ill use and abuse of the Sacraments. Where are the fruits for which God looks? What has become of all those goods with which your Heavenly Spouse endowed your soul? all spoilt and profaned by your iniquities! Think how your ingratitude has amounted even to this, that while God has always followed you step

by step to save you, you have been always flying before Him to lose yourself.

Affections.

1. BE confounded at the sight of your misery : wonder at your deplorable state, say "Not a sense which my wickedness has not misused ! not a power of my soul which my sins have not profaned and corrupted ! not a day of my life passed without producing some evil results ! Is this the fruit of the blessings I have received from my Maker, this the price of the Blood of my Redeemer ?"

2. Ask pardon for your sins, and cast yourself at the feet of your SAVIOUR, as the prodigal son at the feet of his Father, as S. Mary Magdalene at the feet of her SAVIOUR, as the adulteress at the feet of JESUS her Judge, say, " O LORD, pity this sinful soul ! O divine Heart of JESUS ! Source of compassion and bounty, pity my misery."

Resolutions.

1. RESOLVE to live better. O my LORD, I will never give myself up to sin, I detest it with all my heart ; I cling to Thee, O FATHER of mercies. I will live and die in Thee. I will confess my sins, and ask for absolution with humility and a contrite heart, without any reserve or dissimulation. I will do all I can to root them out, particularly . . . . , I will adopt all means recommended to me and never think that I have done enough to repair such grievous faults.

Conclusion.

1. CONCLUDE by thanking GOD for waiting for your conversion until now, and for giving you these good dispositions.
2. Offer Him your resolutions to serve Him strictly.
3. Ask Him to give you His grace and power to fulfil them.

ADVICE AS TO MAKING RESOLUTIONS.

1. IT is better not to form too many at once, but rather make one only which shall remain engraven on the heart.

2. Things which are easy must precede those which are difficult: "He that is faithful in that which is least, is faithful also in much."

3. The resolution should take effect at once. There should be something done on the very day of meditation, as a consequence of the meditation. Even if the resolution have reference to some future emergency which we foresee, we should not merely let it wait, lest it be forgotten; we must keep it steadfastly in mind.

4. We must avoid resolutions which are dependent upon improbable contingencies. Do not resolve to do this or that, with wealth or other opportunities of action which you do not possess.

5. Our resolution must not only be possible for us under actual circumstances, but it must be consistent with our actual duty. We cannot properly resolve to serve GOD in any way that does not suit with the calling which GOD has given us.

Prayer before Meditation.

O MY GOD, I come into Thy presence, do Thou teach me. My sins are more in number than the hairs of my head, yet do Thou show me the light of Thy countenance and I shall be whole. I adore Thee, O my GOD; Thou art the Truth, and to know Thee is life eternal, accept this my meditation, and grant that my secret thoughts may be acceptable to Thee in the presence of the whole company of Heaven, that Thou mayest be glorified in my prayer. I surrender myself to Thy holy will, grant me patience to persevere in prayer, notwithstanding the dryness and desolation I may find therein. Give me Thy grace that I may use all the powers of my mind for Thy glory. I can do nothing of myself, O LORD; yet teach me by Thy HOLY SPIRIT to pray to Thee as I ought. Show me what Thou wilt have me to do. Dispose of me, and of all that is mine according to Thy good pleasure, and give me Thy grace that I may love Thee with all my heart, and at length attain to a happy death; through JESUS CHRIST our LORD. Amen.

Devotions for Occasional Offices.

HOLY BAPTISM.

A Thanksgiving.

BLESSED art Thou, O GOD of mercy, Who hast vouchsafed to bestow on me the purification of Thy Holy Baptism, the gift of Thy regeneration, the inheritance of Thy chosen ones. I thank Thee, O Loving FATHER, that I am indeed Thy child, able to cry, Abba, Father. I thank Thee, O most Loving SAVIOUR JESUS CHRIST, that Thou hast made me a member of Thy Sacred Body, to be ever united in closest bonds unto Thyself, to receive of Thy grace and fulness. I thank Thee, O most Loving SPIRIT, that Thou hast regenerated me with Thy Own life, that Thou hast sanctified my soul and my body for Thine Own abode. May these Thy tender mercies constrain me to live henceforth unto Him Who died for me and rose again; to glorify Thee in my body and in my spirit, which are Thine. Amen.

Renewal of Baptismal Vow.

MOST HOLY TRINITY, FATHER, SON, and HOLY GHOST, One GOD, I mourn and lament my most sinful neglect of the sacred promise and vow which was made in my name at my Baptism. I lament my long continued transgressions, my ingratitude, my coldness and hardness of heart. O LORD, Who art the great Searcher of Hearts, and from Whom no secrets are hid, in Thy presence I do most freely, fully, and unfeignedly, from henceforth and for evermore, repent of and renounce all my sins; I resolve to the utmost of the power Thou givest me, to resist all the temptations of the Devil, the World, and the Flesh, so that I may never willingly follow nor be led by them. I do steadfastly believe, and will, by Thy help, continue in the belief of all the Articles of the Christian Faith; and I am resolved, in all sincerity of heart, through the help of Thy grace, to keep Thy holy Will and Commandments, and to persevere, walking in the same all the days of my life. Enlighten and strengthen me, O GOD, by Thy HOLY SPIRIT, to perform this my vow and covenant unto the end. Preserve me as a living and faithful Member of CHRIST, a dutiful and dear Child of GOD, and an Heir of the Kingdom of Heaven; that through Thy mercy I may in Thy good time obtain the end of my faith, even the salvation of my soul. Amen.

For a Child Unbaptized.

O LORD JESUS CHRIST, Who hadst compassion upon little children, taking them up in Thine arms, and blessing them; bless the Child now born into the world, grant that it may be brought unto Thee in the Laver of Regeneration, to be born again in Thee and to be numbered among Thy people, Who livest and reignest with the FATHER and the HOLY SPIRIT, One GOD, world without end. Amen.

For One lately Baptized.

O LORD our GOD, our true Life, Who by the font of Baptism dost illuminate the baptized with heavenly radiance, Who hast vouchsafed to Thy servant by Water and the SPIRIT, remission of *his* sins, voluntary and involuntary; lay Thy mighty hand upon *him*, and protect *him* with the power of Thy goodness; preserve *him* from losing the earnest of glory; be pleased to bring *him* to eternal life and to Thy good pleasure; for Thou art our Sanctification, and to Thee we render praise and thanksgiving, FATHER, SON, and HOLY GHOST, now and ever, and unto ages of ages. Amen.

CONFIRMATION.

On Anniversary of Confirmation.

THANKS be unto Thee, O my GOD, for all Thy infinite goodness, and especially for that love that Thou hast shewed unto me at my Confirmation. I give Thee thanks that Thou didst then send down Thy HOLY SPIRIT into my soul with all His gifts and graces. O may He take full possession of me for ever: may His divine Unction cause my face to shine: may His heavenly Wisdom reign in my heart, His Understanding enlighten my darkness, His Counsel guide me, His Ghostly Strength fortify me, His Knowledge instruct me, His True Godliness make me fervent, His divine Fear keep me from all evil. Drive from my soul, O LORD, all that may defile it. Give me grace to be Thy faithful soldier, that having fought the good fight of faith, I may be brought to the crown of everlasting life, for the merits of Thy dearly Beloved SON, our SAVIOUR, JESUS CHRIST. Amen.

Prayer for the Fruits of the Spirit.

O ETERNAL FATHER, Who hast sent Thy Blessed SPIRIT to abide in me, to form me after the likeness of Thy dear SON in all purity and goodness; help me, I beseech Thee, to bring forth in my life those fruits of the SPIRIT which belong to Thy true children; the Fruit of Love, that I may love Thee above all things, and all others in Thee and for Thy sake; the Fruit of Joy, that I may find Thy service my delight; the Fruit of Peace, that, pardoned and accepted through Thy mercy, I may repose in Thy love; the Fruit of Long-Suffering, that I may bear with patient submission to Thy will all crosses and afflictions; the Fruit of Gentleness, that I may subdue all risings of temper, and take calmly and sweetly all trials and provocations; the Fruit of Meekness, that I may forgive freely all who may hurt me either by word or deed, and endure with patience all that may be laid upon me; the Fruit of

Temperance and Chastity, that I may restrain all my desires and keep under my body, bringing it into subjection in all things to Thy holy will. And grant, O Gracious FATHER, that thus striving to please Thee here on earth, I may be found meet to behold the glorious Vision of Thee hereafter; through the merits of Thy dearly Beloved SON JESUS CHRIST our LORD. Amen.

This Prayer, with slight alterations, may be used on behalf of those who have been lately Confirmed.

For One about to be Confirmed.

ALMIGHTY and Eternal GOD, Who hast vouchsafed to regenerate Thy Servant in Holy Baptism by water and the HOLY GHOST, perfect the work Thou hast begun in him. Strengthen him with Thy sevenfold gifts, the Spirit of Wisdom, that he may despise the perishable things of this world, and love the things that are eternal; the Spirit of Understanding to enlighten him and give him a more perfect knowledge of the mysteries of the Faith; the Spirit of Counsel, that he may make a right choice in things belonging to his eternal salvation; the Spirit of Ghostly Strength, that he may overcome all temptations; the Spirit of Knowledge, that he may know Thy will; the Spirit of true Godliness, that he may be faithful and devout in Thy service; and the Spirit of Holy Fear, that he may be filled with a loving reverence, and may fear in any way to displease Thee. Seal him through Thy mercy with the Seal of a disciple of JESUS CHRIST unto life eternal; and grant, O LORD, that bearing the Cross on his forehead, he may bear it also in his heart, so that boldly confessing Thee before men, he may be found worthy to be one day reckoned in the number of Thine Elect: through JESUS CHRIST our LORD. Amen.

HOLY MATRIMONY.

A Husband's Prayer.

O GRACIOUS FATHER, Maker and Preserver of Heaven and earth, Who in the beginning didst institute matrimony, thereby foretelling the mystical union of the Church with our SAVIOUR CHRIST, Who, in the time of His ministry upon earth did honour marriage with His first miracle; enable me, I pray Thee, by Thy grace to live in holiness and purity with the wife whom Thou hast given me. Mortify in me all violence of earthly passion, all selfishness and inconsiderateness (*here name any besetting sin which may be a hindrance to you*), that I may love her as CHRIST loved His Church, cherish and comfort her as mine own body, and have as great care of her happiness as of mine own. Grant that we may live in peace, without debate; in unity, without discord. (Give us, O LORD, discreet hearts and understanding minds, to bring up our children in Thy faith and fear, that they may be obedient to Thee and to Thy commandments and to all that Thou requirest of them in duty towards their parents.) And give us, O LORD, a competency of estate, to maintain ourselves and our family, according to that rank and calling wherein Thou hast placed us, without excess or vainglory, in singleness and pureness of heart. Grant this, for JESUS CHRIST'S sake; to Whom with Thee, and the HOLY GHOST, be all honour and glory, now and for ever. Amen.

A Wife's Prayer.

O MERCIFUL LORD GOD, Who in the beginning didst take Eve out of the side of Adam, and give her to him as a helper; give me grace to live worthy of the honourable estate of matrimony to which Thou hast called me, that I may love my Husband with a pure and chaste love, acknowledging him as my head, and truly reverencing and obeying him in all good things: that thereby I may please him, and live with him in all Christian quietness.

Keep me from all worldliness and vanity. Help me, O LORD, that I may, under him, prudently and discreetly guide and govern his household. Let no fault of mine aggravate the sins by which he is especially tempted; enable me to soothe him in perplexity, to cheer him in difficulty, to refresh him in weariness, and, as far as may be, to advise him in doubt. (Give me understanding so to fulfil my part in the education of our children, that they may be our joy in this world and our glory in the next.) Grant that our perfect union here may be the beginning of the still more perfect and blissful union hereafter in Thy Kingdom; and this I pray, through JESUS CHRIST our LORD. Amen.

Prayer for a Husband and Wife.

O MERCIFUL GOD, we humbly beseech Thee to send Thy blessing continually upon us, and to make us thankful for all that Thou hast already vouchsafed unto us, and as Thou hast made us one in the mystical grace of Matrimony, grant that we may be also inwardly of one heart and of one mind, paying due honour one to another, united in love to Thee and to each other in Thee: living together in peace, and holiness, as faithful members of Thy Church, denying ourselves, and being a mutual help, comfort, and support to each other, all the days of our life. (Give us grace to train our children in Thy faith and fear.) Bless us with health and strength, if it be Thy will; and with whatever else Thy good Providence shall see to be best for our souls and bodies. Fit and prepare us day by day for our departure hence, that we may together inherit eternal life in Thy Heavenly Kingdom; for the merits of JESUS CHRIST our LORD and SAVIOUR. Amen.

A Parent's Prayer.

ALMIGHTY GOD, the Father and Maker of us all, Who of Thy blessing and goodness hast vouchsafed to make me a Father (or Mother) of children; be pleased to accept my hearty thanksgiving and devout praise for the same: grant me Thy heavenly grace and assistance so to train them up in Thy faith, fear, and love, that as they advance in years they may grow in grace, and may hereafter be found in the number of Thine elect children; through JESUS CHRIST our LORD. Amen.

Grant unto those who are grown to man's estate that they may be cleansed from whatever of evil they may have contracted in the world, and may live as befits Thy children; through JESUS CHRIST our LORD. Amen.

Prayer for One about to be Married.

O GRACIOUS FATHER, Who dost bless us by Thy bounty, pardon us by Thy mercy, support and guide us by Thy grace, and govern us by Thy Providence. I give Thee humble and hearty thanks for all the mercies which I have received at Thy hands in time past. And now since Thou hast called me to the holy estate of marriage be pleased to be with me in my entering into it and passing through it, that it may not be a state of temptation or sorrow to me by occasion of my sins or infirmities, but of holiness and comfort, of love and dutifulness, as Thou hast intended it to be to all that love and fear Thy holy Name. Amen.

For Fruitfulness.

O MOST Gracious and Eternal GOD, FATHER and LORD of all, Who didst sanctify marriage in the state of innocence, be pleased to look upon me, Thy handmaid, who waits for Thy mercy, and humbly begs of Thy infinite goodness, to be made a partaker of that blessing which Thou didst design to the sons and daughters of Adam. Thou, O GOD, art the LORD and Giver of life; Thine are the blessings of the breasts and of the womb. . O make me, if it please Thee, a joyful mother of children, that I may serve Thee in increasing the number of Thy redeemed ones; minister blessings to this family into which Thou hast adopted me, and bring comfort to my dear husband. But if, O Gracious LORD, Thou willest not to grant me my desire, be Thou to me more than all Thy gifts, give me the grace to know and feel that Thy will is best, and fill me with Thy Own divine consolations, that

I may love Thee and wholly trust in Thee; through JESUS CHRIST our LORD. Amen.

Prayer for a Woman with Child.

ALMIGHTY GOD, the FATHER of all mercy and comfort, of Whose only gift it is, that the womb becometh fruitful; graciously behold me, Thine humble and unworthy Handmaid; that as by Thy good providence I have conceived a child within my womb into which Thou hast breathed the breath of life, so, by Thy continual aid, I may be preserved with it from all perils; and at the fulness of my time may safely bring it forth into the world, to my great joy and comfort, and to the glory of Thy holy Name, through JESUS CHRIST our LORD. Amen.

Prayer when the Time of Travail approaches.

MERCIFUL LORD, Who, when Thou tookest upon Thee to deliver man, didst not abhor the Virgin's womb, but when the fulness of time was come, wast Thyself made of a woman; I beseech Thee, of Thy tender pity and goodness, to protect and strengthen me against all the dangers and pains of my labour and travail; that, through Thy most mighty aid I may be safely delivered. Vouchsafe, O LORD, that when the Child is born into the world, it may be born again by Baptism, and being brought up in the Catholic Faith, may be finally received into Thine everlasting Kingdom, where with the FATHER and the HOLY GHOST, Thou livest and reignest, ever One GOD, world without end. Amen.

Ejaculations in the Time of Travail.

SAVE me, O GOD, for the waters are come in, even unto my soul.

Save LORD, and hear me, O King of Heaven, when I call upon Thee.

Be not Thou far from me, O LORD; Thou art my Succour, haste Thee to help me.

Look upon my adversity and misery, and forgive me all my sin.

O hide not Thou Thy Face from me; nor cast Thy Servant away in displeasure.

Thou hast been my Succour, leave me not, neither forsake me, O GOD of my salvation.

Thou art my Helper and Redeemer, make no long tarrying, O my GOD.

O be Thou my Help in trouble; for vain is the help of man.

O LORD, let it be Thy pleasure to deliver me; make haste, O LORD, to help me.

I will wash my hands in innocency, O LORD: and so will I go to Thine Altar; That I may shew the voice of thanksgiving: and tell of all Thy wondrous works.

Prayer to be used by a Husband or a Friend.

O BLESSED JESUS, Who didst not abhor the Virgin's womb, but took upon Thee the form of a servant, and was made in the likeness of men; look graciously upon Thy Servant, and be merciful unto her, as Thou art wont to be unto all those who fear Thy Name. Be present with her in her trial, be Thou her helper and deliverer now that her soul is troubled, and her pains take hold upon her. Be pleased to support her and comfort her in all her trial with the consolation of Thy HOLY SPIRIT, until, in Thy good time, Thou turn her heaviness into thanksgiving and her mourning into joy. O Thou that formest Thine Image in the womb, we most humbly beseech Thee give Thy servant strength to bring forth, and let her live to rejoice in the fruit of her womb. Bestow upon her, O Good LORD, patience to await her appointed time, and assist her with Thy most merciful aid and protection in all her necessity; for Thy most tender mercy's sake. Amen.

Thanksgiving after Childbirth.

GRACIOUS GOD, by Whose providence we are all fearfully and wonderfully made, Who beholdest us when we are yet imperfect, and in Whose book are all our members written; I humbly beseech Thee to accept this my acknowledgment of Thy power, and to receive this my most hearty praise and thanksgiving, which I now offer to Thy divine Majesty, for Thy favour and goodness towards me. Behold, O LORD, what Thine Own hands have fashioned; and grant that this infant, which Thou hast made by Thy power, may be preserved by Thy goodness, and forthwith enjoying the benefit of Thy Holy Baptism, may be made a lively member of Thy Church, and be carefully brought up to serve Thee in all godliness and honesty; through the merits of Thy Well-Beloved SON, JESUS CHRIST our LORD. Amen.

Prayer when the Child is Still-born.

O LORD JESU CHRIST, Who wast conceived by the HOLY GHOST, born of the Virgin Mary, and laid when an Infant in the manger, have mercy upon me Thy Servant, whom Thou hast been pleased to afflict with the loss of my offspring; grant me comfort in my sorrow, remission of all my sins, and restoration to bodily health; and vouchsafe that this affliction may work for me an exceeding and eternal weight of glory, through Thy loving-kindness. Who livest and reignest with the FATHER and the HOLY GHOST, ever One GOD, world without end. Amen.

DEVOTIONS FOR THE SICK.

RULES FOR A SICK PERSON.

1. *Receive your sickness from the hands of your Heavenly Father dealing with you as a Son.*
2. *Look on it as a loving correction for your sins, and as a summons to prepare more carefully for death.*
3. *Cultivate the virtues of patience and submission to the will of God; deepen your repentance and offer yourself to God to suffer, if it pleases Him, still greater trials; give thanks for the blessings you enjoy.*
4. *In any dangerous illness let your first care be to send for a Priest.*
5. *Engage your friends to give you timely notice if your illness be dangerous, and not to flatter you with false hopes of recovery.*
6. *Make the best use of the time you have: admit but few visitors, let your conversation be as little as may be of worldly matters.*
7. *Settle your temporal affairs in order to give yourself more entirely to spiritual matters.*
8. *Meditate often on our Lord's Passion.*
9. *Bear in mind S. Augustine's words, "However innocent your life may have been, no Christian ought to venture to die in any other state than that of a penitent."*

PRAYER IN THE BEGINNING OF SICKNESS.

O HEAVENLY FATHER, Who in Thy wisdom knowest what is best for me, glory be to Thee. LORD, if it seem good in Thy sight, remove from me this sickness which I now feel seizing upon me, that I may employ my health to Thy glory, and praise Thy Name. But if Thou art pleased it should grow on me, I willingly submit to Thy afflicting hand, for Thou art wont to chasten those whom Thou dost love, and Thou hast promised not to lay on me any more than Thou wilt enable me to bear. I know, O my GOD, that Thou sendest this sickness on me for my good, even to humble and to prove me; O grant that it may not fail to work that saving effect in me. O LORD, create in me a true penitent sorrow for all my past sins, a steadfast faith in Thee, and sincere resolutions of amendment for the time to come. Deliver me from all forwardness and impatience, and give me an entire resignation to Thy divine will: O suffer not my sickness to take away my senses, and do Thou continually supply my thoughts with holy ejaculations. LORD, bless all the means that are used for my recovery, and restore me to my health, if it be Thy will, in Thy good time; but if Thou hast appointed otherwise for me, Thy blessed will be done. O wean my affections from all things below, and fill me with ardent desires after Heaven: LORD, fit me for Thyself, and then call me, when Thou pleasest, to those joys unspeakable and full of glory, and all this for the sake of Thy Only SON JESUS CHRIST, my SAVIOUR, in Whose holy words I sum up all my wants.

OUR FATHER, Which art in Heaven, Hallowed be Thy Name: Thy Kingdom come: Thy Will be done in earth, as it is in Heaven: Give us this day our daily Bread: And forgive us our trespasses, as we forgive them that trespass against us: And lead us not into temptation: But deliver us from evil. Amen.

A DAILY PRAYER.

O ALMIGHTY GOD, behold I receive this sickness, with which Thou art pleased to visit me, as coming from Thy Fatherly hand. It is Thy will that it should be thus with me. Thy will be done in earth, as it is in Heaven. May this sickness be to the honour of Thy holy Name, and for the good of my soul. For these ends I here offer myself to Thee with entire submission; to suffer what Thou pleasest, as long as Thou pleasest, and in what manner Thou pleasest: for I am Thy creature, and Thy child, who have most ungratefully offended Thee. I have truly deserved Thy chastisement, and far more than Thou layest on me, but, O LORD, rebuke me not in Thine indignation, neither chasten me in Thy heavy displeasure. Look upon my weakness, and be merciful unto me, for Thou knowest whereof I am made, Thou rememberest that I am but dust; deal not with me therefore after my sins, nor reward me according to my iniquities; but according to the multitude of Thy tender mercies have compassion upon me. Assist me, I pray Thee, with Thy heavenly grace, and give me strength, that I may be able to bear with Christian patience all the pains, uneasiness, and trials of my sickness. Preserve me from all temptations so far as Thou seest fit, and be Thou my defence against all the assaults of the enemy that I may in nowise offend Thee; and if it be Thy will that this sickness should be my last, I beg of Thee so to direct me by Thy grace, that I may in no way neglect, or be deprived of those helps which Thou hast ordained for the good of my soul, to prepare it for its passage into eternity; so that, being cleansed from all my sins, I may put my whole trust in Thee, and love Thee above all things; and that finally, of the abundance of Thy mercy and loving kindness, I may be admitted into the company of the Blessed, there to praise Thee for ever, through JESUS CHRIST our LORD. Amen.

ACTS OF MOST NECESSARY VIRTUES FOR THE SICK.

Act of Resignation.

LORD, I accept this sickness from Thy Fatherly Hands; I entirely resign myself to Thy blessed will, whether it be for life or death. Not my will, but Thine be done; Thy will be done in earth, as it is in Heaven.

Act of Submission.

LORD, I submit to all the pains and uneasiness of this my illness: my sins have deserved infinitely more. Thou art just, O LORD, and Thy judgment is right.

Act of Self-Oblation.

LORD, I offer up to Thee all that I now suffer, or may have to suffer to be united to the sufferings of my SAVIOUR, and to be sanctified by His Passion.

Act of Adoration.

I ADORE Thee, O my GOD and my All, as my First Beginning and my Last End; I desire to pay Thee the best homage that I am able, and to bow down all the powers of my soul to Thee.

Act of Praise.

LORD, I desire to praise Thee for ever, in sickness as well as in health; I desire to join my heart and voice with the whole Church of Heaven and Earth, in blessing Thee for ever.

Act of Thanksgiving.

I GIVE Thee thanks, O LORD, from the bottom of my heart, for all the mercies and blessings which Thou hast bestowed upon me and on Thy whole Church through JESUS CHRIST Thy SON; above all, because Thou hast loved me from all eternity, and hast sent Thy SON to redeem me with His precious Blood. O let not that Blood be shed for me in vain.

Act of Faith.

LORD, I believe all those heavenly truths

which Thou hast revealed, and which Thy Holy Catholic Church believes and teaches. Thou art the Sovereign Truth, Who neither canst deceive, nor be deceived. Thou hast promised Thy Spirit of Truth to guide Thy Church into all truth. In this Faith I resolve, through Thy grace, both to live and die. O LORD! strengthen and increase this my faith.

Act of Hope.

O MY GOD, all my hope is in Thee! Through JESUS CHRIST, my Redeemer, through His Passion and Death, I hope for mercy, grace, and salvation from Thee. In Thee, O LORD, have I put my trust: let me never be confounded. O Sweet JESU, receive me into Thy arms in this day of my distress; hide me in Thy Wounds, bathe my soul in Thy precious Blood.

Act of Love.

I LOVE Thee, O my GOD, with my whole heart and soul, above all things: at least I desire so to love Thee. O come now and take full possession of my soul, and teach me to love Thee for ever. I desire to be dissolved and to be with CHRIST. O when will Thy Kingdom come? O LORD, when wilt Thou perfectly reign in all hearts? When shall sin be no more?

Act of Love of One's Neighbour.

I DESIRE to love my neighbour with perfect charity for the love of Thee. I forgive from my heart all who have in any way offended or injured me, and I ask pardon of all whom I have in any way offended or injured.

Act of Contrition.

HAVE mercy upon me, O GOD, after Thy great goodness: according to the multitude of Thy mercies do away mine offences. Oh! who will give water to my head, and a fountain of tears to my eyes, that, night and day, I may bewail my sins! Oh! that I had never offended so good a GOD! Oh! that I had never sinned! Happy those souls that have always preserved their baptismal innocence! LORD, be merciful to me a sinner; Holy JESUS, SON of the Living GOD, have mercy upon me.

Act of Commendation to God.

I COMMEND my soul to GOD my Maker, Who created me from nothing; to JESUS CHRIST my SAVIOUR, Who redeemed me with His Blood; to the HOLY GHOST, Who sanctified me in Baptism. Into Thy hands, O LORD, I commend my spirit.

Act of Renunciation of Evil.

I RENOUNCE, from this moment, and for all eternity, the Devil and all his works. I abhor all his suggestions and temptations. Suffer not, O LORD, this mortal enemy of my soul to have any power over me, either now or at my last hour. Let Thy holy Angels ever keep me and defend me against all the powers of darkness.

PRAYER FOR PARDON.

O LORD JESUS CHRIST, in union with Thy sorrow, whereby Thou tookest upon Thyself the cause of my sorrow; and becamest Thyself a remedy for my sins, and together with all true penitents, I confess to Thee all my sins, the evil that I have done, the good that I have left undone, and what I have done carelessly, or without a pure intention, even as Thou knowest them in number, weight, and measure. O LORD, the deep of my misery calleth to the deep of Thy pity. Shut not up Thy loving-kindness in displeasure, and let not the fountain of Thine inexhaustible mercy be dried up by reason of my sins. O Thou Who hast mercy upon all, Who hatest nothing that Thou hast made, it is Thine to forgive; have pity on me now in the season of mercy and of grace; now, while the time of amendment lasts, grant to me to attain the glory of Thy blessing, that in the Day of Judgment Thy terrible curse smite me not. Let Thy full satisfaction for my sins, O LORD, Thy bitter death, the price of Thy Blood which was shed, the renewal of Thy satisfaction, the venerable Mystery of Thy Body, and Thy Blood, which is daily offered to Thee in Thy church for the salvation of the Faithful, be of avail now and in my last hour to obtain the grace here which I do not merit, and hereafter the eternal rest and glory which Thy most bitter Passion has won for me. O Thou, Who makest atonement for sin, grant that being cleansed from the filth of my sins, and enlightened to know Thee by the eye of faith; I may ever confess Thee, press towards Thee, and pant after Thee with the whole desire of my heart; and at length in death attain to Thee, O CHRIST JESU, Who livest and reignest with GOD the FATHER, in the Unity of the HOLY GHOST, world without end. Amen.

PRAYER FOR PATIENCE.

REMEMBER, O most Pitying FATHER, what this frail and feeble work of Thine hands can bear without fainting; nothing, indeed, of itself, but all things in Thee, if strengthened by Thy grace. Wherefore grant me strength, that I may suffer and endure; patience alone I ask. LORD give me this, and behold my heart is ready, O GOD, my heart is ready to receive whatsoever shall be laid upon me; may it even be a consolation to me, that afflicting me with pain, Thou sparest not here, that Thou mayest spare hereafter. Grant, O LORD, that in my patience I may possess my soul; to that end may I often look upon the Face of CHRIST Thy SON, that as He hath suffered such terrible things in the flesh, I may endeavour to be armed with the same mind. Wherefore I commit my strength unto Thee, O LORD; for Thou art my Strength and my Refuge; Thou dost uphold my life. Behold, O LORD, now am I in the midst of the fire, and how long I shall be there, Thou knowest. Keep me, Thou Who didst preserve unhurt the Three Children in the furnace at Babylon, and bring me forth safely out of this trial when it shall please Thee, as Thou didst deliver them, that I also may bless Thee with all Thy creatures for ever. Amen.

PRAYER IN SUFFERING.

O LORD JESUS CHRIST, accept my sufferings which I desire to unite with Thine. Sanctify this affliction, so that every pang I feel may purify my soul, and bring it nearer to Thee; to be made more one with Thee; grant that I may welcome the sufferings which will make me more like to Thee.

O my LORD, stand Thou by me, with Thy supporting grace; sanctify each pang, sustain my weakness. And then order for me what Thou pleasest. Come now to my help, O LORD, and so purify my soul, that I may be spared the last, the eternal suffering; let me fly to the embrace of Thy love for ever.

LORD JESUS, hast Thou not invited all that labour and are heavy laden, to come to Thee for refreshment? Behold now Thy servant, afflicted and oppressed, comes to Thee for help; relieve me, I beseech Thee, Thou Who art Infinite in mercy.

O Thou Who hast comforted the Martyrs in their torments, and refreshed them with heavenly sweetness on the rack and in the fire, renew Thy mercies to me Thy unworthy servant; defend me against all temptation, suffer not the enemy to take advantage of me, but grant me Thy heavenly strength, the fulness of Thy grace and peace. Amen.

Ejaculation.

O LORD, By Thy Cross and Passion strengthen me: LORD, let this cup pass from me; nevertheless, not my will but Thine be done.

THANKSGIVING ON ABATEMENT OF PAIN.

BLESSED be Thy mercy, O my GOD, Who pitiest me in my misery; as a father pitieth his children, so hast Thou pitied me. LORD, my soul shall love Thee, and sing of Thy mercy; in my distress I will always trust in Thee, and not be afraid, for Thou art our Strength whilst we suffer, and our merciful Deliverer when it seemeth fit to Thee to deliver us. To Thee be glory, through JESUS CHRIST our LORD. Amen.

PRAYER ON WANT OF SLEEP.

O LORD, Thou holdest mine eyes waking, and in the night season I take no rest. Consider, O Merciful GOD, my weariness, which calls aloud to Thee for rest; give rest to my wearied eyes, and make my sleep sweet unto me. While Thou keepest me awake let me commune with mine own heart, and search out my spirit; let me remember Thee on my bed, and meditate on Thee in the night watches; let the consideration of Thy tender mercies be my comfort, till Thy goodness sees fit to give sleep to my eyes and refreshment to my sorrows, through my dearest LORD and SAVIOUR JESUS CHRIST. Amen.

Litany for the Sick.

LORD, have mercy upon us.

CHRIST, *have mercy upon us.*

LORD, have mercy upon us.

O GOD the FATHER, of Heaven, } *Have*

O GOD the SON, Redeemer of the world,

O GOD the HOLY GHOST, the Comforter,

HOLY TRINITY, One GOD, } *mercy upon us.*

O GOD, Who in the beginning didst of Thy righteous

judgment make sickness, pain, and death to be the penalty of sin,

O GOD, Who in the midst of judgment rememberest mercy, and dost not afflict willingly nor grieve the children of men,

O GOD, Who hast graciously promised that though Thou causest grief, Thou wilt yet have compassion according to the multitude of Thy mercies,

O Heavenly FATHER, Who of Thy tender mercy dost assure us that Thou chastenest those whom Thou lovest, and scourgest those whom Thou dost receive for Thy children,

O GOD, Who as a most loving FATHER dost chasten us for our profit, that we may be partakers of Thy righteousness,

O Heavenly FATHER, Who teachest us in Thy Holy Word, that it is Thou that makest sore and bindest up, and that as Thou woundest so Thy hands make whole,

Have mercy upon us.

O Heavenly FATHER, Who dost encourage us in all our troubles to fly to Thee in prayer, and to cast all our care upon Thee Who carest for us,

O Thou, Who at the prayer of Moses didst heal Miriam of her leprosy,

O Thou, Who at the prayer of Elijah didst restore to life the widow's son,

O Thou, Who hadst mercy even on wicked Ahab when he humbled himself before Thee,

O Thou, Who at the prayer of Elisha didst restore to life the son of the Shunamite,

O Thou, Who didst hear the entreaty of Hezekiah, and didst prolong his days,

O Thou, Who in the example of Job hast taught us that if we be patient under affliction, Thou art very pitiful and of tender mercy,

FATHER of mercies and GOD of all comfort, Who comfortest us in all our tribulation,

Have mercy upon us.

BE merciful, spare us, O LORD,

BY Thy holy Incarnation,
By Thy sinless Birth,
By Thy lowly Childhood,
By Thy tender pity for the suffering,
By Thy compassion for the bereaved and afflicted,
By Thy Mission to heal the brokenhearted,
By Thine almighty all constraining Love,
By Thine Own pains and Sufferings,
} *Deliver us, O LORD.*

WE sinners beseech Thee to hear us.

THAT we may confess ourselves to be strangers and pilgrims upon the earth,
That our light affliction, which is but for a moment, may work in us an eternal weight of glory,
That we may not despise the chastening of the LORD, nor faint when we are rebuked of Him,
That we may take cheerfully whatsoever shall be brought upon us, and be patient under suffering.
That in all our diseases and afflictions we may say nothing foolishly against the LORD,
That as we have received good at the hand of the LORD, we may with an equal mind endure evil,
That in the multitude of the sorrows that I have in my heart and in my body, Thy comforts may refresh my soul,
That Thou wouldst vouchsafe to make and smooth all our bed in our sickness,
That diseases and all evils of the body may work together for good to us who love GOD,
That, whether we live, we may live unto the LORD, and whether we die, we may die unto the LORD,
That neither life, nor death, nor any other creature, may be able to separate us from CHRIST,
That to us to live may be CHRIST, and to die gain,
That though we walk
} *We beseech Thee to hear us, Good LORD.*

through the valley of the shadow of death, we may fear no evil, for Thou art with us,

That, being steadfast in the faith, we may in the last conflict resist the roaring lion,

That we may die the death of the righteous, and that our last end may be like his,

That Thou wouldest not deal with us after our sins, nor reward us according to our iniquities,

That we may dwell in the House of the LORD all the days of our life,

That when the earthly house of this Tabernacle is dissolved, we may have a house not made with hands, eternal in the Heavens,

} *We beseech Thee to hear us, Good LORD.*

O LAMB of GOD, Who takest away the sins of the world,
Have mercy upon us.

O LAMB of GOD, Who takest away the sins of the world,
Grant us Thy peace.

O CHRIST, hear us.
O CHRIST, graciously hear us.

LORD, have mercy upon us.
CHRIST, have mercy upon us.
LORD, have mercy upon us.

OUR FATHER.

Let us pray.

O GOD, Who by the patience of Thine Only-Begotten SON, didst crush the pride of the ancient enemy, grant to us, we beseech Thee, worthily to commemorate those things which He suffered for us, and, after His example, patiently to endure all adversity; through the Same JESUS CHRIST our LORD. Amen.

PRAYERS ON THE PASSION.
FOR DELIVERANCE IN THE HOUR OF DEATH.

I.

LORD have mercy upon us.
CHRIST have mercy upon us.
LORD have mercy upon us.
O LORD JESU CHRIST, by

Thine Agony and most holy Prayer in the Garden, when Thy Sweat was as it were great drops of blood falling down to the ground, vouchsafe to offer to Thy FATHER, for my sins, those numberless drops of Blood which Thy exceeding sorrow wrung from Thy sacred Body, and deliver me in the hour of my death from all the pain and anguish which I have most justly deserved by reason of my sins, Who with the FATHER and the HOLY GHOST livest and reignest, One GOD, world without end. Amen.

Our FATHER.

O SAVIOUR of the world, Who by Thy Cross and precious Blood hast redeemed us, save us, and help us we humbly beseech Thee, O LORD.

II.

LORD have mercy upon us.

CHRIST have mercy upon us.

LORD have mercy upon us.

O LORD JESU CHRIST, Who for the salvation of the world, didst die upon the Cross, vouchsafe to offer to Thy FATHER, for my sinful soul, all the bitter pangs of Thy Passion which Thou didst endure upon the Cross, especially in that hour when Thy most holy Soul departed from Thy sacred Body, and deliver me in the hour of my death from all the pangs and torments which I have most justly deserved by reason of my sins, Who with the FATHER and the HOLY GHOST livest and reignest, One GOD, world without end. Amen.

Our FATHER.

O SAVIOUR of the world.

III.

LORD have mercy upon us.

CHRIST have mercy upon us.

LORD have mercy upon us.

O LORD JESU CHRIST, Who by the mouth of Thy holy Prophet hast said, "I have loved Thee with an everlasting love, therefore with loving-kindness have I drawn Thee," vouchsafe to offer to Thy FATHER, for my sinful soul, all that same love which drew Thee down from Heaven to bear all our woes and sorrows; and deliver me, in the hour of my death, from all the pains and sufferings which I have most justly deserved by reason of my sins. Open to me, O LORD, the gate of Life, and make me to rejoice with Thy Saints in glory, Who with the FATHER and the HOLY GHOST livest and reignest, One GOD, world without end. Amen.

Our FATHER.

O SAVIOUR of the world.

IV.

O LORD JESUS CHRIST, Who hast redeemed us with Thy precious Blood, imprint the marks of Thy Wounds upon my soul, that I may learn from them Thy sorrow and Thy love; Thy sorrow for all the pains and sorrows which I confess that I have deserved by reason of my sins; Thy love, that I may be joined unto Thee with an inviolable love, and not be parted from Thee and Thine Elect for ever.

Grant me, O LORD JESU CHRIST, a share in Thy most sacred Incarnation, Thy most holy Life, Thy most bitter Passion, Thy most glorious Resurrection and Ascension.

Grant me, O LORD, a share in Thy most sacred Mysteries and Sacraments.

Grant me, O LORD, a share in all the prayers and sacrifices which are offered in Thy Holy Church.

Grant me, O LORD, a blessed portion with all Thy Saints who from the beginning of the world have pleased Thee in their several generations; and that I may rejoice with them in Thy sight for ever. Amen.

EXERCISE IN PREPARATION FOR DEATH.

MY heart is ready, O GOD, my heart is ready; not my will, but Thine be done. O my LORD, I resign myself entirely to Thee, to meet my death at the time and in the manner that shall please Thee.

I most humbly ask pardon of Thee for all the sins that I have committed against Thy Sovereign Goodness, my neighbour, and myself, by omission or commission, in thought or word, mortal or venial, and I repent of them all from the very bottom of my heart.

I firmly believe whatsoever the Holy Catholic Church believes and teaches; and by Thy grace I will die in this Faith.

I hope of Thine infinite

mercy to inherit eternal life, by the merits of my SAVIOUR JESUS CHRIST.

I desire to love Thee above all things, O my GOD, my chief Good.

I desire, for the love of Thee, O GOD, to love my neighbour as myself, and to forgive from my heart all the injuries that have been done to me.

I most humbly ask pardon of all whom I have in any way offended, knowingly or ignorantly, in word or in deed; I protest that I am most ready to make amends to them so far as I am able, and I earnestly pray, if I have hurt or defrauded any man, that GOD may bring the injury to my remembrance, and give me the sincere will, and the full means of repairing it before I die.

I grieve, O GOD, for my exceeding want of thankfulness, and the poverty of my thanks; and I pray Thee to forgive me; regard not my thanklessness, O LORD, but accept my feeble endeavours in union with those praises and thanksgivings, which cease not day and night to be paid to Thee by the Blessed Virgin, by all Thy Saints, and by the holy Angels, especially my guardian Angel; and which are ever offered to Thee through the merits and intercession of my LORD.

I desire to be grateful to all who have bestowed on me any bodily or spiritual benefit; especially to those to whose care I am committed, or who have instructed, rebuked, or admonished me, or who have given me an opportunity of doing any act of love for Thee, O my most Sweet JESUS.

I desire to live and die, fortified by the merits of the Passion, Death, and Bloodshedding of my LORD and SAVIOUR JESUS CHRIST; and by the prayers of all the whole Church; I present the merits of my SAVIOUR to GOD the FATHER for the remission of all my sins, and I offer to Him the prayers of the Church as a thanksgiving for all the blessings which I have received from His Divine Majesty.

May all the Members of CHRIST's Church in Heaven unite their prayers to mine, and by their effectual prayer through the merits of my SAVIOUR, obtain for me, while I live, and chiefly at the hour of my death, true faith, sure hope, ardent love, unshaken fortitude, deep humility, unconquered patience, and whatsoever other virtues may be needful for me during the rest of my life and at the moment of my death.

I protest that if by GOD'S permission the wicked one assail me during my life or at the hour of my death with any temptation, it is my will not to consent to it, tacitly or expressly, by sign, by word, or by deed: but to cleave faithfully for ever to GOD alone, my Maker, and Redeemer.

O my Divine JESUS, how great is my desire to receive Thy Sacred Body! Come now unto my soul, and grant that I may worthily receive Thee before my death! I desire to unite myself to all the worthy Communions which ever have been or shall be made in Thy Holy Church, even to the end of the world.

And when in the agony of death, my tongue can speak no more, yet in my soul I would desire to be united to my GOD; I offer to Him now for then, my agony, my pains, my sweats, my sufferings, to be united to the Agony and Bloody Sweat, the griefs and Passion, of my most Sweet SAVIOUR, JESUS CHRIST, for the remission of my sins, and His eternal glory: and may the holy Angels, who stand before Him, be with me to guard me and protect me at the moment of my death. Amen.

THE LIFE EVERLASTING.

LIKE as the hart desireth the waterbrooks, so longeth my soul after Thee, O GOD. My soul is athirst for GOD, yea even for the Living GOD; when shall I come to appear before the Presence of GOD? O Thou Fountain of Life, Thou Spring of living waters, when shall I pass from this desert, pathless, barren land to the waters of Thy sweetness to see Thy beauty and Thy glory, and to slake my soul's thirst at the gushing streams of Thy love? I thirst, O LORD: Thou art the Fountain of life; give Thou me to drink. I thirst, O my LORD; I thirst for Thee, the Living GOD: Oh, when shall I come and appear before Thy Face! Shall I in very deed see that day which the LORD hath made, that we may rejoice and be glad in it?

O bright and glorious day, which knoweth no evening, whose sun shall no more go down, in which I shall hear the voice of praise, the voice of joy and thanksgiving, Thy voice saying unto me: "Enter thou into the joy of thy LORD;" enter into joy everlasting, into the House of the LORD thy GOD, where are things great and unsearchable, and wonderful things without number; enter into joy wherein is no sorrow, but untroubled gladness: wherein is all manner of good, and no manner of thing that is evil; where all thine heart's desire shall be satisfied, and all that thou fearest and hatest shall be far from thee; where life shall be calm, glad, and thrilling; wherein the hateful enemy shall not enter, nor any breath of temptation shall come near thee; where is supreme and settled security, and tranquil joy, and joyful happiness, a happy eternity, an eternal blessedness, the Blessed TRINITY, the UNITY in TRINITY, and the TRINITY in UNITY, the blissful vision of the Godhead, the joy of the LORD!

O joy upon joy, joy transcending all joy! when shall I enter into thee, and behold my LORD, Whose dwelling is in thee! I shall go thither and see this great sight. And now what keepeth me back? Woe is me, that my sojourning is prolonged! How long, O LORD, shall it be said to me: Wait, wait, yet awhile? Come, O LORD, delay no longer! Come, LORD JESUS CHRIST, and visit us in peace; come and bring forth Thy captives from their dungeon, that they may praise Thee with a perfect heart! Come, Thou Desire of all nations, show Thy Face, and we shall be saved! Come, my Light, my Redeemer, bring my soul out of prison that it may give thanks unto Thy Name. Blessed are they who have passed over the great and wide sea to the eternal shore, and are now blessed in their desired rest. Blessed are they who have escaped from all evils, and are secure of their unfading glory in thee, thou Kingdom of blessedness! How long shall I be tossed about on the waves of this my mortal life, crying unto Thee, O LORD GOD, while Thou hearest me not? Hear me, O LORD, from this great and wide ocean, and bring me to the everlasting Haven.

O everlasting Kingdom, Kingdom of endless ages, whereon rests the untroubled light and the peace of GOD, which passeth all understanding, where the souls of the Saints are at rest, and everlasting joy is upon their heads, and sorrow and sighing have fled away! Oh, how glorious is the Kingdom in which all Thy Saints reign with Thee, O LORD, clothed with light as with a garment, and having on their heads a crown of precious stones! For there is infinite unfading joy, gladness without sorrow, health without a pang, life without toil, light without darkness, life without death; there the vigour of age knows no decay, and beauty withers not, nor doth love grow cold, nor joy wane away, for there we look evermore upon the Face of the LORD GOD of Hosts.

O CHRIST, our Refuge and Strength, Thou Hope of humankind, Whose light shineth from afar upon the dark clouds which hang around us; behold, Thy redeemed ones cry unto Thee, Thy banished ones whom Thou hast redeemed with Thine Own most precious Blood. Hear us, O GOD our SAVIOUR, Thou Who art the Hope of all the ends of the earth, and of them that remain in the broad sea. We are tossed about on the wild and stormy waves in the dark night; and Thou, standing on the eternal shore, beholdest our peril: save us for Thy Name's sake. Guide us among the shoals and quicksands which beset all our course, and bring us at length in safety to the Haven where we would be. Amen.

EJACULATIONS

FOR THE SICK AND DYING.

I.

GOOD JESU! Physician of souls and bodies;

Make my sickness a healing medicine to my soul;

Soothe by Thy presence each ache and pain;

Hallow my suffering by Thine all holy Suffering;
Teach me to unite my sufferings with Thine;
To be hallowed by Thine.

II.

LORD, offer all my sufferings to Thy Father.
As Thou didst offer all Thine Agonies to Him.

III.

O GOOD JESU, crucified for us:
Nail my will to Thy Cross, for love of Thee.

IV.

GOOD JESU, make me wholly Thine;
And in what way Thou willest;
Bind me faster to Thee.

V.

GOOD JESU, give me a deep love for Thee,
That nothing may be too hard for me to bear from Thee.

VI.

GOOD JESU, Who hast borne the Cross for me,
What Cross willest Thou that I should bear for Thee?
Thou knowest, LORD, that I am all weakness,
Teach me to bear my Cross;
Bear it for me, bear it in me.

VII.

LORD, strengthen me to bear my Cross patiently, humbly, lovingly;
If I sink under it, look on me and raise me up.
Give what Thou commandest, and command what Thou willest.
Only by Thine all-holy Cross and Passion,
Sanctify my Cross to me, and
Keep me Thine for ever.

VIII.

GOOD JESU, nailed motionless by Thy sacred Hands and Feet,
For love of me,
Keep me still, motionless, unmoved, unshaken,
Cleaving fast to Thee.

IX.

O GOOD JESU, my GOD, and my All,
Keep me ever near Thee,

Let nothing for a moment separate me from Thee.

X.

GOOD JESU, to Thee I flee,
Hide me in Thy sacred Side.

XI.

O GOOD JESU, Who keepest Thine Own,
Under the shadow of Thy wings;
Teach me to flee to Thee, and hide me from all evil.

XII.

O GOOD JESU, shelter me from the evil one,
Shed Thy dew upon me to calm my soul,
And dwell in me fully, that I may wholly love Thee.

XIII.

GOOD JESU, Strength of the weary, Rest of the Restless,
By the weariness and unrest of Thy sacred Cross,
Come to me who am weary
That I may rest in Thee.

XIV.

JESU, most Tender, in Thee would I trust,
Let me never be confounded.

XV.

LORD, if Thou increase my pain, increase also my patience,
Thou knowest my weakness.

XVI.

GOOD JESU, Who hast borne so patiently with me,
Make me wholly patient for love of Thee.

XVII.

O GOOD JESU, humbled to the death upon the Cross for me,
Good JESU, mocked and blasphemed for love of us,
Make me truly humble for love of Thee.

XVIII.

O BLESSED JESUS, into Thy hands I commend my soul and my body,
To live or to die as seemeth good to Thee,
And to Thine infinite mercy,

For Thou hast redeemed me, O LORD, Thou GOD of truth!

XIX.

GOOD JESU, Thou knowest that I desire to love Thee,
Who hast so loved me, unworthy.
Thine would I be, Who hast made me Thine;
I would love Thee, be wholly Thine.
Open mine eyes that I may see
All in me which displeases Thee,
All which would please Thee.
Give me grace to cast out all which offends Thine holy Eyes,
And to choose, do, and be all which Thou lovest.

XX.

GOOD LORD, teach me to judge myself as Thou judgest.
Make me more ashamed of sin than of all besides,
Yet not so ashamed as not quickly to come to Thee,
All-merciful, All-loving LORD.

XXI.

GOOD JESU! by Thy Loneliness in the Garden,
By the Desolation Thou willest to come over Thee,
Sanctify mine.

XXII.

GOOD JESU, Who alone orderest all things well,
I cast myself wholly upon Thine infinite undeserved love,
I trust Thee with my all,
Myself, and all whom I love, and all which I desire,
My present and my future, my hopes and my fears,
My time and my eternity, my joys and my sorrows.
Deal with me, as Thou willest, and knowest best,
Only bind me safe to Thine everlasting love.

XXIII.

GOOD JESU! Who didst give Thyself for me,
Give Thyself to me,
Make me wholly Thine, that I may deeply love Thee.

XXIV.

GOOD JESU! bared, racked, reviled, forsaken, motionless on the Cross, for love of us,

Help me to bear all pain meekly, in humble love of Thee,

Bare me, empty me of myself, to fill me with love of Thee.

XXV.

GOOD JESU, lead me that I may follow Thee,

Hold me, that I may hold fast to Thee,

Teach me, that I may choose Thee alone,

Keep me, that I may be Thine for ever.

XXVI.

JESU, most tender, Thou hast been very tender to me,

Make me very tender to all and of all who are Thine,

For the love of Thy most tender love.

XXVII.

O GOOD JESU, Who hast so loved us,

Pour Thy love largely into my soul,

That I may love Thee intensely,

And all besides in and for Thee.

DEVOUT PRAYERS
IN PREPARATION FOR DEATH.

O ETERNAL FATHER! I am that most unworthy servant, whom Thou hast so loved that Thou gavest Thy Well-Beloved SON to die for him. Deal mercifully with Thy servant in this hour, lest that precious Blood be shed for me in vain. For what profit is there to me in my SAVIOUR's Blood, if I go down to the pit?

O JESU CHRIST, I am that lost sheep, for whom Thou didst leave the ninety and nine in the wilderness, and seek so diligently, and set it on Thy shoulders to bring it home again. Thou art the Good Shepherd, Who didst lay down Thy life for Thy sheep. O, seek Thy servant, for I have gone astray like a sheep that is lost. Let not that roaring lion, that goeth about seeking whom he may devour, snatch me and tear me from Thee: save me from the lion's mouth, O LORD.

O JESU, I am that poor traveller, who going down from Jerusalem to Jericho, fell among thieves, and after many blows, was left half dead. Thou art my Physician, and that Good Samaritan Who wast moved with compassion towards me, Who hast bound up my wounds, yea, hast prepared for me the medicine of Thine Own Wounds and Blood. Thou art He Who hast borne our sicknesses, and by Whose stripes we are healed. Pity me LORD, in my last hour; O LORD, make haste to help me, ere my soul die and perish for ever.

O JESU, I am that miserable sinner, who is guilty of many sins: Thou art my Advocate with the FATHER, and the Propitiation for my sins. Thou willest not the death of a sinner, but that he should live. Thou camest into the world to save sinners. Deal mercifully with me in the last hour of my life. Be Thou my Mediator and Advocate with the FATHER. O Good JESU, be gracious to me a sinner. Into Thy Hands, O LORD, I commend my spirit. Amen.

PRAYERS
TO BE SAID AT THE BED-SIDE OF THE DYING.

O JESU, Fount of Love, show Thy love to me, a poor needy creature, help me in this my last necessity.

O JESU, my Maker and Redeemer, set Thy Passion, Cross, and Death between Thy judgment and my soul. I give myself wholly unto Thee, cast me not away; I come to Thee, drive me not from Thee. Now, LORD, deal mercifully with me, according to Thy will, and bid my spirit be taken up in peace.

Thou hast redeemed me, O LORD Thou GOD of truth; O may these soothing words sound in the ears of my soul, "To-day shalt Thou be with me in Paradise."

O Crucified JESU, take me into those loving Arms, which I see stretched out for me upon the Cross, take me into Thy loved embrace and draw my soul to Thee: receive me, Good JESU, of Thy mercy; receive my soul in peace. Amen.

Lighten mine eyes, O Good JESU, that I sleep not in death; lest mine enemy say, I have prevailed against him.

O LORD JESU CHRIST, SON of the Living GOD, set Thy Passion, Cross, and Death, between Thy judgment and my soul.

O Good JESU, remember not my old sins, but have mercy upon me and that soon, for I am come to great misery.

O most Sweet LORD JESU CHRIST, for the honour and virtue of Thy blessed Passion, bid me be written among the number of Thine Elect.

Enter not into judgment with Thy servant, most Pitiful JESU, for in Thy sight shall no man living be justified.

One thing have I desired of the LORD which I will require, even that I may dwell in the House of the LORD all the days of my life.

Bring my soul out of prison, that I may give thanks unto Thy Name: lo, the righteous wait for me till Thou recompense me.

O stablish me according to Thy word, that I may live, and let me not be disappointed of my hope. Amen.

A Commendatory Office.

At the Last Agony.

INTO Thy merciful hands, O LORD, we commend the soul of this Thy servant, now departing from the body: acknowledge, we meekly beseech Thee, a work of Thine Hands, a sheep of Thine Own fold, a lamb of Thine Own flock, a sinner of Thine Own redeeming. Receive *him* into the blessed arms of Thine unspeakable mercy, into the sacred rest of Thine everlasting peace, and into the glorious estate of Thy chosen Saints in Heaven.

✠ GOD the FATHER, Who hath created thee, GOD the SON, Who hath redeemed thee, GOD the HOLY GHOST, Who hath poured down His grace upon thee, be now and evermore thy defence, assist thee in this thy last trial, and bring thee into the way of everlasting life. Amen.

CHRIST, Who redeemed thee with His Agony and bloody Death, have mercy upon thee and strengthen thee in this agony of death. Amen.

CHRIST JESUS, Who rose the third day from the dead, raise up thy body again in the resurrection of the Just. Amen.

CHRIST, Who ascended into Heaven, and now sitteth at the Right Hand of GOD, bring thee unto the place of eternal happiness and joy. Amen.

✠ GOD the FATHER preserve and keep thee. GOD the SON assist and strengthen thee. GOD the HOLY GHOST defend and aid thee. GOD the HOLY TRINITY be ever with thee, that thy death may be precious in the sight of the LORD, with Whom mayest thou live for evermore. Amen.

When the Soul has Departed.

MAY the Holy Ones of GOD succour *him;* may the Angels of GOD receive and bear *his* soul and present it before the Face of the most High.

℣ May CHRIST, Who has called thee, receive thee; may the Angels carry thee into Abraham's bosom.

℟ Receive *his* soul, and present it before the Face of the most High!

℣ Grant *him* eternal rest, O LORD; and let perpetual light shine upon *him*.

℟ May the Angels of GOD receive and bear *his* soul, and present it before the Face of the most High!

LORD, have mercy upon *him*.
CHRIST, have mercy upon *him*.
LORD, have mercy upon *him*.

OUR FATHER.

℣ And lead us not into temptation.
℟ But deliver us from evil.
℣ Grant *him* eternal rest, O LORD.
℟ And let perpetual light shine upon *him*.
℣ From the gates of Hell,
℟ Deliver *his* soul, O LORD.

℣ May *he* rest in peace.
℟ Amen.
℣ O LORD, hear our prayer.
℟ And let our cry come unto Thee.

Let us pray.

WE commend to Thee, O LORD, the soul of Thy Servant N., that being dead unto the world, *he* may live unto Thee: and whatsoever sins *he* has committed through the frailty of *his* mortal nature, do Thou of Thy merciful lovingkindness, blot out for ever; through CHRIST our LORD. Amen.

PRAYERS FOR MOURNERS.

I.

O ALMIGHTY GOD, Who knowest the weakness and frailty of our nature: We beseech Thee to give unto us, Thy servants, whom Thou hast stricken with this sorrow, such measures of Thy grace as shall enable us to bear it with humility, resignation, and submission to Thy Divine Will. Grant that no impatient murmuring or repining thoughts may find a place in our hearts: that we may not sorrow as those who have no hope. Let not our grief exceed the bounds of reason and religion; but so temper it, we beseech Thee, with the consolations of Thy HOLY SPIRIT, that whatever we may want in outward consolation, we may find in the inward rest of perfect submission to Thy holy will, O GOD, and unshaken trust in Thy loving mercy; through JESUS CHRIST our LORD. Amen.

II.

ALMIGHTY and most Merciful FATHER, Who lovest those whom Thou chastenest, and turnest away Thine anger from us, look down in pity upon our distress and sorrow, and grant that the affliction which it has pleased Thee to bring on us may be a means of drawing us nearer to Thee. Strengthen us, O LORD, that we may not languish in fruitless and unavailing sorrow, but by the assistance of Thy HOLY SPIRIT, may truly repent, meekly submit, and effectually be comforted, that we may obtain that peace which the world cannot give, and pass the residue of our life in humble resignation, and cheerful obedience: teach us to set our affections on things above, not on things on the earth; on those joys which never fade, the pleasures that are at Thy Right Hand for evermore. Amen.

III.

O ALMIGHTY GOD, Judge of the quick and the dead, so fit and prepare us, we beseech Thee, by Thy grace, for that last account which we must one day give, that when the time of our appointed change shall come, we may look up to Thee with joy and comfort, and may at last be received together with *him* whom Thou hast now taken from us, and with all that are near and dear to us, into that place of rest and peace where Thou shalt Thyself wipe away all tears from all faces, and where all our troubles and sorrows shall have an end: Who with the FATHER and the HOLY GHOST livest and reignest One GOD world without end. Amen.

SORROW'S CREED.

I BELIEVE, O GOD, That my time is in Thy hand.

That going through the vale of misery, I may use it for a well of everlasting life.

That they that sow in tears shall reap in joy.

That blessed are they that mourn, for they shall be comforted.

That in all our affliction CHRIST is afflicted, and that the Angel of His presence saveth us

That heaviness may endure for a night, but joy cometh in the morning.

That CHRIST will not leave me comfortless.

That as one whom his mother comforteth, so will the LORD comfort me.

That our light affliction, which is but for a moment, worketh for us a far more exceeding and eternal weight of glory.

That like as a Father pitieth his own children,

even so the LORD careth for us.

That He will bring me unto the Haven where I would be.

That there remaineth a rest for the people of GOD.

That He healeth those that are broken in heart, and giveth medicine to heal their sickness.

That His loving Spirit will lead me forth into the land of righteousness.

That the GOD of all comfort comforteth us in all our tribulations, that we may be able to comfort them which are in any trouble, by the comfort wherewith we ourselves are comforted of GOD.

That she that is a widow indeed and desolate trusteth in GOD, and continueth in supplications and prayers night and day.

That we are compassed about with a great cloud of witnesses.

That in our FATHER'S House are many mansions.

That He hath there prepared a place for us.

That when we walk through the valley of the shadow of death we will fear no evil, for He is with us.

That GOD will be our guide unto death.

That death is swallowed up in victory.

That I may not sorrow as those which have no hope.

That this corruptible must put on incorruption, and this mortal must put on immortality.

That since by man came death, by Man came also the resurrection of the dead.

That CHRIST shall change our vile body, that it may be like unto His glorious Body.

That when our earthly house of this tabernacle is dissolved, we have a building of GOD, an house not made with hands, eternal in the Heavens.

That we shall not all sleep, but we shall all be changed.

That mortality shall be swallowed up of life.

That we shall be like unto CHRIST, for we shall see Him as He is.

That His Saints in Paradise hunger no more neither thirst any more, for the Lamb feeds them and leads them unto living fountains of waters.

That GOD shall wipe away all tears from our eyes, and that there shall be no more death, neither sorrow, nor crying, neither shall there be any more pain, but that all these things shall pass away.

That Heaven and earth shall pass away, but His words shall not pass away.

That He cometh quickly, even so come LORD JESUS. Amen.

Let us pray.

O ALMIGHTY GOD, Who hast knit together Thine elect in one communion and fellowship, in the mystical Body of Thy SON, CHRIST our LORD; Grant us grace so to follow Thy blessed Saints in all virtuous and godly living, that we may come to those unspeakable joys, which Thou hast prepared for them that unfeignedly love Thee; through JESUS CHRIST our LORD. Amen.

PRAYERS IN GREAT SORROW.

I.

O MOST Mighty, most Merciful FATHER, have mercy on me; have mercy on me, Good LORD. O do Thou bear me up, succour me, strengthen me in my hour of tribulation. Thou hast smitten me to the dust. Thou hast afflicted me very sore; my heart fainteth within me, I am brought very low. I know not, O LORD, how to bear such sorrow: I am overwhelmed with sorrow. I fly to Thee for help, for Thou only canst give me help. Help me, O FATHER, help me, and that right soon; help me for Thy mercies' sake. Make haste to help me for Thy dear SON's sake, JESUS CHRIST our LORD. Amen.

II.

O ALMIGHTY GOD, I fall down before Thee in the agony of my soul. Thou hast taken my beloved one from mine eyes, I have none to help me, my heart is desolate. O comfort me, for I am very greatly troubled. Teach me, O GOD, in this awful hour of affliction, in this great bereavement, in this most bitter, yea, exceeding bitter day, to have patience and Christian resignation. Teach me to bow meekly to Thy will, that my affliction may not utterly break me down, that I may be able to bear it. Thou knowest my sufferings, my sorrows, my tears; look upon me and succour me. Enable me to bear this weight of trial, for of myself I am unable to bear it. O pity me, Good LORD; pity me, most Gracious FATHER: for CHRIST'S sake turn Thou Thy face towards me, and mercifully accept my prayer. Amen.

III.

O LORD GOD, Who chastenest those whom Thou dost love, teach me in this sore trial, this dark day of very heavy chastisement, to know Thy love. LORD, I believe that Thou lovest me; help Thou mine unbelief. Teach me to see Thy love, though Thou seemest to turn Thy Face from me. Increase Thy love towards me, O GOD, now that Thou hast smitten me, lest I be consumed; be very pitiful, speak comfortably to my soul. Give me of Thy comfort, for what can I do, whither can I turn, O LORD? Thou only, Who hast afflicted, can comfort me; I have none beside Thee.

I come to Thee in my loneliness, my desolation of heart, my anguish. Hold Thou me up; give me of Thy love; I kneel at Thy feet, I cast myself down before Thee; even weeping do I beseech Thee to receive my prayer for JESUS' sake. Amen.

For the Departed.

O LORD, Holy FATHER, Almighty Everlasting GOD, we pray Thee in Thy pity, in Thy love, wash in the Sacred Fountain of eternal Life, and clothe with the white robe of everlasting Beatitude, the soul of our dear *Brother*. Among the shining Jewels of Paradise may *he* rest, gazing into the unfathomable mysteries of Thy wondrous love, in sweet and silent adoration; absorbed in the soft light of the ever abiding Presence of JESUS, *his* LORD and *his* Redeemer, till the Day of the Resurrection, when Thou wilt bring *him* through the golden gates into the Heavenly City, to Thy dear Feet, there to see Thee Face to face in Thy unveiled splendour, there to join the Choir of Thy redeemed ones in the new song, the Song of Songs, there to unite with Seraphim and Cherubim, with Angels and Archangels, in one unending chant of praise through all the ages of Eternity. Amen.

May the Judge before Whom thou must appear, accept thee, purge thee from all earthly stain, purify thee with the purification of the Sanctuary, and draw thee into His bosom of endless rest, forgiven, blessed for evermore. Amen.

May the place of waiting be to thee refreshment, light, perfect cleansing, endless growth of divine beauty; the Face of GOD transforming thee more and more into Himself. Amen.

THE COMMUNION OF THE SICK.

Exercise before Communicating.

O FATHER of mercies, and GOD of all comfort; behold I Thy creature, made after Thine Image and redeemed by the Blood of Thy Only-Begotten SON, appear before Thee my Creator; by Whom and for Whom I was created, by Whose grace I have hitherto lived; unto Whom henceforth, so long as Thou seest good, I would wish to live; for Whom, and in Whom, I desire to die: I humbly adore Thee, Whom my soul desireth and longeth for; I cry to Thee, Whom alone I love above all things, O Thou my Rest, my Hope, my Love, my Desire, my heart's only Good.

O most Loving FATHER, although I am the least of all Thy sons, yea, unworthy to be called Thy son, because I have not honoured Thee as a Father; yet I come to Thee with full confidence, and throw myself upon the breast and into the arms of Thy most sweet Love and Mercy, grieving from my inmost soul that I have ever forsaken Thee my GOD, the Fountain of all good; that I have departed from Thee, my most sweet Father; and have forgotten Thee, Who, as though there were none else to care for, every moment rememberest me. O that I had never offended Thee, my

GOD and my all: accept at least this the ardent wish and desire of my inmost heart: look Thou upon me, and be merciful unto me now in the time of pity; Thou knowest, O LORD, that I love Thee, or desire to love Thee, more than myself, more than all that claims or can claim my love. I know Whom I have believed, and that Thou art able to keep that which I have committed to Thee: I know too that a broken and contrite heart, O GOD, Thou wilt not despise.

I hope, O LORD, that Thou wilt never cast me away from Thy Presence, Thou Who dost so lovingly invite us to Thyself, saying, "Come unto me all ye that labour and are heavy laden, and I will give you rest." Behold, I come, O LORD; Thou that castest not out any that come to Thee, receive me according to Thy word, and I shall live, and let me not be disappointed of my hope. Bring my soul out of this prison, that I may give thanks unto Thy Name. O blessed Hour, when I shall be delivered from the body of this death; when I shall come to Thee! when Thou wilt come to me and comfort me; when I shall no more see, through a glass darkly, but see Thee face to face! when I shall put off this corruptible body that presseth down the soul, and praise Thee without hindrance! when Thou wilt let Thy servant depart in peace, to serve Thee wholly! But before I go hence and am no more seen, I desire, in this vale of tears, to begin with all my soul to join in offering to Thy Divine Majesty the Sacrifice of praise, that henceforth I may praise Thee for ever. Wherefore I give Thee infinite thanks because Thou hast vouchsafed to think of me so lovingly from all eternity, for creating me in time after Thy Image, and when the fulness of time was come, for redeeming me by the Blood of Thy Only-Begotten SON, for sparing me so often when sinning, and calling me so often out of the darkness of sin into Thy marvellous light.

What reward shall I give unto Thee, LORD JESU, for Thy toilsome Life and most bitter Death, for vouchsafing so often to feed me with Thy Body and Thy Blood? what reward shall I give unto Thee for all the benefits Thou hast done unto me, O beloved

Spouse of my soul? The deep of my nothingness and my misery calleth to the deep of Thy goodness and Thy boundless love, because of Thy Wounds: in them is all my hope and my confidence: through them, and the boundless ocean of Thy love that flows from them, I come in confidence to Thee, wretched though I am, and poor and naked; for Thou art rich towards all, and my goods are nothing unto Thee. I will take cheerfully at Thy hand, the Cup of Salvation which Thou givest me to drink, bitter though it be, and I will drink it with Thee, Who didst drain it first for me, when Thou didst so earnestly thirst for my salvation. I will call upon the Name of the LORD, and offer to Thee the Sacrifice of thanksgiving. O that in return for this I could embrace Thee with all the love of the heavenly company, Angels and Saints, and above all, of Thy blessed Mother; and, with the voices and affections of all these and all Thy creatures, could praise and magnify Thy Name.

Accept, LORD, my heart as a burnt sacrifice; I give it all to Thee: I give Thee mine eyes, to see Thee alone and all things in Thee: my ears, to hear Thy Word: my mouth, my lips, and tongue, to be filled with Thy praise, and to sing of Thy glory and honour all the day long: my hands, to be stretched forth in prayer to Thee in Heaven, or in alms to the poor, and to do Thy will: my feet to be led into the way of peace: all my members and my bones, that they may say, LORD, who is like unto Thee? Bless the LORD, O my soul, and all that is within me, bless His holy Name: bless the LORD, O my soul, and forget not all His benefits. I now renounce all these earthly things, for in Thee alone I have all things: I renounce myself, for I am Thine: I live, yet not I, but Thou, CHRIST JESU, liveth in me. I love Thee with all my heart, with all my mind, with all my soul and with all my strength. Amen.

Prayer after Communicating.

GLORY be to Thee, O CHRIST, Who hast vouchsafed to visit and refresh my poor soul with Thy sweetness. Now, LORD, lettest Thou Thy servant depart in peace according to Thy Word. I hold Thee now, my Love and Sweetness, and will not let Thee go: I gladly bid farewell to the world and all therein; and now I come with joy, my GOD, to Thee. Henceforth nothing, O Good JESU, shall part me from Thee: I am joined to Thee, O CHRIST, I will live in Thee and die in Thee, and if Thou wilt, abide in Thee for ever. Now I live, yet not I, but CHRIST liveth in me. I am weary of my life; I desire to depart and to be with CHRIST; to me, to live is CHRIST, and to die is gain. I will fear no evil as I walk through the valley of the shadow of death, for Thou, O LORD, art with me: as the hart desireth the waterbrooks, so longeth my soul after Thee, O GOD; my soul is athirst for GOD, yea, even for the Living GOD; when shall I come to appear before the Presence of GOD? Bless me, most Loving JESU, and let me now depart in peace, for I am Thine; and I will never let Thee go for ever. O that I were now joined to Thee in a blessed union for ever! O that I were wholly taken up, wholly absorbed and buried in Thee! O that my soul, resting sweetly in Thy Arms, were altogether taken up in Thee, and blissfully enjoyed Thee, her loving GOD! What more have I to do with the world, my most Loving JESU? Lo, there is none upon earth that I desire in comparison of Thee. Into Thy Hands, LORD JESU, I commend my spirit. Receive me, my Love and Sweetness, that it may be well with me for ever, and that I may gently lay me down in peace in Thee, and take my rest. Amen.

Act of Spiritual Communion.

O MOST Loving JESU, I believe that Thou art truly Present in the most Holy Sacrament of the Altar. I adore Thee; I love Thee. Since I cannot now be present at the Holy Eucharist, and receive Thee sacramentally, I most earnestly desire to partake of Thee spiritually. Come to my poor soul. Unite Thyself to me. O my JESU, my soul rejoices in Thee; my soul blesses Thee. O never leave me. Amen.

THANKSGIVING FOR RECOVERY.

IN the Name ✠ of the FATHER, and of the SON, and of the HOLY GHOST. Amen.

Glory be to Thee, O Heavenly FATHER, for the sickness Thou hast in mercy sent me. LORD, the stripes Thou didst lay on me were the stripes of love; glory be to Thee. Before I was troubled, I went wrong; but now will I keep Thy word. It is good for me that I have been in trouble, that I might learn Thy statutes.

Glory be to Thee, O LORD; glory be to Thee, for delivering me from the terrors of death, and restoring me to my health again; glory be to Thee. I called upon the LORD in my trouble, and the LORD heard me at large. I shall not die but live, and declare the works of the LORD. Praise the LORD therefore, O my soul: as long as I have my life, which at first GOD gave me, and which He has now restored to me, I will sing praises unto my GOD.

O LORD GOD, Who hast in Thy tender mercy prolonged my days in this world, give me grace to spend this life, which Thou hast now lengthened, in Thy service. Oh, give me grace to perform all my resolutions of new obedience, and so to live in the filial fear of Thee all the remainder of my time, that I may at last die at peace with myself, at peace with the whole world, and at peace with Thee; and that for the sake of Thy Well-Beloved SON, and my SAVIOUR, in Whose holy words I sum up all my wants.

OUR FATHER.

✠ The blessing of GOD, the FATHER, the SON, and the HOLY GHOST descend upon me and all belonging to me, and dwell in my heart and be with me in my going out and coming in now and for ever. Amen.

Index.

	PAGE
Act of Adoration	85, 108, 287.
,, of the Blessed Trinity	222.
Amendment	18, 24, 102.
Commendation to God	289.
Contrition	9, 16, 102, 135, 167, 192, 288.
Faith, Hope, Love	29, 102, 120.
,, ,, ,, and Contrition	16, 288.
Faith	16, 29, 102, 120, 287.
Hope	16, 30, 103, 120, 288
Humility	104.
Love	16, 30, 103, 120, 288.
,, of one's neighbour	288.
Oblation to God the Father	109, 226.
,, to God the Son	230.
,, to God the Holy Ghost	237.
Praise	287.
the Presence of God	12
Renunciation of Evil	289.
Reparation	104.
Resignation	287.
Self-Oblation	8, 109, 287.
Spiritual Communion	104, 317.
Submission	287.
Virtues for the Sick	287.
Advent, Devotions for	151.
Affliction or Pestilence, Prayer in	65.
Amendment, Prayer for Pardon and	138.
Angels, Memorial of	40, 248.
Prayers for Guardianship of	10, 25.
Ascension Tide, Devotions for	211.
Aspirations at Holy Communion	105, 106.
in honour of our Lord's life	231.
Beatitudes, The Eight	4.
Benefactor, Prayer for	61.
Bishops and Clergy, Prayer for	59.
Bishop of the Diocese, Prayer for	60.
Brotherhoods, Prayer for	60.

	PAGE
Child-birth, Prayers in	282.
Christmas, Devotions for	155.
Church, Litany for the	262.
Prayer for the	58.
Seasons, Devotions for	151.
Circumcision, The, Devotions for	159.
Clergy, Prayer for the	59.
Commemoration of the Living	86.
of the Departed	87.
of the Saints	86.
Commendatory Office	307.
Confession, Forms of	8, 22, 133, 134.
Prayers for	133.
Confirmation, Devotions for	277.
Contrition, Considerations to excite, see Act	131.
Conversion of Sinners, Prayer for	64.
Daily Devotions	7.
Death, Prayer for a Happy	25, 33.
— Prayers in preparation for	295, 297, 305, 306.
Departed, Commemoration of	87, 313.
Memorial of	39.
Prayers for the	65, 301, 313.
Dying, Prayers on behalf of the	64.
Easter, Devotions for	206.
Ejaculations	25.
for Sick and Dying	301.
in time of Travail	282.
Penitential	132.
in Suffering	26, 291.
Ember Weeks, Prayers for	152, 172, 218, 223.
Enemies, Prayer for	63.
Epiphany, The, Devotions for	162.
Evangelical Counsels, The Three	5.
Evening Prayer	17, 21, 24.
Forgiveness, Prayers for	168.
Four last things, The	5.
Friends, Prayer for	61.
Fruits of the Holy Ghost, The Twelve	3.
Prayers for	277.
Gifts of the Holy Ghost, The Seven	3.
Prayers for	238.
Grace before Meals	27, 32.
after Meals	32.
Prayer for	9, 108.

Index

	PAGE
Heathen, Prayer for	64.
Heretics, Prayer for	63.
Holy Baptism, Devotions for	275.
Holy Communion, Devotions for	67.
Memorial of	40.
of the Sick, Devotions for	314.
The Holy Ghost, Memorial of	39.
Oblation to, Act of	237.
Prayer to	239.
Seven Gifts of	3.
,, Prayers for	238.
Six Sins against	5.
Twelve Fruits of	3.
,, Prayer for	240.
Holy Innocents Day, Prayers for	156.
Holy Matrimony, Devotions for	279.
The Holy Trinity, Devotions to	221.
Memorial of	38.
Prayer to	23.
Holy Week, Devotions for	189.
Hours, Prayers for the Third, Sixth, Ninth and Compline	42.
Husband's Prayer	279.
Husband and Wife's Prayer	280.
Hymns—	
Adoro Te devote	118.
Ave verum corpus	85.
Lauda, Sion, Salvatorem	114
Nunc, sancte nobis Spiritus	42.
O Esca Viatorum	117.
Pange lingua gloriosi	116.
Rector potens verax Deus	46.
Rerum Deus tenax vigor	50.
Te lucis ante terminum	56.
Veni Creator	15.
Verbum supernum prodiens	117.
Intercessory Prayers	10, 13, 19, 23, 24, 58.
Jews, Prayer for	64.
Journey, Prayer before	32.
Kindred, Prayer for	61.
Lent, Devotions for	166.
Prayers to keep	165.
Light, Prayer for	17, 21, 24.
Litany for Advent	152.
of the Word Incarnate for Christmas	157.
of the Holy Name for the Circumcision	159.

	PAGE
Litany of the Holy Child for the Epiphany	162.
of the Passion for Lent	184.
of the Resurrection for Easter	207.
of the Ascension	212.
of the Holy Ghost for Whitsun Tide	218.
to the Holy Trinity, for Trinity Season	223.
to God the Father, for Trinity Season	227.
to God the Son, for Trinity Season	234.
to God the Holy Ghost, for Trinity Season	241.
the Golden	248.
for the Church	262.
for the Holy Communion	110.
of Repentance	141.
for the Sick	292.
Master's Prayer	62.
Meditation	269.
Subjects for Daily	6.
Memorial of the Incarnation	8, 41.
of Saints' Days	244.
for a Week	38.
Missions, Prayer for Home and Foreign	61.
Morning Prayer	7, 11, 14.
Mourners, Prayers for	309.
Ejaculation for	29.
Mysteries of the Incarnation, or The Five Joyful	255.
of the Redemption, or The Five Sorrowful	258.
of the Resurrection, or The Five Glorious	260.
Notable Duties, The Three	5.
Occasional Offices, Devotions for	275.
Prayers	31.
Orphans, Prayer for	62.
Pardon and Amendment, Prayer for	138.
Prayer for	18, 22, 24, 289.
Parent's Prayer	280.
Parent, Prayer for	61.
Parish, Prayer for	60.
Priest, Prayer for the	60.
Passion, The, Prayers on, for Daily Use	166.
Prayers on, for Deliverance in Death	295.
S. Bridget Prayers on	175.
S. Bernardine Prayers on	174.

	PAGE
Passion, The, S. Gregory Prayers on	173.
Readings for the Hours of	189.
Patience, Prayer for	290.
Penitential Devotions	119.
Pestilence, or Affliction, Prayer in	65.
Precepts of the Church	2.
Psalms, Gradual	5.
Penitential	5, 144.
Queen, Prayer for	59.
Repentance, Three Parts of	5.
Rogation Days, Devotions for	210.
Saints, Commemoration of	86.
Prayer for the Intercession of	10.
Days, Devotions for	244.
Memorial of	39, 244.
Schism, Prayer for Removal of	63.
Self-Examination, Method of, by Ten Commandments	121.
Method of, by Deadly Sins	128.
Prayers before	119.
Questions of	18, 22, 24.
Septuagesima, Prayers for	165.
Servant's Prayer	62.
Service, Prayer before	26, 31.
Prayer after	31.
Seven Words from the Cross	5.
Devotions on	201.
Sick, Devotions for	285.
Ejaculations for	25, 26.
Prayer for Recovery of	65.
Rules for	284.
and Dying, Prayer for	64.
Sin, Nine Ways of Participating in Another's	4.
Ejaculation after falling into	28.
Sins, The Seven Deadly	4.
Prayers against	139, 180.
Six, against the Holy Ghost	5.
Sisterhoods, Prayer for	60.
St. John Evangelist Day, Prayers for	156.
St. Stephen's Day, Prayers for	156.
Study, Prayer before	33.
Sufferers in Mind or Body, Prayer for	63.
Teaching, Prayer before	33.
Tempted, Prayer for the	27, 28, 63
Thanksgivings	8, 17, 21, 24, 29, 287.
at Holy Communion	108.

	PAGE
Thanksgiving after Child-birth	283.
after Confession	135.
for Seven Effusions of our Lord's Blood	180.
for Baptism	275.
for Recovery from Sickness	318.
on Abatement of Pain	292.
Travellers, Prayer for	62.
Ejaculation for	26.
Trinity Season, Devotions for	221.
Unity of the Church, Prayers for	59, 87.
Virtues, The Four Cardinal	3.
The Three Theological	3.
Prayer for	34–36.
Vocation, Prayer for Choice of	33.
War, Prayer in Time of	65.
Way of the Cross, The	191.
Whitsun Tide, Devotions for	217.
Widow, Prayer for a	62.
Wife's Prayer	279.
Work, Prayer before Commencing a	32.
Ejaculation before or after	27–29.
Works of Mercy, The Seven Spiritual	4.
The Seven Corporal	4.
Wounds of our Lord, Devotions on the	182.

www.ingramcontent.com/pod-product-compliance
Lightning Source LLC
Chambersburg PA
CBHW021152230426

43667CB00006B/368